CHRISTIAN ETHICS AND THE
MORAL PSYCHOLOGIES

RELIGION, MARRIAGE, AND FAMILY

Series Editors

Don S. Browning
John Witte, Jr.

CHRISTIAN ETHICS AND THE MORAL PSYCHOLOGIES

Don S. Browning

WILLIAM B. EERDMANS PUBLISHING COMPANY
GRAND RAPIDS, MICHIGAN / CAMBRIDGE, U.K.

Wm. B. Eerdmans Publishing Co.
255 Jefferson Ave. S.E., Grand Rapids, Michigan 49503 /
P.O. Box 163, Cambridge CB3 9PU U.K.

Printed in the United States of America

11 10 09 08 07 06   7 6 5 4 3 2 1

Library of Congress Cataloging-in-Publication Data

Browning, Don S.
Christian ethics and the moral psychologies / Don S. Browning.
p.   cm.
Includes bibliographical references.
ISBN-10: 0-8028-3171-0 / ISBN-13: 978-0-8028-3171-2 (pbk.: alk. paper)
1. Christian ethics. 2. Psychology, Religious.
3. Christianity — Psychology. I. Title.

BJ1251.B77 2006
241.01′9 — dc22

2006004253

www.eerdmans.com

Contents

Series Foreword

The Religion, Marriage, and Family series has a complex history. It is also the product of some synergism. The books in the first phase evolved from a research project located at the University of Chicago and supported by a generous grant from the Division of Religion of the Lilly Endowment. The books in this new phase of the series will come from more recent research projects located in the Center for the Study of Law and Religion in the School of Law of Emory University.

This second phase of the series will include books from two of this Center's projects, both supported by generous grants from The Pew Charitable Trusts and Emory University. The first project was called Sex, Marriage, and Family in the Religions of the Book and began with an Emory University faculty seminar in 2001. The second project was called The Child in Law, Religion, and Society and also was initiated by a semester-long Emory faculty seminar that met during the autumn of 2003.

Although the first phase of the Religion, Marriage, and Family series primarily examined Christian perspectives on the family, it also included books on theological views of children. In this second phase, family in the broad sense is still in the picture but an even greater emphasis on children will be evident. The Chicago projects and the Emory projects have enjoyed a profitable synergistic relationship. Legal historian John Witte, director of the two Emory projects, worked with practical theologian Don Browning on the Chicago initiatives. Later, Browning worked with Witte on the research at Emory. Historian Martin Marty joined Witte and Browning and led the 2003 seminar on childhood.

Some of the coming books in the Religion, Marriage, and Family series will be written or edited by Emory faculty members who participated in the two seminars of 2001 and 2003. But authors in this new phase also will come from other universities and academic settings. They will be scholars, however, who have been in conversation with the Emory projects.

This series intends to go beyond the sentimentality, political manipulation, and ungrounded assertions that characterize so much of the contemporary debate over marriage, family, and children. In all cases, they will be books probing the depth of resources in Christianity and the other Abrahamic religions for understanding, renewing, and in some respects redefining current views of marriage, family, and children. The series will continue its investigation of parenthood and children, work and family, responsible fatherhood and motherhood, and equality in the family. It will study the responsibility of the major professions such as law, medicine, and education in promoting and protecting sound families and healthy children. It will analyze the respective roles of church, market, state, legislature, and court in supporting marriages, families, children, and parents.

The editors of this series hope to develop a thoughtful and accessible new literature for colleges, seminaries, churches, other religious institutions, and probing laypersons. In this post-9/11 era, we are all learning that issues pertaining to families, marriage, and children are not just idiosyncratic preoccupations of the United States; they have become worldwide concerns as modernization, globalization, changing values, emerging poverty, changing gender roles, and colliding religious traditions are disrupting families and challenging us to think anew about what it means to be husbands, wives, parents, and children.

DON S. BROWNING *and* JOHN WITTE, JR.

Preface

This book evolved out of a project located at the School of Law at Emory University. More specifically, it was stimulated by a research program administered by legal historian John Witte titled "The Child in Law, Religion, and Society," funded by a generous grant from the Pew Charitable Trust. Many other books from this project will be published, and some of these will appear in Eerdmans' Family, Marriage, and Religion Series.

I want to thank Professor Witte for his support of this project, his remarkable collegiality, and his tireless efforts to pull out the best efforts of others on issues of vital importance to the intersection between religion, law, ethics, and a variety of issues affecting children and families. I also want to thank Eliza Ellison, Amy Wheeler, Janice Wiggins, and April Bogle, who make up the "dream team" that supported the Child in Law, Religion, and Society Project.

At the Divinity School of the University of Chicago, I want to give special thanks to Kevin Jung, who helped prepare the manuscript and gave excellent advice about how to improve it at various stages of its development. Sarah Schuurmans has aided in the task of securing permissions and preparing the index. And my long-time secretary Judy Lawrence was always in the background ready to lend a helping hand when we needed it.

This book consists of a rather extensive revision and further development of a series of articles I wrote and published in the 1990s and early 2000s on the relation of Christian ethics and the moral psychologies. I want to express my thanks to the publishers listed below for permission to reprint material from my previously published articles:

"Altruism and Christian Love," *Zygon* 27, no. 4 (December 1992), used by permission.

"The Challenge and Limits of Psychology to Theological Ethics," *The Annual of the Society of Christian Ethics* 19 (1999).

"An Ethical Analysis of Erikson's Concept of Generativity," in *The Generative Society: Caring for Future Generations,* ed. Ed de St. Aubin, Dan P. McAdams, and Tae-Chang Kim. Copyright © 2004 by the American Psychological Association. Adapted by permission.

"Human Dignity, Human Complexity, and Human Goods," from *God and Human Dignity,* ed. Kendall Soulen and Linda Woodhead (Grand Rapids: Eerdmans, 2006), used by permission.

"Moral Development," from *The Blackwell Companion to Religious Ethics,* ed. William Schweiker (Malden, Mass.: Blackwell Publishing, 2005), used by permission.

"Moral Education and Practical Theology in the Thought of Johannes van der Ven," from *Hermeneutics and Empirical Research in Practical Theology: The Contribution of Empirical Theology by Johannes A. van der Ven,* ed. Chris A. M. Hermans and Mary E. Moore (Leiden: Brill, 2004), used by permission.

"Ricoeur and Practical Theology," copyright 2002, from *Paul Ricoeur and Contemporary Moral Thought,* ed. John Wall, William Schweiker, and W. David Hall (New York, 2002), reproduced by permission of Routledge/Taylor & Francis Group, LLC.

"Science and Religion on the Nature of Love," from *Altruism and Altruistic Love: Science, Philosophy, and Religion in Dialogue,* by Stephen G. Post, Lynn G. Underwood, Jeffrey P. Schloss, et al., copyright 2002 by Oxford University Press, Inc. Used by permission of Oxford University Press, Inc.

"Violence, Authority, and Communities of Reconstruction," from *Divine Justice, Human Justice,* ed. J. S. Dreyer and J. A. van der Ven (Pretoria: University of South Africa, 2002), used by permission.

Introduction

Christian theology has had a long-standing interest in psychology. Various psychologies are implicit in the understandings of human existence, sin, freedom, and redemption in the Hebrew and Christian Scriptures. As early as the writings of Paul, Stoic psychology influenced Christian theology, marking Paul's understandings of lust, passion, and control. Platonic psychology influenced the writings of the church fathers, especially Augustine. When Aristotle was rediscovered by the medieval church, his philosophical psychology profoundly shaped the theological anthropology and ethics of Thomas Aquinas, and it still influences Roman Catholic thinking today. In the nineteenth and twentieth centuries, phenomenological psychologies, existential psychologies, and the psychologies associated with philosophical pragmatism had their influence on the moral thought of Christian theology. In recent decades, psychoanalytic, Jungian, humanistic, Kohlbergian, and, most recently, evolutionary psychologies and cognitive neuroscience have all found a place in the theological and ethical writings of various Christian theologians.

In recent decades, much of the influence of modern psychology on theology has come from psychotherapeutic psychology. The processes of therapeutic communication — listening, acceptance, empathy, constancy — seem to change troubled and broken individuals and have analogies to the love, forgiveness, and acceptance attributed to Jesus and hence to God. Gradually, however, ethicists and theologians have begun to analyze more carefully the images of human health and fulfillment implicit in theories of psychotherapeutic change. Questions have arisen as to what psychological health actually means and whether it is, in fact, compatible with what Christians call righteousness, redemption, or sal-

I

vation, and, if not, just how health relates to these more specifically theological concepts.[1]

The questions pertaining to the meaning of such ideas as health, human fulfillment, and optimal human development are difficult to confine to the disciplines of psychology; they venture into the field of ethics. They raise the issue of who is the good person. Most everyone agrees that the concepts of health and moral goodness are not identical, but it is very easy for discussions of health to slide into the moral field. Furthermore, in recent decades, a robust new field of moral psychology and moral development has emerged. Sigmund Freud, Erik Erikson, Jean Piaget, Lawrence Kohlberg, Carol Gilligan, Owen Flanagan, and Elliot Turiel have been leading contributors. At the same time, the moral implications of allegedly psychological concepts such as health, human fulfillment, and human development have become a matter of new concern to the field of ethics, both philosophical and religious.

In recent decades, critiques of the ethical implications of the modern psychologies have been advanced by Philip Rieff, Martin Gross, Isaac Frank, Christopher Lasch, and many others.[2] These criticisms have forced new questions: Can the normative disciplines of moral philosophy and Christian ethics learn something for their purposes from insight into the workings of psychotherapy and the nature of moral development? More specifically, can Christian ethics trust these new psychologies? Or should moral theologians critique these psychologies and perhaps cleanse both theology and the wider culture of the possible mistaken images of moral responsibility proffered by them? These are the questions that will be examined in this book.

A full answer to these questions will be developed throughout the remaining chapters of this book, but to give you some idea of what will follow in these pages, here is the brief answer: *Yes, contemporary moral psychology can contribute to Christian ethics, but only when it does its research with competent pre-scientific or pre-empirical understandings of morality.* By pre-scientific or pre-empirical, I mean the kind of philosophical and conceptual clarification of the meaning of morality that all good empirical

1. Don Browning, *Religious Thought and the Modern Psychologies* (Minneapolis: Fortress, 1987; second ed., 2004); Paul Vitz, *Psychology as Religion* (Grand Rapids: Eerdmans, 1977).

2. Philip Rieff, *The Mind of the Moralist* (Chicago: University of Chicago Press, 1979), and *The Triumph of the Therapeutic* (New York: Harper and Row, 1966); Martin L. Gross, *The Psychological Society* (New York: Random House, 1978); Isaac Frank, "Self-Realization as Ethical Norm: A Critique," *Philosophical Forum* 9, no. 1 (Fall 1977): 9; Christopher Lasch, *The Culture of Narcissism* (New York: Warner, 1979).

moral psychology requires in order to do its observations, tests, and experiments. Modern moral psychology has not always launched its work with such careful pre-empirical and philosophical clarifications and definitions. Hence, Christian ethics must critique these psychologies at the same time that it learns from them. Christian ethics itself must also help develop more adequate pre-empirical and philosophically sound models of morality. The chapters to follow will develop these points.

A Dialogue Partner: *Hardwired to Connect*

Although this book explores primarily the relation of two academic disciplines — moral psychology and Christian ethics — I also will investigate the concrete issue of the moral formation of children and youth. Of course, the nature of adult moral maturity will also have to be addressed. In examining moral development in children and youth, I will engage both appreciatively and critically a significant new scholarly report that is influencing, and should influence even more, American schools, social service institutions, and churches. Entitled *Hardwired to Connect: The New Scientific Case for Authoritative Communities,*[3] it was the result of a consultative study by thirty-three leading American scholars studying the well-being of children and youth. These researchers come from diverse fields of study including developmental psychology, neuroscience, evolutionary psychology, biology, psychiatry, sociology, and theology. They present a troubling picture of today's youth, revealing a significant rise among them in depression and anxiety, drug use, alcoholism, and sexual activity. Although these trends have moderated in recent years in some respects, the report indicates that they are still considerably worse than they were in 1975.[4] Some commentators, such as Steven Mintz in his recent *Huck's Raft: A History of American Childhood,* argue that in comparison to young people in the mid 1800s, today's American youth are far better off.[5] But as Catherine Wallace says in her perceptive review, Mintz misses the point. In spite of the slight improvements over the last decade, children and youth are on the whole worse off than thirty years ago. And this

---

3. *Hardwired to Connect: The New Scientific Case for Authoritative Communities* (New York: Institute for American Values, 2003). This report was prepared by a panel of thirty-three leading scholars from several disciplines and was sponsored by Dartmouth Medical School, YMCA of the USA, and the Institute for American Values.

4. *Hardwired to Connect,* p. 9.

5. Steven Mintz, *Huck's Raft: A History of American Childhood* (Cambridge, Mass.: Belknap, 2004).

is true in a time of otherwise expanding social wealth and health.[6] Children may be better off now than they were in the mid 1800s, but not, as both *Hardwired* and Wallace contend, than they were just a few decades ago.

What is the explanation for these trends? *Hardwired to Connect* argues that they are caused by the failure of technology-driven modern society to meet the deep needs (hardwired needs) of the young to connect with people, institutions, community, and meaning. The cure, the report insists, is not more therapy, more professional intervention, more treatment, or more mental-health resources, although the authors are certainly not opposed to these resources. This report advocates moving from the medical model to a prevention model, from professional intervention to healthy guidance from strong families and communities. *The cure, in short, is the restoration of authoritative communities.* These are communities with a shared memory, a history, some continuity through time, and a comprehensive moral tradition and interpretation of life.[7] These communities support parents, neighborhoods, and schools in their socialization tasks. They meet the deep needs for attachment and connection that children, adolescents, and even the adults themselves bring to living. They help "moralize" and "spiritualize" these needs for connection and attachment.[8]

But will any strong and cohesive community do? Apparently not. The authors of the report make a big distinction between authoritarian and authoritative communities. This point of view is what makes the report intriguing. Authoritarian communities promote tradition, authority, and communal cohesion but have no critical principle that tests their shared practices according to some idea of justice. Ann Hulbert in her splendid *Raising America* points out that today, the field of child psychology has in many ways been taken over by experts such as Dr. James Dobson, who are representatives of authoritarian communities and their views of child rearing and discipline.[9] By contrast, authoritative communities, as the authors of *Hardwired* define them, must be communities with a critical principle, something close to what we will find in Paul Ricoeur's concept of the "deontological test" — an idea that I will amplify in the pages to come.[10] This means the report goes beyond the biological, psychological, and so-

6. Catherine Wallace, "Kids These Days: The Changing State of Childhood," *The Christian Century* 122, no. 6 (March 22, 2005): 26.

7. Wallace, "Kids These Days," pp. 33-40.

8. Wallace, "Kids These Days," p. 29.

9. Ann Hulbert, *Raising America: Experts and Parents, and a Century of Advice about Children* (New York: Alfred Knopf, 2003), p. 329.

10. *Hardwired to Connect,* p. 39.

cial sciences and actually makes normative proposals. It also goes beyond naive communitarianism, which celebrates communal solidarity as the dominant moral ideal, and develops a critical principle of justice by which to judge communities. Although deeply informed by the social sciences, this report moves into moral and political philosophy, if not the philosophy of religion and the borderline of theology. In fact, it spans the long distance between biology, neuroscience, and more explicitly normative disciplines. In this respect, it is a rare bird. But it is also an important one.

Has the report covered all its bases? Does it truly and adequately synthesize an approach to moral psychology, civil society, moral philosophy, and religion that meets the criteria that I will be developing in this book? Not quite. In spite of its considerable value, it underestimates the role of interpretation in maintaining and critically re-creating viable authoritative communities. I will amplify the crucial role of interpretation — in fact, a community of interpretation — in the chapters that follow. Furthermore, one might get picky and say that the report is somewhat misleading in its use of the word "hardwired" to characterize our deep human need to connect to both individuals such as parents and various kinds of authoritative groups. These inclinations and needs, as important and even biological as they are, can be easily derailed, repressed, or distorted. Hence, it might have been better to speak of our being "softwired" to connect. But I will not push that point too far. These needs are deep, but they also need to be nurtured and guided. That is the point of the report. I suggest, however, that we leave the title as the authors gave it to us.

Themes

Before going too far with a discussion of the moral formation of children and youth, I want to develop a perspective on the relation of modern moral psychology and Christian ethics. The chapters in this book have taken shape over the last decade and reflect common concerns and preoccupations. The reader will notice the following themes discussed throughout the pages to come, often in slightly different contexts and with different issues at stake.

The Context of Moral Psychology

First, I argue that the field of moral psychology cannot stand alone. It must always be developed in close association with pre-empirical and philosophical (perhaps even theological) assumptions, arguments, and insights about the nature of ethics and morality. This points to the dilemma of almost all fields of modern psychology. Psychology aspires to be a science. But what does that mean? Does it mean that in order to be objective and advance publicly replicable knowledge about human behavior it must forget the history of the human race, wipe it away from the minds of psychologists, who must study behavior as though they had never learned anything from the past? Some psychologists think that is what objectivity means.

I don't hold that view. I argue that moral psychology must build its empirical work on pre-empirical philosophical and even theological assumptions. As I will point out in Chapter 2, this was the wisdom of the moral development theories of Lawrence Kohlberg; he did some important, although ultimately inadequate, pre-scientific philosophical reflection about the nature of morality. Western philosophy and theology have been investigating human behavior for centuries, and most of the great theories of morality already had been identified before the advent of modern scientific psychology. These models of morality constitute part of the "classics" that make up our cultural history, or what I, with a bit more sense of gravity, will call in Chapter 4 our "effective history."[11] Most good contemporary moral psychologists acknowledge that they are testing and clarifying models of ethics and morality that already have been developed in the past. Good scientific work allows past accomplishments to guide and enrich the empirical tests of modern academic psychology.

Foundationalism vs. Anti-Foundationalism

Second, the debate between foundationalism and anti-foundationalism in the philosophy of science helps clarify the relation of contemporary moral psychology to Christian moral theology. This discussion is about the nature of science and its relation to human wisdom. Much of modern philosophy and science has been driven by the idea that only a proposition that is totally objective — that is, totally unconditioned by subjectivity, tradition, or cultural bias — can be said to be true. Images of objectivity differ in the various sciences, but objectivity has been the common goal nonetheless. Many scientists think that objectivity is achieved by starting an inquiry on some neutral foundation or beginning point. Valid

11. Hans-Georg Gadamer, *Truth and Method* (New York: Crossroad, 1982), p. 267.

knowledge might require beginning with sense experience — what one can see, hear, smell, or feel. Or it might come, as Descartes argued, from starting with a statement that one cannot doubt, such as the fact that "I am" (that "I exist"), and then deriving all other achieved knowledge from that foundational beginning point.[12] Others have argued that objectivity can be achieved only through controlled experimental procedures that can be replicated publicly by competent experts. Edmund Husserl, the great European phenomenologist, thought objectivity had to be based on rigorous descriptions of how the phenomena of the world appeared to consciousness, with one's subjectivity and naive belief in the existence of these phenomena bracketed or kept under control.[13] All of these beginning points can be classified as foundationalist perspectives on science and knowledge.

Anti-foundationalists or nonfoundationalists question the possibility of finding some absolutely neutral beginning point for the enterprises of science, philosophy, and morality. Not only is it impossible, they argue, it is culturally nihilistic and arrogant, especially when it comes to the field of morality.[14] Think what it would mean to start from a neutral foundation in raising children. Parents and teachers would be saying, in effect, that our community and the human race have nothing to learn from our history about the good and the right and that we must discover it all over again — a very confusing experience, I would think, for a two-year-old. The foundationalist attitude, I will argue, alienates us from the wisdom of tradition, assumes that our ancestors never learned anything that was true or valid, and assumes that to learn how to design a society or live a good life, we literally must invent the world anew.

The foundationalist/anti-foundationalist discussion has been with us, one way or the other, for decades if not for centuries. In trying to locate modern moral psychology in relation to Christian ethics, I take a somewhat anti-foundationalist point of view. This means I think that moral psychology as a science must begin with our moral traditions and

---

12. For a discussion of this Cartesian beginning point, see Richard Rorty, *Philosophy and the Mirror of Nature* (Princeton, N.J.: Princeton University Press, 1979), pp. 8-9; also see Richard Bernstein, *Beyond Objectivism and Relativism* (Philadelphia: University of Pennsylvania Press, 1983).

13. For an excellent introduction to the phenomenology of the German philosopher Edmund Husserl, see Paul Ricoeur's *Husserl: An Analysis of His Phenomenology* (Evanston, Ill.: Northwestern University Press, 1967).

14. Paul Ricoeur, *Hermeneutics and the Human Sciences* (Cambridge: University of Cambridge Press, 1982), p. 60.

moral history. These traditions constitute the source for the authoritative communities that the *Hardwired* report talks about so forcefully, and they include our Jewish and Christian traditions, which have been the most powerful influences on our religious authoritative communities in Western civilization. Notice, however, that I say that my position is "somewhat" anti-foundational. I say this because within my respect for the relevance of tradition to moral psychology, I also believe there is an enormous role for what the philosopher Paul Ricoeur calls the "distanciating" contributions of both philosophical reflection and various forms of science.[15] Science rightfully and helpfully tries to get distance from its beginning points in commonly held cultural and tradition-shaped assumptions. But it can never, and should never, achieve total objectivity and detachment from culture and tradition. Just what the concept of distanciation means is something I will explain, more than once, in the following chapters, especially in Chapter 4. My view is nonfoundationalist because I begin with history and moral tradition, but there still remains, from my perspective, a subordinate place for the distanciating attitudes and procedures of science.

A Critical Hermeneutical Ethics

Third, the pre-empirical model of ethics and morality used in these chapters is "critical hermeneutical" in character. These unfamiliar words can be explained fairly simply. I follow philosophers Hans-Georg Gadamer and Paul Ricoeur — especially Ricoeur — in holding that ethics begins with our aspirations for the goods of life. All humans bring their organic desires and instincts to the evaluation and identification of these goods, but no human society relies on only these raw organic responses to discern the good. Early in life, the communities and traditions that socialize us teach us our first reliable understanding of what these goods *really are,* how they should be ordered in relation to one another, and which objects will be truly satisfying. In contrast to some modern views of ethics, I believe we never rely only on what feels good in making our moral judgment, although that in some sense is relevant. Rather, we rely on tested practices that teach us what goods, and what actions leading to them, are truly reliable and satisfying.

Nonetheless, the goods of life can conflict with one another. Even our

---

15. Ricoeur, *Hermeneutics and the Human Sciences,* pp. 64-65.

relatively tested and culturally accepted goods can, under certain circumstances, conflict with each other. They conflict within ourselves and between us and other people. To address these conflicts requires going beyond our ethical striving for the goods of life to *morality* in the more mature sense of the word. Mature moral reflection and action must necessarily begin with but also go beyond our conventional patterns of striving for the good. Mature morality entails a deeper interpretation of our conventional practices. In order to accomplish this, one must search the classic moral teachings, texts, and monuments of a tradition for their deeper meaning. We as individuals and groups must try to understand more deeply their real intentions, meanings, and what they have to teach about the tested goods of life. The move into *morality,* in contrast to mere *ethical striving* after the goods of life, requires acts of interpretation about the traditions and communities that have formed us.

But this interpretive process is not enough. Our traditions — their practices, views of the goods of life, and stories — must be *critiqued*. We must ask, are these insights valid and lasting, and can they be generalized to others? In other words, can they fairly and justly organize the goods of life for other persons as well as for myself? Just how that appreciative criticism of the classic resources of a tradition's authoritative communities can be accomplished will be a central concern of this book.

These interpretive and critical acts, however, are still not enough. Fully moral action and reflection must return to the original situation of our ethical conflicts over the good. We must reflect on what our deeper interpretation of the classics behind our practices and our critical principle of generalization actually means for the unique conditions and conflicts of the original context that provoked our moral crisis in the first place.

In summary, serious moral action and reflection are something of a circle that (1) starts with our present ethical dilemmas, (2) goes backward to study and interpret the classics and traditions that have shaped us morally, (3) critiques these sources, and (4) then moves back once again to the original situation. It is a circle, true; but, as I will say several times in the chapters that follow, *it is also a circle with a critical moment in the middle.* That critical moment helps keep the circle from becoming vicious — that is, circular, closed, and unable to evolve. It is also best to think of moving through this circle *in dialogue with other people* and even in dialogue with others who may, in fact, be a source of the conflict that creates the moral issue. It is best to think of this interpretive and critical circle as a dialogue we should have with others rather than a monologue that goes on internal to the solitary mind.

Once the reader understands what this critical interpretive or hermeneutic circle is all about, we can apply it to the field of Christian ethics,
and it can help us understand the task of Christian ethics. Moreover, we
can use it to locate for Christian ethics the contributions and limits of the
modern psychologies — psychoanalysis, humanistic psychology, cognitive
moral psychology, evolutionary psychology, neuroscience — as well as to
find a place for the insights of moral philosophers such as Aristotle, Kant,
John Rawls, Alasdair MacIntyre, and Jürgen Habermas.

One of my scholarly friends accused me of using this model to subordinate psychology to theology. He was, in fact, a professional psychologist
and valued the autonomy of psychology as a scientific discipline. He did
not want theology telling moral psychologists what to think. I responded
that I was not so much trying to subordinate psychology and social sciences to theology as I was trying to locate both disciplines — psychology
and theological ethics — within a larger theory of experience or praxis. I
hold that the effective history of a tradition — that is, its memory of the
resolution of past moral crises and hence its possible wisdom — is always
needed to make moral sense of the discrete facts of scientific discovery. A
moral tradition should not dictate to the scientist what the facts really
are, even though a tradition may provide the psychologist some good,
testable hypotheses about these facts. But science alone cannot establish
the broader theory of experience and praxis required to give the more discrete facts of science their full meaning.

In the chapters that follow, especially Chapters 5, 6, and 9, I will examine the nature of love, both Christian love and other kinds of love, within
the framework of this model. My thesis is rather simple: The modern
moral psychologies can help us clarify the teleological inclinations of love,
that is, the range of premoral human desires and needs that humans
bring to love and upon which love builds. The modern moral psychologies can even clarify some of the conditions required for the critical tests
of genuine love — what I will call, following Paul Ricoeur and Johannes
van der Ven, the "deontological test" (Chapters 2 and 3). But the modern
moral psychologies cannot explain or justify some of the assumptions
about the status of humans required to ground love as equal-regard for
both other and self as well as equal concern to actualize the good for
other and self. I will argue that genuine Christian love makes love as
equal-regard central, but also includes a necessary submoment of self-
sacrificial love symbolized by the Christian concept of the cross.

In the end, the full range of conditions needed to sustain and stabi-
lize the naturalistic dimensions of love (the desires and needs that go into

love) is provided only by the higher reaches of love as equal-regard and sacrificial giving, and even then only when these are manifest in a living and vibrant community. Since Christian love is so central to my discussion of the relation of moral psychology and Christian ethics, I will engage the thought of some of the preeminent views on love to be found in Christian circles — the views of the apostle Paul, St. Thomas Aquinas, Martin Luther, Anders Nygren, Reinhold Niebuhr, Gene Outka, Louis Janssens, Stephen Pope, Timothy Jackson, and several contemporary theological feminists.

A Critique of Contemporary Moral Psychology

Fourth, although contemporary moral psychology can contribute to our understanding of ethics and morality when it is placed in dialogue with the Western philosophical and religious traditions, it also merits fairly severe criticism. I will argue that we can learn much from the modern psychologies about what moral philosophers call the "teleological" aspects of ethics and morality. By teleological dimensions of love, I do not mean love's ultimate metaphysical goals. This is precisely what the modern psychologies cannot clarify, since they disdain metaphysics and questions of ultimate concern. These psychologies sometimes lazily lapse into metaphysical speculations, but they also fear that intentionally doing so will compromise their status as true science. But there is another form of teleology that the moral psychologies can clarify; this is the matter of the finite motivations and strivings for the good that humans bring to their morality and their loves. This means that the moral psychologies can help us clarify and rank the nature of the finite goods of life (I will often refer to them as premoral goods) that we try to realize or accomplish in our ethical strivings.

But even these insights can be confusing unless they are situated within some more pervasive features of moral action that modern psychology often fails to address or understand. Much of modern moral psychology is overly individualistic, egocentric, and insensitive to the contributions of community and tradition in shaping the moral life. To this extent, much of modern moral psychology sides with the forces of modernity that undercut and fragment traditional communities. It tends not to understand fully the role of family, community, and the classics of a tradition in forming the moral self. At the same time, it has not properly located the role of critique in cleansing the moral distortions almost always found in a tradition. I argue that our choice is not tradition *or* critique; the way forward is tradition *and* critique. Both are important. But these two emphases need to be properly positioned in relation to one another. Critique becomes formal and empty unless it is preceded by the careful interpretation of a tested and powerful moral tradition.

Differing Understandings of Premoral Goods

Fifth, many, but not all, of the modern moral psychologies differ in their understanding of the premoral goods of life. I claimed above that the scientific moral psychologies can contribute to understanding the premoral inclinations (and the goods that they seek) that contribute to the formation of Christian love. But I hold that they cannot capture some of the unique and distinctive aspects of this love, especially the self-sacrificial moment required to renew and sustain the essence of Christian love as equal-regard. I will argue at length in Chapters 1 and 2 that the premoral level of human experience and praxis is only one of five levels of the multidimensional nature of any praxis — even the praxis of love. The premoral level is important, but it is not the fullness of what is happening in any experience, including the experience of love.

Nonetheless, much of contemporary social science specializes in measuring the premoral consequences of various modes of intervention. The field of economics tries to conceptualize and measure economic goods and consequences. Medicine and much of modern psychology study the goods of health, both physical and mental. Some social sciences such as anthropology and evolutionary psychology study how various strategies of action yield, or fail to yield, adaptive goods and consequences in the struggle for survival. It is best to think of these kinds of goods as premoral or nonmoral; they are not fully moral. Health, wealth, adaptive power and survival, and such basic goods as food, water, clothes, shelter, employment, or even education are goods, but they are goods in the premoral sense of the word. Persons or societies are not necessarily moral just because they enjoy a plentitude of these goods; they may have stolen, killed, or maimed defenseless women, children, and the elderly to get them. But most everyone agrees that moral persons and societies are in some way about the business of producing and distributing these goods according to some theory of justice.

The competing moral psychologies conflict not only because they hold different understandings of the essential goods of life; they also hold different implicit principles of moral obligation. There are moral psychologies that clearly hold an ethical-egoist view of obligation. There are moral psychologies that are primarily utilitarian in orientation. There are the deontological or Kantian models of moral obligation such as that found in the celebrated moral psychology of Lawrence Kohlberg. And there are moral psychologies that are primarily virtue psychologies woven together by very vague principles of obligation. But wait, there is more. These two differences among the different psychologies on premoral goods and principles of obligation are often compounded by different worldviews or visions of life that are implicit in the psychologies. Furthermore, they often disagree on how to interpret the main social and cultural trends of modern life. In short, they often differ on nearly all of the dimensions of practical reason that I will elaborate throughout these pages. No wonder they disagree on which practices are the best for raising children, choosing a mate, staying married, or becoming a good and moral person. As if these differences were not confusing enough, the conflicts between the modern moral psychologies are partially due to the fact that many of the judgments on the various dimensions of practical reason are unconscious and beyond the control of the scientists who promote them. Part of what I will do in this book is to scan various schools of moral psychology and ferret out the hidden assumptions that so-called behavioral scientists unwittingly insert into their theories but for which they take no direct responsibility.

The Naturalistic Submoment

The discussion of premoral goods and values points to a fifth theme that runs through these chapters: the importance of what I call a "naturalistic" submoment in ethical and moral judgments. What does this mean? First we must ask, how do we come to know the premoral goods of life? Some people would say we examine our feelings — our wants, desires, and what we find pleasurable or satisfying in the direct and unmediated testimony of experience. I say, not so fast. Clearly our bodily experiences tell us much about the goods of life, but seldom as directly as we think. We read our bodily experience through the linguistic customs of the communities that socialize us and the traditions that they carry. Or, to say it differently, we learn about the premoral goods of life through our traditions and their codification of goods and values. A child may have a bodily need for protein and calcium, but whether the parent turns to milk or tofu to satisfy this, and whether there is a language to speak about one or the other of these goods, is probably a matter of custom. I never heard the word "tofu" when I was growing up. Do kids have a need for milk and is milk a universal premoral good? Not really. Children have a need for protein and calcium, but any number of foods might do the job, although a mother's milk might indeed do it best in the very early months. The Chinese, I am told, don't do well with cow's milk. Their practices don't include downing a quart every day as many American teenagers do.

So, how do we discover the most abiding and durable premoral goods of life? We first analyze our inherited practices, with all the symbolic overlay that they carry — images and narratives about how specific goods of life like milk fit within the more overarching goals of life, and so on. These traditions are full of linguistic codes that help us make logical distinctions between premoral and moral goods; for example, "The steak that Bill is eating tastes good, but Bill himself is not good; he is morally rotten to the core." But, in situations of conflict between premoral goods, we ask, what are the really real premoral goods, the ones that actually meet basic needs and the ones that can be easily and harmoniously organized with other needs and the goods that meet them? For instance, the steak may taste good, but science tells us it contains cholesterol and requires excessive amounts of the world's corn to produce it. So, the practice of consuming a steak is at best an ambiguous premoral good requiring additional moral reflection to truly justify. Are steaks really good for our bodies and is it really fair to eat too many of them when other people don't even have corn?

Notice that I consulted science — biology, medicine, the health sciences — when I suggested that steak may contain too much of the wrong kind of fat. This opens a place for science in ethics and a role for what Paul Ricoeur calls "diagnostics" in making moral decisions (see Chapter 4). Foundationalists would say we cannot build a new and reliable ethic until science determines the really reliable goods of life. At least, this would be the claim of the sociobiologist E. O. Wilson.[16] But my moral psychology and theology works the other way around. *We first come to know our moral and premoral goods by interpreting a tradition; science can then play a secondary diagnostic role in helping us to clarify goods and threats to them when conflict and obscurities within our cultural and religious traditions require additional testing.* For example: the beef tastes good and builds muscles, but

---

16. See E. O. Wilson, *Consilience: The Unity of Knowledge* (New York: Alfred A. Knopf, 1998).

what is it doing to my blood? So, possibly it is a matter of both health (a premoral good) and justice (a moral good) for all of us to eat less beef and more fruits and vegetables, which it is also a part of our practice to consume.

What is the point? I claim that science, like a good doctor, can help us interpret and clarify some of our basic needs, certain threats to them, and the conditions under which they flourish. But science can do this as a supplement to, not as a replacement for, the wisdom of tradition. I will expand this idea in the rest of the book.

Strong Families Are Important but Not Sufficient

Finally, strong and cohesive families are important but not completely sufficient relative goods for creating moral persons. Showing how this statement is true will help illustrate some of the arguments of this book. Other examples of contemporary moral issues also could be used to make this point. But family is a good example for my purposes. Over the last decade, I have headed a large, multidisciplinary study of families in modern societies called the Religion, Culture, and Family Project of the University of Chicago. Hence, I come to the writing of this book full of ideas about both family issues and the relevant methodological approaches required to think about families both descriptively and normatively. Some of these issues have clear implications for the relation of moral psychology to Christian ethics. From time to time, therefore, I will use examples from the field of family studies to illustrate my points. A warning, however, is in order; this is not a book about families or family issues. It is primarily a theoretical discussion of the field of contemporary moral psychology in relation to the claims of Christian ethics. The field of the family is used as an illustration.

I conclude this introduction with one more statement about the limits of this book. Over the years, I have taken many stands of a socially progressive kind.[17] They are, to my mind, a result of exercising what I will call, following Paul Ricoeur, the "deontological test for justice." But I will say very

17. For a summary of the liberal social policies I have argued for, see Don Browning, Bonnie Miller-McLemore, Pam Couture, Bernie Lyon, and Robert Franklin, *From Culture Wars to Common Ground* (Louisville, Ky.: Westminster John Knox, 1997, 2000), chap. 11; see also Don Browning and Gloria Rodriguez, *Reweaving the Social Tapestry: Toward a Public Philosophy and Policy for Families* (New York: W. W. Norton, 2001).

little about the details of social policy in these pages. I mention this matter now to make sure that the strong emphasis on community and tradition (albeit critically conceived) is not perceived by the reader as ignoring the need for a just society. Indeed, a just society also helps produce and socialize just youths and adults. But a just and liberal society also needs communities of tradition and shared memory for reasons I will soon develop. In fact, we need both — a just society and one full of communities of tradition. The kind of Christian community that I will argue for is also one that fits into — and, indeed, helps make possible — a just society. But in these pages, I will say more about the moral person in the Christian community than I will about the edifice of the just society.

Chapter 1

Multidimensionality of Praxis
and Christian Ethics

I made several points in the introduction that we should keep in mind as the book unfolds. I argued that contemporary moral psychology requires a pre-empirical understanding of morality out of which it should do its empirical work. I asserted that past frameworks — whether Kantian, utilitarian, or ethical-egoist — had inadequate views of human moral action. I claimed that moral experience or praxis is thick or multidimensional. Once we acknowledge this multidimensionality, it becomes easier to determine what moral psychology has to offer Christian ethics and how Christian ethics can critique and recontextualize, but also employ certain insights from, moral psychology. I also shared my belief that the main contribution to ethics of the contemporary moral psychologies is clarification of the premoral dimension of the five dimensions of all moral praxis, including the moral praxis of Christian individuals and communities.

In the introduction, I began developing what I called a critical hermeneutical perspective on human action. This view sees humans as embodied creatures who also have the capacity to interpret their existence. They are creatures of interpretation. Furthermore, when properly understood, this critical hermeneutic view (sometimes called hermeneutic realism) implies a multidimensional view of morality. In the following chapters, I will develop a multidimensional view of practical moral reason that can serve the needs of interdisciplinary collaboration in our time. This view of practical reason also will have implications for a proper understanding of love.

Most modern views see practical reason as very thin. Some philosophers have seen it as a matter of reasoning about efficient means to accomplish various desires for the self.[1] This view of practical reason is quite popular in the social sciences today, especially in many schools of psychology and in the field of rational-choice economics. The great eighteenth-century moral philosopher Immanuel Kant rejected this view of practical reason, but put in its place another theory which though very important was still quite thin. Practical reason was for him a matter of generalizing those moral maxims that could be applied universally to all rational persons.[2] Utilitarians came up with another broad but still rather slender principle built around reasoning — or calculating — which action would bring the greatest good to the largest number of people.[3] When individuals use their reason to calculate goods primarily for themselves with little regard for the wider community, they are indulging in what moral philosophers call an ethical-egoist view of practical rationality.[4]

All of these typically modern views of practical reason are one-dimensional. The utilitarians and ethical-egoists (whose views are commonly called "teleological" because they see practical reason as promoting various forms of premoral good) have little to say about how to derive the theory of goods that their calculus is supposed to distribute. Kant and his followers have even less to contribute to defining the goods or values that justice should distribute. In addition, all three of these modern perspectives tend to ignore the role of communities of tradition in moral thinking. Such communities mediate to us tested practices about pursuing the good, images of the good life, and stories or narratives that orient us to the purpose of life. These elements of human action contribute something to our ethical and moral life that the modern, but rather gaunt, theories of practical reason may be missing.

But asserting that there is a role for community and tradition raises the question: how can we reason about the practices, images, and narratives of a communal tradition? And how can we do so critically in such a

1. One interpretation of Aristotle sees him as promoting this narrow means-end view of practical rationality, although he is also seen to have a second and larger view closer to the one developed in this book. See Norman Dahl, *Aristotle and the Weakness of the Will* (Minneapolis: University of Minnesota Press, 1984), pp. 23-34; see also David Hume, *An Inquiry Concerning the Principles of Morals* (Indianapolis: Hackett, 1983); and for a more contemporary Humean who tends to reduce practical reason to means-end thinking, see Gary Becker, *A Treatise on the Family* (Cambridge: Harvard University Press, 1991).

2. Immanuel Kant, *Foundations of the Metaphysics of Morals* (Indianapolis: Bobbs-Merrill, 1959), p. 18.

3. John Stuart Mill, *On Liberty* (New York: Liberal Arts Press, 1956).

4. For a discussion and critique of ethical egoism, see William Frankena, *Ethics* (Englewood Cliffs, N.J.: Prentice-Hall, 1973), pp. 117-20.

way as to not fall into unreflective conformity or uncreative traditional-ism? This is a question that haunts the perceptive contemporary moral psychologist Elliot Turiel. In his recent *The Culture of Morality,* Turiel seems to divide contemporary moral psychologists and philosophers between those who uphold the importance of conformity to tradition and those who anchor morality in the rationality of individuals in free interaction with one another.[5] Turiel sides with those who suppress tradition and em-phasize the moral rationality of interacting persons. In this, he seems to side with Alan Wolfe in his *Moral Freedom,* though Wolfe, in fact, empha-sizes moral autonomy and freedom from tradition even more than Turiel.[6] I contend that if we can develop a sufficiently complex understanding of practical reason, we need not follow Turiel and Wolfe in pitting moral au-tonomy and moral rationality against the wisdom of tradition.

I argue that practical reason is indeed complex and has, in fact, five identifiable dimensions or levels. I have developed this thick view of practical reason over the last couple of decades, partially in dialogue with Paul Ricoeur and partially in conversation with Jürgen Habermas. This view holds that our practical reason is first informed by the ethical prac-tices of the family, religion, and community into which we are born and raised; it is *first* shaped by a history of practices — practices that always have a moral horizon. We eat, sleep, make love, teach, learn, and worship in certain ways, following certain practices. These practices often imply certain virtues — for example, a capacity and readiness to regularly and habitually enact honored practices — and they channel our pursuit of tested goods in a variety of situations. These identifiable goods embed-ded in practices are the *second* dimension of practical reason. When asked why we do something this way rather than another, we will sooner or later justify our practices with some statement that uses the uniquely ethical word "should" — for example, "this is the way it should be done." This statement of should — this statement of obligation — points to a *third* dimension of practical reason. *Fourth,* our practical action also will always assume some vision or story of life that makes what we are doing have meaning within the whole of life. *Fifth,* our practical action and rea-son will always implicitly or explicitly assume, or make assessments about, some view of the natural, social, and cultural context that con-strains or channels our practical action. To act morally, we have to make

---

5. Elliot Turiel, *The Culture of Morality* (Cambridge: Cambridge University Press, 2002), p. 290.

6. Alan Wolfe, *Moral Freedom* (New York: W. W. Norton, 2001).

judgments at all of these levels or dimensions. This is the thickness — the multidimensionality — of practical reason.

Our inherited practices and virtues help us pursue the goods of life — food, health, pleasure, wealth, companionship, safety, and so on. But our various practices and goods can conflict with one another. We cannot have all the goods of life at the same time. Sometimes the goods of health conflict with the goods of food, and quite often the goods of pleasure conflict with the goods of wealth. Our individual efforts to secure these various goods frequently conflict with the efforts of others to obtain them for themselves. It is within the context of these conflicting situations that practical reason begins to reflect on these practices, interpret them more deeply, and make more intentional judgments for each of these dimensions.

If I reflect carefully, I discover that all of my habitual practices are quite thick — quite multidimensional. Take this situation. Assume that you are a father or mother with three children. You go to the fridge and discover there is milk for only one person. Yet all of you, including your spouse if you have one, are hungry and thirsty. What should the parent do? Drink the milk, leaving the others out? Share it equally so that each gets a taste, but not enough to really satisfy? Go to the store and buy some more? Look for a cow to milk?

This is a very simple example, but it is really quite rich, quite thick. First, there are *customary practices* — the practice of drinking milk, going to the store, possibly milking a cow. Second, there is the *good or goods* at issue — in this case, milk that is not only full of calcium but will satisfy both thirst and hunger (if, that is, it is really good milk and not dirty, spoiled, or simply white water). Third, there is the *principle of distribution* — who should get what. Should the parent drink it first or sacrifice for the children? Or should the youngest get it first on the assumption that older children and adults can go hungry and thirsty for longer periods of time? Fourth, there is the *vision of life* that guides the action of the parent. Are children valued and seen as intrinsic goods that should be preserved at all costs? Is it important for them to grow and, if so, grow in order to become what and to do what? Should parents serve children or children serve the needs of parents? If parents should sacrifice for their children, why? What is the overarching purpose of life that justifies parental self-sacrificial love? Fifth, and finally, what are the *conditions that constrain and pattern* the parent's action? Where does clean milk come from? Does one go to stores to purchase it? If so, does it require money? Does it require an automobile to get there? Or does it require a cow? And what happens if the parent runs out of money, has no way to get to the store, or does not have a cow?

Our practices take place in various social and natural environmental contexts, patterns, and systems that shape and limit them. Practical reason must make judgments about these factors at the same time that it attends to the more dominant factors of what life is about and to more general principles of obligation. And what does practical reason have to do with love? My answer is this: every act of love assumes a justification provided by practical reason and every exercise of practical reason is somehow shaped by the investments of love. This explains the juxtaposition time and again throughout this book of love and practical reason.

Practical reason implicitly or explicitly makes judgments about all of these five dimensions when it is considering a moral action. More specifically, *practical reason has the task of connecting these various dimensions, weaving its various subdimensions together into a working whole.* If it is critical or reflective practical reason, it has the task of testing and possibly reconstructing assumptions that are brought from the various dimensions into the final synthesis that feeds our deliberative decisions. Sometimes it simply retains traditional assumptions about each of these dimensions. At other times, however, it consciously deepens, tests, and reorganizes assumptions at each of these levels.

When practical reason thinks critically about each of these dimensions, it goes backward — becomes both reflective and historical — and asks: Is milk really all that important, all that good? Is it possible to eat or drink (practice consuming) something else? Is going to the store the only way to get it? Does the parent really understand the nature of parental obligation? Does he (or she) really hold the right vision of the purpose of life, and is he interpreting his beliefs properly? And, finally, does he understand the constraints and possibilities of the situation accurately? All of this retrospective reflection is done in order to move forward *into the future.* Practical reason is about the future, but it takes a lot of thinking about the past to get to the future — a fact of life that future-oriented Americans tend to overlook.[7]

Most contemporary moral psychologies shortchange this reflective process and thereby fail to contribute all that they could. But even if they do not explicitly address all of these dimensions, one can often find hidden assumptions about the ignored dimensions floating in the background of their more thematized theoretical statements. We will find unacknowledged visions about the nature of life in psychoanalytic,

---

7. Although David Brooks rightly shows how Americans are incurably future-oriented, he fails to notice how much thinking about the past is required to properly act toward the future. See his *On Paradise Drive* (New York: Simon and Schuster, 2004).

humanistic, and evolutionary psychological views of moral development. We will notice in the various moral psychologies different implicit principles of obligation and different theories about the premoral — sometimes called nonmoral — goods of life that more explicitly moral principles should try to organize. We will see this particularly through the multidimensional nature of Erikson's view of moral maturity in his concept of generativity discussed in Chapter 7.

Multidimensionality in Niebuhr's Christian Ethics

So far, what I have said is fairly formal. I have not tipped my hand as to how I view the main substance of Christian ethics or, to say it differently, practical reason within a Christian narrative vision of life. I should now give the reader a taste of how I view the content of Christian ethics before discussing its relation to contemporary moral psychology. I will do this in a way that illustrates how the multidimensional view of praxis and practical reason sketched above works out in the Christian faith, at least as seen through the eyes of Reinhold Niebuhr, one of North America's most influential and widely read theologians. I also will repeatedly make use of the French philosopher Paul Ricoeur and create something of a dance — a clarifying dance, I hope — between Niebuhr and Ricoeur. I will use Ricoeur to do what philosophy can do for theology, that is, to help clarify and give added plausibility to a religious substance which philosophy as such cannot provide.

In my book *A Fundamental Practical Theology*, I examined the theological ethics of Reinhold Niebuhr from the perspective of these five dimensions of practical reflection.[8] Niebuhr is generally not perceived to have elaborated a multidimensional theological perspective. And indeed, he did not explicitly do so. But the dimensions are in his thought nonetheless, as they are, at least implicitly, in all manifestations of the human experience and action. Niebuhr will give us a good example of what a Christian ethic looks like from the perspective of these five dimensions. In order to fit the contours of an explicitly Christian theological view of praxis, however, I will discuss the five dimensions in a slightly different order. I will move from practices to goods, and then to narratives, principles of obligation, and contexts. Hence, in contrast to the order given the di-

8. Don Browning, *A Fundamental Practical Theology* (Minneapolis: Fortress, 1991), pp. 95-109.

mensions above, and the order given when I discuss Ricoeur on the five dimensions, I will here present the narrative dimension prior to the obligational dimension. Why? Because in Christian theology, moral obligation is derived *in part* from the perspective of the Christian narrative that tells us about God's creation of humans in the *imago Dei,* that is, in relation to God and in the image of God. Hence, the narrative helps ground our obligations to our neighbor.

The First Dimension: Practices

First, Niebuhr had little to say theoretically about the importance of practices, habits, virtues, and the rules that govern them. He was not a theoretician of practices in the sense of Alasdair MacIntyre or Pierre Bourdieu.[9] From another perspective, however, it can be said that he was analyzing the thickness of concrete practices on almost every page of his writings. Niebuhr's respect for insights in Marxism and philosophical pragmatism demonstrates his appreciation for both the power and distortions of concrete practices. He was aware as well of their perpetual need for critique. The industrial practices of modern societies, the labor practices that isolated poor populations in inner societies, the practices of nations in the exercise of power, the practices of democratic citizens in pursuit of their self-interests, and the distortions of family practices in the pursuit of security and intimacy — these repeatedly were his point of departure in his multidimensional theological ethics or, to say it differently, his multidimensional and theologically qualified understanding of practical reason. In his own way, he was aware of one of the central points of these first two chapters, that human practices are both important and theory-laden. Practices are encoded with many additional dimensions of meaning that have both moral and religious significance.

The Second Dimension: Premoral Goods

Second, Niebuhr animates his theological ethics with a portrait of humans as finite and desiring creatures striving for the goods of life. We see

---

9. Alasdair MacIntyre, *After Virtue* (Notre Dame, Ind.: University of Notre Dame Press, 1988); Pierre Bourdieu, *The Logic of Practice* (Stanford, Calif.: Stanford University Press, 1990), pp. 53-54.

this in the first volume of *The Nature and Destiny of Man* when he depicts a human being as "a child of nature, subject to its vicissitudes, compelled by its necessities, driven by its impulses and confined within the brevity . . . which nature permits."[10] From one perspective, such words suggest the finitude of human existence. From another, they show how Niebuhr was aware of the creaturely, desiring, and teleological aspects of humans — vitalities that were also for him a source of both form and creativity.[11]

In the language of Ricoeur and my five dimensions, these features of the human being demonstrate how Niebuhr understood our creaturely search for the premoral goods of life. Indeed, he mentioned a few tendencies that were firmly anchored in our animal nature. Most of these were gleaned from biblical insights but secondarily from a reading of Darwin and Freud — two scholars who also influenced much of modern moral psychology. He thought humans had survival instincts and primal needs for attachment (he would have liked contemporary attachment theory, used by *Hardwired,* as he indeed liked the work of psychoanalyst Erik Erikson, whom I discuss in a later chapter). He believed humans have sexual urges that express themselves through the differentiation of male and female. Humans have needs for material acquisition and needs for group relatedness. For Niebuhr, our basic human instincts were not just sources of vitality; they were also sources of some degree of form and direction.[12]

But Niebuhr makes no simple distinction between instinct and the higher levels of the human spirit. For him, the levels of language, culture, and history interpenetrate with the vitalities of instinct much as they do — we will soon learn — in the thought of Paul Ricoeur. This synthesis of nature and history, instinct and language, contributes to the higher accomplishments of spirit but also to the ambiguities of human creativity. Niebuhr writes,

> The natural impulse of sex is, for instance, an indispensable condition of all higher forms of family organization as it is the negative force of destructive sex aberrations. In the same way, the natural cohesion of tribe and race is the foundation of higher political creations as also the negative determinant of interracial and international anarchy.[13]

10. Reinhold Niebuhr, *Nature and Destiny of Man,* 2 vols. (New York: Charles Scribner's Sons, 1941-1943), vol. I, p. 3.

11. Niebuhr, *Nature and Destiny of Man,* vol. I, pp. 26-27.

12. Niebuhr, *Nature and Destiny of Man,* vol. I, p. 27.

13. Niebuhr, *Nature and Destiny of Man,* vol. I, p. 27.

It is important to note that Niebuhr believed that all of these tendencies were *premorally good* when viewed from the perspective of the ontology, that is, the view of being, implicit in the Christian doctrine of creation. But it is also well-known that Niebuhr viewed desiring and finite humans as living in dialectical tension with their capacity for freedom and self-transcendence.[14] It is from the anxiety of this freedom that sin emerges — the prideful and sensual drive to protect oneself from the anxiety of freedom rather than trust in God. It is difficult for secular psychology to understand this view of sin. Sin is not for Niebuhr, first of all, wrong or evil willful acts. It is, at its most profound level, a response to the pervasive insecurity of being a finite and free human being. Sin is our tendency to overreach or, indeed, underreach in an effort to secure ourselves in the face of human finitude. The category of sin is relevant, I will argue, for the dialogue between moral psychology and Christian ethics. And Niebuhr's understanding of sin, when rightly understood, viewed it as a more empirical concept — in the sense of the broadly descriptive radical empiricism of William James — than contemporary psychology understands or is willing to admit.

The Third Dimension: The Christian Narrative

Surrounding this view of the human as a desiring, free, anxious, and sinful creature is a third dimension of Niebuhr's ethics: a narrative — cosmological in scope — about the nature and action of God in relation to the world. Moral psychologists should not get too nervous when the idea of narrative is introduced to clarify ethics and morality. I will contend in Chapter 8 that some kind of narrative envelope or framework, often implicit but still discernible, surrounds almost all of the modern psychologies, including the moral psychologies. So, if the modern psychologies have their implicit, and untested, narratives about the deep meanings of life, why should we not give consideration to the Christian narrative, a narrative that has achieved classic status in societies around the world and been tested both existentially and conceptually over many centuries?

Niebuhr unfolds his view of the Christian narrative around a group of deep metaphors taken from the Jewish and Christian Scriptures and further elaborated throughout their respective histories. In these sources, God is repeatedly presented as Creator, Governor, Redeemer, and

14. Niebuhr, *Nature and Destiny of Man,* vol. 1, pp. 3-4.

Sustainer.[15] Niebuhr believes that these features of God are dimly revealed in general experience and explicitly manifest in the revelation of Jesus Christ. These metaphors provide the terms within which God's relation to the world and to humans is played out; they constitute the framework that defines the broad trajectory of Christian anthropology. God as Creator means that the world is created as good, and even the material world and basic human desires are good in the premoral sense of goodness. This goodness includes our sexual and acquisitive desires, our need for attachment, our need to protect ourselves, and even our aggressive tendencies. From the standpoint of God the Creator, all of these human tendencies have their proper place in human life and indeed in the entire created world. Furthermore, humans are dependent for all these goods on their *relation to God*. This relationality, in fact, is an important part of the image of God in humans. This is one of the meanings of the idea that humans are made in "the image of God" (Gen. 1:27); they are irrevocably related to God and dependent on God for the goods of life.

According to the biblical narrative, the human condition of finitude, freedom, and basic anxiety (in contrast to neurotic anxiety) is also good — but in the premoral sense of the word. Sin and moral evil enter the world not through our basic desires and needs but through the way we handle them in relation to the anxiety precipitated by freedom and finitude as well as the threats of other people. This point will be very important for understanding the insights and limitations of contemporary moral psychology — especially evolutionary psychology — in comprehending the place in human life of the premoral motivations of attachment, kin altruism, self-actualization, assertion, and pleasure.

In Niebuhr's view of the Christian narrative, God emerges as Governor in the face of sin and the broken world that follows from it. God as Governor judges injustice and maintains the moral framework of the world. The metaphors of Governor communicate God's concern for justice but also God's continuing creative goodness. We will see how the tension between God's justice and God's goodness is maintained in Christian symbolism as the book unfolds. But this same narrative contains an image of God the Redeemer — a Redeemer who works through all history but acts decisively in Jesus the Christ. These initiatives by God as both Judge and Redeemer provide both the judgment against sin and the grace and the forgiveness needed to overcome in principle sin's prideful and idolatrous response to anxiety and freedom.

---

15. Niebuhr, *Nature and Destiny of Man,* vol. 1, p. 132.

Finally, the Christian story also sees God as Sustainer. This refers to the continuing presence of God the Spirit with the redeemed and indeed with the wider world beyond the church. God the Sustainer inspires and sustains humans to endure in hope and faith in spite of the losses of life. As I will say in more detail in Chapter 9, moral action helps humans reconcile some of the conflicting goods of life. But complete harmony of the goods of life can never be fully accomplished. Finitude, disease, death, and natural evil (in contrast to moral evil) are always with us. The narrative of God the Sustainer, the promise of Christian eschatology, and the assurance of the resurrection give meaning, courage, and hope in face of the impossibility of ever achieving the full harmony of the goods of life in this world. Disappointment and loss are inevitable. As I write these lines, the dramas of the deaths of the allegedly brain-dead Terri Schiavo and of Pope John Paul II have just recently been played out before the world's consciousness. Among the various lessons that both deaths conveyed was one of the inevitability of death and the loss of the goods of life. Moral action can reconcile some of the conflicts of life, but moral action cannot preserve us forever. More is needed; at the least, more is yearned for. And the struggle to find hope and a broader meaning beyond the inevitable moral clashes of finite goods was portrayed with dramatic clarity before the eyes of a questing and seeking world population. The idea of God the Sustainer gained heightened plausibility during this time.

I often refer to this narrative as the "envelope" that surrounds, contains, and largely, although not totally, shapes Niebuhr's ethic and its several dimensions. But the full content of Niebuhr's theological-ethical view of the human is not derived from this narrative alone. In this, I think that Niebuhr is faithful to the Christian tradition. The Christian faith time and again absorbed and celebrated insights into the human that were not entirely derived from this narrative. In the case of Niebuhr, his view of humans as a dialectic between nature and spirit was derived in part from a kind of phenomenological analysis of the situation of being human. More specifically, it was a product of radical empiricism in the sense that William James used that term. Or, to say it more simply, Niebuhr believed this dialectical view of humans could be derived from the general testimony of experience in addition to the insights of revelation.[16] Niebuhr held that

16. Reinhold Niebuhr, *The Self and the Dramas of History* (New York: Scribner, 1955). It is often overlooked that Niebuhr had a healthy respect for experience when it is conceived in its broadest dimensions. He was critical of narrowly scientific approaches to experience that measure it in terms of discrete data. Experience in the larger sense — as William James

the reality of sin itself is also evident from experience even though its deeper meaning is both revealed and measured by God in the dramas of judgment and redemption. Insofar as experience testifies to sin, Niebuhr thought that modern psychology should pay attention to it in its own empirical research. And as we have already seen, his insights into certain natural tendencies of humans were informed by evolutionary theory and psychoanalysis, somewhat analogously to the way, as we will see, the great medieval Roman Catholic theologian Thomas Aquinas used the psychobiology of Aristotle. This observation about Niebuhr is important to highlight; it shows he held that the multiple dimensions of the human *cannot* be fully derived from any one of them, even the narrative dimension. This is why he was able to absorb, even while modifying, insights from experience and from disciplines and sources other than Scripture and theology — even those from the discipline of modern psychology.

The Fourth Dimension: Moral Obligation

The fourth dimension of Niebuhr's theological ethics is the more distinctively moral dimension. But it does not stand alone. It assumes the natural creaturely needs of the human being and the deep metaphors of the Christian narrative — in other words, the second and third dimensions discussed above. This is one of the more problematic areas of Niebuhr's view of the human. It has to do with his understanding of Christian love and what this means for Christian ethics and obligation. Niebuhr believed that self-sacrificial love, exemplified by Christ's death on the cross, is the highest expression of Christian morality. We are called by God to be ready to lay down our lives for our neighbor.[17] For Niebuhr, this is the perfect — the ideal — love which Christians should live by. Because of finitude, sin, and human weakness, however, this is a perfection that "is not attainable in history."[18] At best, it is an ideal by which life is measured but which can be attained only in momentary and fragmentary ways. As the reader can imagine, such a view of Christian love and obligation would raise the most profound skepticism of almost every conceivable branch of

---

used the term — testified to the ubiquitous reality of anxiety and sin. Jamesian radical empiricism provided for Niebuhr some of the values that European phenomenology would provide for a slightly later generation. We should be reminded, however, that Husserl himself got many of his first insights into phenomenology from William James.

17. Niebuhr, *The Nature and Destiny of Man,* vol. 2, p. 74.
18. Niebuhr, *Nature and Destiny of Man,* vol. 2, p. 68.

modern moral psychology. To put it bluntly, in contemporary moral psychology, self-sacrifice is out, and self-affirmation is in. There are some nuances to this generalization about psychology today, but there are few exceptions.

But even Niebuhr seemed to think that it was unrealistic, if not impossible, to live in a mode of perpetual self-sacrificial love. So, he claimed that at the level of actual historical existence, love and justice in the form of a reciprocal kind of give and take were the highest that humans realistically could attain.[19] Love as self-sacrifice was for him an ideal that was needed to keep love and justice as reciprocity from deteriorating into crass self-serving egoism. Love in the real world, in Niebuhr's view of Christian ethics, required a realistic balance of power.

As the reader will learn, I use Niebuhr in close association with Paul Ricoeur and the Catholic moral theologian Louis Janssens for my conversation between moral psychology and Christian ethics. But even though I rely significantly on Niebuhr, I also criticize him a bit, just as I do Ricoeur and Janssens. It is not my goal here to give a full review and evaluation of the multiple criticisms, especially by feminists, of Niebuhr's elevation of sacrificial love over mutuality and justice as the touchstone of his Christian ethics — his Christian practical reason.[20] But let me at least say this; in my view, Niebuhr makes two mistakes. Correcting them is important for a successful exchange between Christian ethics and the moral implications of the contemporary psychologies.

First, he debases a full theory of love as mutuality and equal-regard (concepts I borrow from Janssens) by reducing it to conditioned reciprocal exchange. There are forms of mutuality and equal-regard, we will soon learn, that take the other as an end in himself or herself, just as they expect the other to take oneself as an end. Mutual love does not necessarily mean a tit-for-tat exchange between persons and communities in which giving is always conditional on receiving something in return. Love as mutuality and equal-regard can itself be unconditional. This is true even in this finite and broken world.

Second, Niebuhr identifies Christian love as *agapē* too completely with self-sacrificial love. He never adopts the truly strong *agapē* — the strong self-sacrificial view of love — associated with the great Anders Nygren, whom I discuss later. But he modifies Nygren's view only slightly.

19. Niebuhr, *Nature and Destiny of Man,* vol. 2, p. 69.
20. For one of the more articulate critiques, see Barbara Andolsen, "Agape in Feminist Ethics," *Journal of Religious Ethics* 9 (Spring 1984): 69-81.

I argue, following Janssens, that a more balanced view of Christian love (the obligational dimension for Christian ethics) is to understand it as mutuality and equal-regard for both *other* and *self.* The center of Christian love is a strenuous form of mutuality that regards the other as seriously as I do myself but that also expects the other to do the same toward me. The modern moral psychologies, as we will see, actually have something to contribute on this point. I further will argue that Christian love defined by the concept of love as equal-regard is more justifiable both biblically *and* philosophically.

It follows from this view, however, that we should think of self-sacrificial love not as the Christian ideal as Niebuhr does, but as a moment in the fullness of love, required, in the midst of sin and brokenness, to renew love as mutuality.[21] But this is a concept that I will expand later in the book. In championing the equal-regard view of Christian love as a slight correction to Niebuhr, I will be relying extensively not only on the moral theology of the Catholic Janssens but also on that of the Protestant Gene Outka and on the feminist theologies of Christine Gudorf and Barbara Andolsen.

It is not, as I have indicated, my goal to solve immediately the difficulties with the obligational dimension of Niebuhr's view of Christian ethics. I mean rather to show how, even within his own formulations, his theory of obligation — his view of love and justice — is qualified by, but has a degree of autonomy from, his view of the Christian narrative. In spite of sin's corruption of reason, Niebuhr believed we retain sufficient moral reason to make universal and just ethical judgments. This means that even as sinners, we have the moral capacity to view moral conflicts from the perspective of our neighbor's interests and to imagine universally generalizable solutions. According to Niebuhr, sin does not destroy our moral-cognitive capacity to make such reasoned judgments. *Instead, sin simply impairs our capacity to fulfill them in action.*[22]

This means, as we will see, that like the ethics of Kant, Kohlberg, Rawls, and Ricoeur, Niebuhr's Christian ethics held that humans enjoy a realm of moral reason not totally derived from either revelation or tradition and not completely corrupted by sin. Moral cognitive capacity is a genuine dimension of the human, even though, as Ricoeur has forcefully argued, it always works dialectically in relation to the materials of narra-

---

21. See Louis Janssens, "The Norms and Priorities of a Love Ethics," *Louvain Studies* 6 (spring 1977): 207-38.

22. Niebuhr, *Nature and Destiny of Man,* vol. 1, pp. 284-85.

tive and tradition, on the one hand, and the materials of affection and desire, on the other. Human beings, corrupted by sin as they are, *think* better morally than they *act*. All of this is quite important for the discussion between Christian ethics and moral psychology, especially those moral psychologies influenced by the commanding cognitive moral theories of Lawrence Kohlberg, as I will show in Chapters 2 and 3.

The Fifth Dimension: The Contextual

Finally, the fifth dimension has to do with Niebuhr's awareness of the social and natural systems shaping the human. Niebuhr was both weak and strong at this dimension of his theological ethics or, to say it differently, his theologically shaped practical reason. To my knowledge, he had nothing directly to say about environmental or ecological factors that condition and constrain human action; these concerns had not emerged in academic theology during Niebuhr's era. On the social side, he was aware of the challenges of industrialization, especially how the demands of efficiency and profit affected the wages, health, and freedom of the working classes and supported the privileges of the managerial classes.[23] He was even more aware of how philosophical and religious ideals can function to legitimate both class domination and class rebellion — how, for example, Platonism and Aristotelianism helped legitimate feudalism, or how Romanticism fueled the imagination of Marxism and the lower classes.[24] Even though Niebuhr had not worked out fully the influence of social systems on humans, the attention he did give to this issue provides us with the space to apply and further develop this dimension of praxis within Christian ethics.

It is important for Christian ethics to understand and differentiate the thickness of human experience and praxis. It is important for scientific moral psychology to understand the full thickness — the full multidimensionality — of the human experience it studies from the psychological perspective. I will try to amplify these remarks in the chapters that follow. It is the multidimensional nature of human experience that will provide us with the resources for helping Christian communities to function as authoritative communities — communities faithful to the Chris-

23. Niebuhr, *Nature and Destiny of Man*, vol. 1, pp. 49-51.
24. Niebuhr, *Nature and Destiny of Man*, vol. 1, pp. 49-53.

tian story yet able to provide an element of critique to their own life and the life of the larger society.

This brief attempt to illustrate how Christian anthropology can be understood as containing five interacting dimensions will be useful in the chapters to come. It will help us understand in what areas contemporary moral psychology can contribute to Christian ethics. It will also help us grasp the ways in which Christian ethics can and should critique the modern moral psychologies.

Chapter 2

Moral Psychology and
Critical Hermeneutics

It is now time to talk more concretely about human development as seen by various perspectives in contemporary moral psychology. I begin with reflections on the concept of "moral development." For many educated people, the study of moral development by definition belongs to the field of moral psychology. Moral psychology is the academic discipline that is often thought to have the most profound insight into the processes of moral formation. Others, however, think of traditional religion; religious communities, they hold, are the primary carriers of the ethical truths and processes of socialization needed to create moral people. Immediately, then, the rather harmless idea of moral development plunges us into the conflict between religion and science. Psychology, it is thought, is a science; religion, it is held, is about our relation to the ultimate — something about which science, some believe, can tell us very little.

Science versus Tradition

Behind the conflict between science and religion on the moral development of persons is the deeper philosophical tension between foundationalism and nonfoundationalism or anti-foundationalism. The foundationalism versus anti-foundationalism discussion is absolutely central to the question of relating moral psychology to Christian ethics. This distinction refers to a debate in the philosophy of science about how genuine knowledge, both moral and scientific, should be acquired. Foundationalists, as I mentioned in the introduction, believe that true knowledge comes from rejecting or bracketing alleged forms of knowledge handed down by tradition, custom, or history, and building knowledge on something certain and objective. Candidates proposed by philosophers for such certain beginning points have been the clear and distinct evidence of sense data (what we can see, touch, or smell), scientific experiment (what we can publicly replicate in a controlled manner), irrefutable *a priori* ideas (assumptions without which thinking and experience would not make sense), or phenomenologically described pervasive structures of consciousness of the kind that the German philosopher Edmund Husserl tried to grasp. Nonfoundationalists, on the other hand, believe that cultural and religious traditions are the carriers of reliable knowledge, and that, at best, science or *a priori* intuitions add only certain minor clarifications to what our traditions already tell us.[1]

When it comes to the question of how humans develop morally, foundationalists believe that true knowledge about this will be discovered scientifically, most likely from the various fields of psychology, whether psychoanalytic, humanistic, cognitive, or evolutionary psychological. Nonfoundationalists are more likely to believe that our religious and cultural traditions already have discovered both what moral persons are and how to form them. This book argues that *the nonfoundationalists are right, but only if they acknowledge the important role the sciences can play in the criticism, refinement, and appropriation of the moral wisdom of our traditions.*

Modern Psychology: The Foundationalist Turn

Most of the modern psychologies of moral development have been foundationalist to the core. They have aspired to find an objective, value-free, and tradition-free way of talking about moral development. This means erecting views of moral development that would be free of tradition — and not only free of the dominant Christian views that have shaped so much of Western culture, but free of every other tradition as well.

But total objectivity in the field of moral psychology has proven to be something very difficult actually to achieve. It is difficult to imagine what morality is without some reference to a culture's various traditions of moral thinking. Because much of moral psychology has aspired to premature objectivity, much of the field is in a state of crisis. Its scientific aspira-

---

1. Richard Bernstein, *Beyond Objectivism and Relativism* (Philadelphia: University of Pennsylvania Press, 1983), pp. 1-20.

tions toward objectivity are now widely thought to have been highly problematic. It did much of its research with unstated or inadequate pre-empirical models of what mature moral action and reflection are really like.

Let's look at some examples of how this happens. Take Sigmund Freud: he believed that his psychoanalytic insights into moral development were scientific and value-free. Morality is formed, he taught, by infants and children emotionally identifying with the powerful parental figures in their lives, especially the father. In order to retain the father's love, children identify with the negative prohibitions of the father and internalize them into their inner psychological lives, creating what Freud called the superego.[2] But this made moral development primarily an unconscious process of taking in the values — and often the prejudices — of parents. It is true that many people never go beyond their parents' moral teachings; indeed, many young people struggle to achieve even that. Although Freud's view suggested that the morally mature person would sometime and somehow become autonomous from the parental superego, he gave us no criteria for judging how such autonomy could be regarded as moral.[3] Freud's description of moral development teetered on the edge of foundationalism; it suggested that the autonomous moral person would be rational and experimental, something like the modern research scientist. Tradition, in the sense of the internalized superego, was dethroned, but no clear alternative was put in its place except some vague sense of autonomy plus a firmer grasp of reality.

Both Niebuhr and Ricoeur, as we will learn, in their different ways learned much from Freud, but they rejected his foundationalist conclusion that morality could, in the end, be fashioned on the experimental and neutral grounds of science itself. Both gained reinforcement from Freud, however, for a truth that they first had learned from Judaism and Christianity and, in the case of Ricoeur, also from Aristotle. This truth is that humans are creatures of nature with desires, impulses, wants, and needs. Although they did not deny this, they both would make something quite different out of this insight than did Freud. Both of them made much out of how tradition and the classics of a tradition provide patterns, habits, and linguistic codes which make it possible for these desires, wants, and needs to find truly reliable and lasting — truly good — satisfaction.

2. Sigmund Freud, *The Ego and the Id* (London: Hogarth, 1957), pp. 34-53.

3. See Philip Rieff, *Freud: The Mind of the Moralist* (Chicago: University of Chicago Press, 1979).

A branch of psychology called humanistic psychology also wanted to find a ground for moral development that was both scientific and liberated from religious and cultural traditions. Humanistic psychology was widely popular from 1960 to 1990 and is still influential on some psychotherapies and certain programs in moral education.[4] It is an approach to personality development and psychotherapy identified with the names of Carl Rogers, Abraham Maslow, and Fritz Perls.[5] All of these psychologists taught that the moral development of persons is a matter of learning how to listen to, reflect on, and evaluate one's own organismic experience and capacity for self-actualization. Religious and cultural traditions — whether mediated by parents, religious traditions, or local communities — should be at best advisory to the final center of authority found in the biologically grounded self-actualization tendencies of the individual person. Much of what these psychologists said was attractive. "Trust your feelings," they told us; "they are full of moral wisdom." We heard from these psychologists that our feelings tell us what we really want, and that what we really, really want — down deep — is good and easily harmonized with the desires of others.

Only gradually did it become apparent that this view of morality was a form of what moral philosophers call "ethical egoism," according to which morality is what satisfies and fulfills the individual.[6] This implicit moral principle lacked the main feature of genuine morality, namely, the capacity to mediate conflicts between the needs and desires of the individual and the needs and desires of others.[7] In face of the inevitable conflict between wants within ourselves as well as the conflict between our wants and others' wants, the humanistic psychologists had to sneak into their writings two unstated and undefended assumptions. They had to assume a final metaphysical harmony between all authentic feelings of the self and all authentic desires of all other people, or they had to assume that

---

4. For a review of the moral and religious horizon of the modern psychologies, see Don Browning, *Religious Thought and the Modern Psychologies* (Minneapolis: Fortress, 1987); for the influence of humanistic psychology on the values-clarification approach to moral education, see Johannes van der Ven, *Formation of the Moral Self* (Grand Rapids: Eerdmans, 1998), p. 235.

5. For representative works of the humanistic psychologists, see Carl Rogers, *Client-Centered Therapy* (Boston: Houghton Mifflin, 1951); Abraham Maslow, *Motivation and Personality* (New York: Harper and Brothers, 1954); Frederick Perls, Ralph Hefferline, and Paul Goodman, *Gestalt Therapy* (New York: Dell, 1951).

6. Browning, *Religious Thought and the Modern Psychologies*, p. 72.

7. William Frankena, *Ethics* (Englewood Cliffs, N.J.: Prentice-Hall, 1973), p. 19.

when conflict was real and unbending, other people had to relent and give way to our own self-actualizations.[8] The first assumption about the hidden harmony of all authentic feelings requires, however, a huge metaphysical leap of faith — a quasi-religious hypothesis about the ultimate nature of the universe as being in concord and free of conflict. In the name of getting rid of religion, humanistic psychology opened the door for a highly romantic and harmonious religious worldview to come creeping back into the horizon of its thinking. The second assumption — the right to put one's own self-actualization before all others — gave birth to a new ethical egoism and a culture of interpersonal conflict and dominance, all in the name of therapeutic health.

In spite of these striking inadequacies, humanistic psychology has influenced the images of health and human fulfillment in much of modern psychotherapy and even the program in moral education called "values clarification" — an approach widely used in schools, prisons, and churches throughout the United States and in other countries as well.[9]

The humanistic psychologies, with their biologistic understanding of moral development, have affinities with the more recent claims of evolutionary psychology. This school of psychology believes that moral values are embedded in the biological processes of sexual selection: the mechanisms of kin altruism and natural selection. Kin altruism is the primal inclination shared by all reproducing creatures to protect, care for, and sometimes even empathize with those beings who carry and extend their own genes (offspring and relatives).[10] This universal tendency in the insect and animal world, which includes humans, implies another concept — that of inclusive fitness. Evolutionary psychology's concept of inclusive fitness claims that creatures procreating through sexual selection are concerned about the survival and well-being of not only their own genes but also the offspring and relatives that carry their genes.[11] This is not just a selfish process, as Richard Dawkins has argued.[12] It can also be seen as the

---

8. Browning, *Religious Thought and the Modern Psychologies,* pp. 74-75.

9. Sidney Simon, Leland Howe, and Howard Kirchenbaum, *Values Clarification: A Handbook of Practical Strategies for Teachers and Students* (New York: Hart, 1971).

10. For a lucid discussion of kin altruism in evolutionary psychology, see Robert Wright, *The Moral Animal* (New York: Pantheon, 1994), pp. 158-61.

11. The central breakthrough redefining the meaning of fitness to entail inclusive fitness, instead of just the fitness of the individual gene, was accomplished by William D. Hamilton, "The Genetical Evolution of Social Behavior, II," *Journal of Theoretical Biology* 7 (1964): 17-52.

12. Richard Dawkins, *The Selfish Gene* (New York: Oxford University Press, 1976).

ground of sympathy and identification with others, as primatologist Frans de Waal and biologist Shelley Taylor have contended.[13] The processes of natural selection, the theory goes, have tended to retain creatures with these sympathetic capacities because of their adaptive qualities for themselves and their genetic family line.

In *The Moral Sense,* James Q. Wilson develops a link between evolutionary psychology and the moral sentiment theories of Scottish philosophers Francis Hutcheson, David Hume, and Adam Smith.[14] He argues that kin altruism and inclusive fitness give rise to moral sentiments that can become elaborated into an adult sense of sympathy, fairness, self-control, and even duty.[15] These sentiments develop and mature within the context of the deep investments of family life but can gradually be extended analogically and universalized to others outside the family.[16] The moral philosopher Peter Singer, without special reference to the Scottish school of moral sentiments, has also argued that morality is the analogical extension of the inclinations of kin altruism beyond the immediate circle of close kin to other humans and indeed other creatures.[17]

But this claim about the relation of kin altruism to morality is not necessarily a new idea. Without the benefit of modern evolutionary theory, Thomas Aquinas, as far back as the thirteenth century, argued that morality was the analogical extension outward to non-kin of parents' love for their own flesh and blood and their children's love of them in turn.[18] In the case of Aquinas, however, the idea of kin altruism as the ground of morality was supplemented by an additional idea. This was a theological symbolism that conveyed the concept that all humans everywhere were children of God the divine parent and for this reason should be treated as kin through our analogically extending outward to all persons the biologically based love first found in the affection between natural parents and their children. The logic went like this: since I am a child of God and all other

13. Frans de Waal, *Good Natured: The Origins of Right and Wrong in Humans and Other Animals* (Cambridge, Mass.: Harvard University Press, 1996), pp. 78-83; Shelley Taylor, *The Tending Instinct* (New York: Henry Holt, 2002), p. 158.

14. James Q. Wilson, *The Moral Sense* (New York: Free Press, 1993).

15. Wilson, *The Moral Sense,* pp. 29-120.

16. Wilson, *The Moral Sense,* pp. 192-200.

17. Peter Singer, *The Expanding Circle: Ethics and Sociobiology* (New York: Farrar, Straus, and Giroux, 1981), pp. 93-108.

18. For the classic argument to support the analogical extension of parental investment in their own flesh-and-blood children to the love of other children as children of God, see Thomas Aquinas, "Of the Order of Charity," *Summa Theologica* (London: R. and T. Washbourne, 1917), II, ii, Q. 26.

persons are children of God, I should treat all people in some sense as I would my own children or, at least, with the love with which my parents treated me. Later in the book, I will say more about this similarity and this great difference between Aquinas and evolutionary psychology. I also will show similarities between Aquinas, Niebuhr, and Ricoeur, at least in their deep respect for the vitalities and attachments of nature. But I can say this for now: both evolutionary psychology and Aquinas (as well as Niebuhr and Ricoeur) saw morality as in some sense growing out of biology.

Both humanistic psychology and evolutionary psychology are doubtless correct in holding that our organismic experience or deep inclinations toward gene immortality, kin altruism, and inclusive fitness *under certain conditions* contribute to morally relevant inclinations and sentiments. *As we will see more fully below, however, neither school of moral development understands the difference between such premoral organismic valuations or kin altruistic inclinations and more properly moral inclinations, sentiments, values, or principles.* Nor do they understand the social, cultural, and hermeneutic conditions under which our morally relevant (yet still premoral) biological inclinations are selected, nourished, or enhanced and our morally suspect inclinations are channeled, sometimes suppressed, but finally redirected toward more morally worthy ends.

The authors of *Hardwired to Connect* are more sophisticated. They believe, as do the humanistic and evolutionary psychologists, that ethics has its foundations in our biological substratum — our desires, as Paul Ricoeur would say. But the desires, although basic to the development of morality, are not in themselves sufficient. Take the desire or need to connect or attach. *Hardwired* sees this as one of our most fundamental human desires, far more basic in the end than Freud's desire for sexual or pleasurable release. Alan Schore, of the University of California School of Medicine, has done a great deal of research within the field of neuroscience to extend the ground-breaking work of John Bowlby on attachment.[19] From the standpoint of this book, Bowlby's work is important because, in a unique way, even though it transcended the psychological insights of Freud, it also combined them with the biological insights of Darwin.[20] This ended in giving us a thicker and richer understanding of the nature of human instincts, desires, and needs — one that made the

---

19. For further discussion of attachment theory since the seminal work of John Bowlby in his three-volume *Attachment and Loss* (New York: Basic, 1969, 1973, 1981), see Allan Schore, *Affect Dysregulation and Disorders of the Self* (New York: W. W. Norton, 2003), pp. 55-70.

20. Schore, *Affect Dysregulation and Disorders of the Self*, pp. 57-58.

need for attachment even more basic than the need for pleasure or aggression. Schore, who has researched the animal and human need to attach or connect, summarizes his work with the following words: "The idea is that we are born to form attachments, that our brains are physically wired to develop in tandem with another's, through emotional communication beginning before words are spoken."[21] Schore goes on to say, "If these things go awry, you're going to have seeds of psychological problems, of difficulty coping, stress in human relations, substance abuse, those sorts of problems later on."[22]

What kind of evidence does Schore have in mind that leads him to put so much weight on our premoral needs for connection? Some of it comes from research on animals rather than humans. For instance, Larry Young of Emory University has found that, for rats, early nurturing experience has a significant effect on their capacity to handle later stressful situations.[23] This same research shows something even more astounding. Not only does good nurturing increase the pup's emotional resilience, it can also be passed on to future generations, developing a line of psychological strength.[24] Such findings seem to relate to humans as well. The authors of *Hardwired* write,

> In fact, the presence in humans of many of these same hormones connected to sexual bonding, birth, and lactation suggests that they may also be relevant to human behavior and relationships. Available human data, as well as these and other similar findings from animal studies, suggest that our deep need for attachment and connectedness to others can be traced back to the brain's deepest centers of reward and gratification.[25]

I will summarize more research like this as the book proceeds. But I want to make a specific point related to my discussion of Freud, humanistic psychology, and evolutionary psychology. All of these psychologies overstate the contribution of biology to ethics and morality. *Hardwired*'s position is more nuanced. First, it holds a more complicated theory of bi-

21. As quoted in *Hardwired to Connect* (New York: Institute for American Values, 2003), p. 16.

22. As quoted in *Hardwired to Connect*, p. 54. These quotes were taken from an interview of Schore by Benedict Carey and reported in "Shaping the Connection," *Los Angeles Times*, March 31, 2003.

23. *Hardwired to Connect*, p. 17.

24. *Hardwired to Connect*, p. 18.

25. *Hardwired to Connect*, p. 18.

ological needs. Rather than simply speaking of sexual desires (Freud), organismic experience (humanistic psychology), or inclusive fitness (evolutionary psychology), it talks about our needs for attachment and connection as well. Second, it holds that our biological needs for connection and attachment constitute the psychological raw material which community, culture, tradition, and spirituality build upon and transform into what Paul Ricoeur calls our ethics and morality.

At one point, *Hardwired* makes a very interesting distinction that Freud, humanistic psychology, and evolutionary psychology frequently overlook: "The beginning of morality is the biologically primed moralization of attachment."[26] Note that word "moralization." This is a subtle point that inadvertently brings up a distinction that I will use, with the help of Ricoeur, quite frequently. Our biology, in this case our need for attachment, contributes to our teleological quest for the good. But these yearnings, in their brute biological facticity, need to be met and further guided by ethical and moral communal practices. When biological inclinations become nurtured and defined by culture, they contribute to our efforts to realize the good life, what Ricoeur calls the field of ethics. This is what happens when our need for attachment gets "moralized," to use the language of the report. But, as we will later see at length, there may be more in the move from our need for connection to a fully mature morality than even this perceptive formulation realizes. This move will point to an even deeper understanding of the role of authoritative communities in bringing the young to fuller adult health and morality — authoritative communities based on something like the critical Christian moral theology that Niebuhr, Ricoeur, Janssens, and Aquinas will help us understand.

Kohlberg: Structuralism as Foundationalism

Some modern psychologies de-emphasize tradition by resorting to a foundationalism based on biology. Other schools of psychology, however, turn to another kind of foundationalism, one based on our cognitive capacities.

The most powerful contemporary psychological perspective on moral development can be found in the cognitive theories of Lawrence Kohlberg. Kohlberg, who wrote during the decades of the 1960s, 1970s, and 1980s, believed along with the Swiss psychologist Jean Piaget that

---

26. *Hardwired to Connect*, p. 25.

moral development proceeded by using the same cognitive capacities used in the realms of science and mathematics.[27] Morality, he thought, consisted of solving conflicts between humans and required deliberative skills that invariably use these cognitive capacities. Kohlberg was stimulated to do his work because of accumulating evidence that moral training of the kinds associated with Boy Scout merit badges and Sunday School moral instruction did not help young people learn to cope with the kinds of moral conflicts and dilemmas we increasingly face in our complex, diverse, and rapidly changing society.[28]

Kohlberg was sophisticated enough to realize that social scientists cannot adequately do empirical work in the field of moral development unless they first make some important pre-empirical decisions about the nature of morality. Kohlberg made such decisions quite self-consciously, and this partially explains both the successes and the shortcomings of his extensive research program. He decided that the moral theories of Immanuel Kant and the neo-Kantian perspective of John Rawls provide the most adequate philosophical framework for the scientific study of the moral development of persons.[29] Morality, Kohlberg concluded, is primarily a matter of *moral thinking;* it is the capacity to think universally and reversibly. To think universally meant to Kohlberg what it meant to Kant: the capacity to guide our actions by maxims that we can will to be a universal law, a law for each of us to follow, both in our actions toward the other person and in that person's actions toward us — in short, all action by all people toward other and self.[30] To think reversibly means to be able to place oneself in the shoes of the other and think what one's actions might mean to them as well as to oneself. It also means, as John Rawls suggested, being *blind* to how one's action might benefit oneself in light of one's race, wealth, class, abilities, gender, education, or age.[31] Notice that basing morality on our rational capacities for moral thinking tends to downplay the role of history, tradition, communal practices, and particular characteristics such as education, gender, and race.

If Kohlberg came to his empirical work with these philosophical pre-

---

27. Lawrence Kohlberg, *The Philosophy of Moral Development,* vol. 1 (San Francisco: Harper and Row, 1981); Jean Piaget, *The Moral Judgment of the Child* (New York: Free Press, 1965).

28. Kohlberg, *Philosophy of Moral Development,* vol. 1, pp. 8-9.

29. Kohlberg, *Philosophy of Moral Development,* vol. 1, pp. 135, 193-99.

30. Kohlberg, *Philosophy of Moral Development,* vol. 1, p. 274; Immanuel Kant, *Foundations of the Metaphysics of Morals* (New York: Bobbs-Merrill, 1959), p. 19.

31. Kohlberg, *Philosophy of Moral Development,* vol. 1, p. 197; John Rawls, *A Theory of Justice* (Cambridge, Mass.: Harvard University Press, 1971), pp. 136-37.

commitments, what then did he actually learn from his scientific observations? He learned that the development of moral thinking is measurable, that one actually can find people thinking with some approximation of Kant's view of universality and Rawls's view of reversibility, and that there is a developmental timetable for the emergence of one's capacity for fully moral thinking. Moral thinking, he claimed, moves through three overarching stages characterized by structures, forms, or styles of thinking. There is first the *preconventional* and egocentric stage of early childhood, according to which the right thing to do is that which is satisfying and avoids pain and punishment. Then comes the *conventional* thinking of late childhood and early teens, according to which right action is what parents and the community say we should do and what will maintain our reputations as good or bad boys and girls. Finally, for some people, although not all, comes the *postconventional* thinking of late teens and adulthood, according to which right action follows the principle of the greatest good for the largest number or, higher still, the principle of treating all persons as ends and never as means alone according to the universal and reversible thinking advocated by Kant and Rawls.[32] Not everyone moves to the higher stages because experience does not force them to do so; in fact, most do not get beyond some level of conventionality, and some are arrested at preconventional levels.

As I indicated above, Kohlberg believed his empirical studies demonstrated that moral development parallels, and is aided by, the natural sequence of human cognitive development. Hence, neither a five-year-old nor a thirteen-year-old can consistently think morally at postconventional levels; their cognitive capacities have just not sufficiently matured to attain these levels of abstraction. Finally, he claimed to have learned some of the empirical conditions that actually facilitate the growth, elaboration, and complexification of higher levels of moral thinking. In short, his data suggested that it was *not* a homogeneous socialization process within a consistent community that produced high levels of moral thinking, as the communitarians might have it.[33] Rather, he believed that moral development is provoked by diverse and conflicting social experiences that compel us to restructure our moral cognitive categories so that they become more attentive to and inclusive of the claims of other people, even those outside our traditional circles.[34]

---

32. Kohlberg, *Philosophy of Moral Development,* vol. 1, pp. 17-18.
33. Kohlberg, *Philosophy of Moral Development,* vol. 1, p. 59.
34. Kohlberg, *Philosophy of Moral Development,* vol. 1, p. 305.

Research has continued on Kohlberg's insights.[35] He also has been influential on the discourse ethics of the continental social philosopher Jürgen Habermas. Habermas, however, is joined by feminist theorist Seyla Benhabib in advancing a more intersubjective view of universal and reversible moral thinking than that found in the Kohlbergian model.[36] In fact, both Habermas and Benhabib accuse Kohlberg of having a monological view of the universalizing process, seeing it as something that goes on within the mind of the individual moral actor rather than as a dialogical process between invested but competent moral actors in some kind of actual social situation. The moral psychologist Elliot Turiel takes his use of Kohlberg in this direction as well.

But Kohlbergian views have not only influenced social and political theory. Models of moral development of the kind advocated by Kohlberg have had impact on some religious ethicists; this can be seen especially in Ronald Green's use of Rawls's theory of justice as reversible fairness.[37] Green thinks that models of moral thinking (or practical reason) built on universality and reversibility reflect the mind of God as this is represented in Scriptures.[38] God thinks universally and reversibly in perfect and flawless ways; this means that God treats all humans fairly and knows their needs better than they do themselves. The task of the religious life, according to Green, is to challenge us to become like God and yet help us at the same time to handle our inevitable failures in accomplishing this goal.[39] God, according to Green, is the perfect exemplification of the abstract features of practical reason as practical reason is envisioned by the likes of Kohlberg, Rawls, and before them, Kant.

Today, however, it is widely believed that Kohlberg's view of moral development was far too narrow. He confined morality to moral thinking and paid no systematic attention to the premoral goods (of the kind emphasized by humanistic psychology, evolutionary psychology, and attachment theory) that moral thinking should order. Closely related to this point is the feminist critique of Kohlberg; Carol Gilligan has argued that

---

35. For a summary of the ongoing research on Kohlberg, see Owen Flanagan, *Varieties of Moral Personality* (Cambridge, Mass.: Harvard University Press, 1991), pp. 185, 212.

36. Jürgen Habermas, *Communication and the Evolution of Society* (Boston: Beacon, 1979), p. 90; Seyla Benhabib, "The Generalized and the Concrete Other: The Kohlberg-Gilligan Controversy and Feminist Theory," in *Feminism as Critique: On the Politics of Gender,* ed. Seyla Benhabib and Drucilla Cornell (Minneapolis: University of Minnesota, 1987), pp. 77-91.

37. Ronald Green, *Religious Reason* (New York: Oxford University Press, 1978).

38. Green, *Religious Reason,* pp. 128-30.

39. Green, *Religious Reason,* p. 109.

Kohlberg advanced a model of moral thinking that fits men more than women. Hence, it was a gender-biased model.[40] Kohlberg's view of moral thinking, she argues, emphasizes justice and rights and neglects elements of care and nurture, features that Gilligan believes are, at least in Western societies, more often found in the way women approach moral issues.[41]

Finally, communitarians have advanced criticisms of Kohlberg. They complain that he neglects other aspects of morality, principally the role of virtue, narrative, tradition, and community. Theologians such as Stanley Hauerwas have criticized Kohlberg's preoccupation with an ethics of principle. He joins philosopher Alasdair MacIntyre in believing that morality mainly has to do with a way of life shaped by the narratives and virtues of a particular tradition.[42] The field of psychology itself has been influenced by this line of thinking. Owen Flanagan, whom I discuss in Chapter 8, argues for the importance of narrative, in both psychology and moral philosophy, for the formation of moral character and virtue.[43] The turn to narrative and virtue in moral psychology, philosophy, and theology is a clear rejection of foundationalism of either the biological or rationalist kind.

Associated with this turn is the emergence of character education in schools and communities in the United States and other countries. In the early 1990s, the general public in several countries became concerned about the increase in crime, cheating, out-of-wedlock pregnancies, sexually transmitted diseases, and alcohol and drug consumption among school-age populations. Many people promoted intentional programs in moral education in both schools and communities. It is interesting to note, however, that neither Kohlberg's view of moral development nor the highly popular values-clarification model of the 1960s and 1970s became the most widely used model. Rather, the leading approach centered around various programs in character education. These initiatives generally entail school, community, and religious institutions such as churches, synagogues, and mosques having discussions that first try to arrive at a consensus about which character traits or virtues are thought by the

40. Carol Gilligan, *In a Different Voice* (Cambridge, Mass.: Harvard University Press, 1982).

41. Gilligan, *In a Different Voice,* p. 62.

42. Stanley Hauerwas, "Character, Narrative, and Growth in the Christian Life," in *Toward Moral and Religious Maturity,* ed. James O'Donohoe, James Fowler, and Antoine Vergote (Morristown, N.J.: Silver Burdett, 1980), pp. 441-84; Alasdair MacIntyre, *After Virtue* (Notre Dame, Ind.: University of Notre Dame Press, 1981).

43. Flanagan, *The Varieties of Moral Personality,* pp. 139-40.

whole community to be truly essential. Lists of virtues such as respect, responsibility, integrity, caring, self-discipline, trust, worthiness, fairness, and citizenship are often settled on through this extensive process of consensus-building.[44] The fact that this process can be done at all demonstrates a very interesting social reality, namely, that diverse individuals and traditions can agree, at least at this preliminary level, on common highly valued virtues. Then, there is a widespread process of discussing the meaning — the actual content and behavior manifestation — of these virtues. Ministers, priests, and rabbis preach on their meaning. Church schools and scout troops discuss them as well. Parents and other community officials take part. Community involvement and reinforcement are thought to be crucial to the success of such programs. Sometimes the programs begin in the schools and spread outward to other sectors of the community.[45] Sometimes they start with religious institutions or other community organizations and finally involve the schools. But the point is to involve the entire community. This total community involvement is a very good idea and something that any effort to revive the power of communities of authority should try to accomplish.

This approach is apparently powerful in producing a higher level of civility among students and community members, an accomplishment in itself which should be valued. Some critics, however, believe that this approach to character education does little to illuminate either the goods at stake in moral issues or the principles of obligation that should guide deliberation and action in new situations. Skeptics claim that character education may produce more day-to-day decency but does little to increase genuinely critical moral thinking and action. Furthermore, sociologist James Davison Hunter believes that character education's concentration on lists of specific virtues may actually function to disconnect these virtues from living traditions and the powerful narratives, rituals, and communal patterns that animate them. This may produce only superficial conformity rather than a vital and transformative moral life.[46]

I must admit: looking at moral development, as I will below, from the perspective of Paul Ricoeur's critical hermeneutics and the theological ethics of Niebuhr, Janssens, and Aquinas gives me considerable sympathy for the accomplishments of character education. From the standpoint of

44. For a very helpful review of the character education movement, see Robert Browning and Roy A. Reed, *Forgiveness, Reconciliation, and Moral Courage* (Grand Rapids: Eerdmans, 2004), pp. 155-60.

45. Browning and Reed, *Forgiveness, Reconciliation, and Moral Courage*, pp. 157-58.

46. James Davison Hunter, *The Death of Character* (New York: Basic, 2000).

Ricoeur's critical hermeneutic model of moral reflection, character education finds a firm place for beginning the process of reflection on the classic practices of virtues and habits that have come to us from the past. Yet, Hunter's critique of character education, as it is practiced in many institutions in our society, also may contain a bit of truth. This approach may be a good place to begin the process of moral reflection and learning, but it may also short-circuit the larger hermeneutical task — the larger task of interpretation, critique, and return to the concrete situation of conflict.

A Critical-Hermeneutic Understanding of Moral Development

Modern scientific psychology with its foundationalist philosophy has contributed bits and pieces of insight into the nature of the moral development of persons. It has not, however, delivered a dominant model that has been accepted widely or that has improved decisively our understanding of moral development beyond the wisdom of inherited religious and philosophical resources. Yet, the bits and pieces — the partial insights — can prove valuable if we resist the temptation to inflate a limited finding or theory into a representation of the entire field of moral deliberation and action. The problem with social-scientific research into moral development is that it has been guided by inadequate pre-empirical models of morality. Kohlberg gravitated too rapidly toward Kant and Rawls, even though they are both important. Other social scientists have done even worse.

But recently, new philosophical models of ethics and morality have emerged that should be examined for their usefulness for understanding the fullness of moral development. These new philosophical models are relevant for understanding the contributions to the ethics of particular religious traditions, especially the version of Christian ethics that I present in this book. Paul Ricoeur is especially helpful in placing Niebuhr in a larger philosophical context and thereby helping me explain Niebuhr to wider philosophical and empirical communities. These new philosophical sources also may have much to contribute to the social-scientific study of moral development. I will illustrate these new pre-empirical models by briefly outlining the critical hermeneutic view of ethics and morality found in the writings of Paul Ricoeur. Although Ricoeur is a philosopher, his hermeneutic model has great relevance to the empirical study of morality and the field of religious and theological ethics. Because he is a promoter of hermeneutic philosophy, he sides with the nonfoundationalists in honoring tradition and the challenge of interpreting tradition. Since he also has a critical moment within his hermeneutic theory, he can appreciate aspects of the foundationalist project in moral psychology and philosophy — especially the Kantianism of Kohlberg, Rawls, and Habermas — even though he places this critical moment within a wider framework of tradition and narrativity.

Ricoeur's model is stated most fully in what he calls his "little ethics" in *Oneself as Another*.[47] In his hermeneutic or interpretive model, development toward mature moral reflection can include yet go beyond the internalization of the prohibitions of the father (Freud), deepened trust in one's own organismic valuing process (humanistic psychology), kin altruism analogically applied to non-kin (evolutionary psychology), attachment needs met by parents and community (Bowlby, Schore), universalizable moral thinking (Kohlberg), and the assimilation of virtues (character education), even if these virtues are connected with the narratives of a great tradition (Hauerwas, MacIntyre). In other words, Ricoeur's hermeneutic model can find a place for the important points of most of the other contemporary schools of moral psychology. In the process, however, his model prevents these schools from claiming more completeness than they actually have earned. Standing by themselves, most of these schools are reductionistic in one way or another. Placed within a more multidimensional and sophisticated theory of both ethics and morality, however, their partial insights can be retained and yet supplemented by a more satisfying pre-empirical model of moral existence. In turn, this new and better philosophical model should stimulate new and better empirical research.

According to Ricoeur, the development of persons toward mature moral reflection and action includes many of these elements — many of these bits and pieces — but has a larger structure; it has the fuller structure of the self in its interpretive and dialogical action with its world. Ricoeur believes that the self in dialogue with its world has a three-step rhythm — the steps of *describing, narrating,* and *prescribing*.[48] This happy formula will help us understand Ricoeur's complex theory of moral maturity.

Mature moral thinking and action, according to Ricoeur, develop along the following lines. He first makes a distinction between *ethics* and *morality* — a distinction I already have referred to briefly when discussing *Hardwired to Connect*. In fact, he goes even further and asserts the temporal

---

47. Paul Ricoeur, *Oneself as Another* (Chicago: University of Chicago Press, 1992). Ricoeur's "little ethics" can be found in chapters 5 to 10.

48. Ricoeur, *Oneself as Another,* p. 20.

priority of ethics over morality in the full arch of moral reflection — a point relevant to moral development. This is what Ricoeur means when he writes, "The present study will be confined to establishing the primacy of ethics over morality — that is, of the aim over the norm."[49] This means, for Ricoeur, that the field of ethics springs from our desiring selves and from our efforts to realize some good in our lives. Here is where Freud, the humanistic psychologies, evolutionary psychology, and attachment theory throw some light on moral development.[50] Morality builds on, tries to fulfill, yet properly orders our ethical striving toward the goods of life. Niebuhr's strong view of humans as desiring creatures fully anchored in nature points in this same direction, but, as we will see, Janssens and Aquinas will agree on this point with Ricoeur even more, arguing that morality builds on our desire for the goods of life.

But how do we understand and learn about these aspirations toward the good? Do we learn about them by *directly* feeling and following our raw desires, needs, and actualization tendencies, somewhat the way humanistic evolutionary psychology sees it? Ricoeur thinks not, especially if we truly want to pursue the good life. First, Ricoeur reminds us that we always experience our needs and desires in a mediated way, through some inherited language and tradition of evaluation. Second, if ethics is to get off on the right track, we should interpret our desires and needs through some tested and excellent tradition that has proven to really satisfy or realize them. We should, first of all, try to *describe* (the first of the three steps) our culture's and tradition's classic *practices* for pursuing these goods and realizing these needs. Ricoeur writes, "The properly ethical character of these precepts is ensured by what MacIntyre calls 'standards of excellence,' which allow us to characterize as good a doctor, an architect, a painter, or a chess player."[51] Such practices crystallize our enduring goods and the appropriate means to acquire them. In this emphasis on practices as revealing the goods of our ethical strivings in their marks of excellence, we see shades of the teleologically oriented modern psychologies but also, at the same time, shades of MacIntyre and communitarianism. This view says, in effect, that the goods of life are discovered through the inherited practices of a community and its traditions.[52] Ricoeur accepts, up to a point, MacIntyre's under-

---

49. Ricoeur, *Oneself as Another,* p. 171.

50. Paul Ricoeur, *Freud and Philosophy* (New Haven, Conn.: Yale University Press, 1970), pp. 291-92; Jean-Pierre Changeux and Paul Ricoeur, *What Makes Us Think?* (Princeton, N.J.: Princeton University Press, 2000), pp. 195-201.

51. Ricoeur, *Oneself as Another,* p. 176.

52. MacIntyre, *After Virtue,* p. 177.

standing of the relation of goods and practices, which MacIntyre illustrates vividly in the following quotation:

> If, on starting to listen to music, I do not accept my own incapacity to judge correctly, I will never learn to hear, let alone to appreciate, Bartok's last quartets. If, on starting to play baseball, I do not accept that others know better than I when to throw a fast ball and when not, I will never learn to appreciate good pitching let alone to pitch. In the realm of practices the authority of both goods and standards operates in such a way as to rule out all subjectivist and emotivist analyses of judgment. De justibus *est* disputandum.[53]

But teaching persons in their search for the good how to *describe* and act on the inherited practices of a tradition is, according to Ricoeur, just the beginning of ethics and only the first step toward the moral development of persons. It does not exhaust the full meaning of morality. Furthermore, the descriptive task is itself complex. If we are socialized beings at all, the more excellent forms of our desires are projected into hierarchies of linguistic codes that give intelligibility to our practices. By hierarchies of linguistic codes Ricoeur has in mind codes of coordination (simple patterns of means to various ends), codes of subordination (such as plowing *in order* to farm), constitutive rules (moving the pawn to play the game of chess), plans of life (far-reaching goals and aspirations), images of the "good life" (general evaluative models as to what are truly valuable aspirations for life as a whole), and, finally, larger narratives that give unity and meaning to our life in the midst of disappointments and conflicts.[54]

From a Christian perspective, this larger narrative would include the action of God in relation to the world, conveyed in those four great metaphors that we discussed in the introductory chapter — the metaphors of God the Creator, Governor, Redeemer, and Sustainer witnessed in the life and ministry of Jesus the Christ. All of these layers of inherited linguisticality — from the efficiency-oriented codes of coordination and subordination to the grand narratives of life — function to pattern our desires into practices that carry us toward the goods of life. They *lead us to the doorstep of morality.* These valuable and tested practices also require a great deal of description and interpretation by parents, educators, neighborhoods, communities of faith,

---

53. MacIntyre, *After Virtue,* p. 177.

54. Paul Ricoeur, "The Teleological and Deontological Structures of Action: Aristotle and/or Kant?" in *Contemporary French Philosophy,* ed. A. Phillips Griffiths (Cambridge: Cambridge University Press, 1987), pp. 100-103.

and finally oneself in order to be understood and appropriated. Thus, ethics understood as the pursuit of the goods of life requires a grand and complex process of education, socialization, and critical interpretation on the excellent practices of a tested and established tradition.

Notice that "narration" was the last of the long list of ways that our practices, which embody the goods we seek, are encoded by language and tradition. Also remember that *narration* was Ricoeur's second step in his threefold understanding of the moral self as an interpretive and dialogical self. Some narrative — some story about life — holds together and integrates the hierarchies of our encoded ethical practices. Some narrative gives the final meaning to our means-end actions, our if-then actions, our plans of life, and our images of the good life. This is true not only for Christians but for everyone. If it is not one narrative, it is another. If it is not the Christian narrative — some form of it — it is another narrative. Ricoeur's phenomenology of human action suggests that our practices are always surrounded by — always assume — some story about the meaning of life. To develop as a moral person, one must assimilate the classic narratives of one's tradition, those that over time have proven most capable of giving meaning to our ethical struggles and losses. In the words of Hans-Georg Gadamer, from whom Ricoeur has learned so much, development toward morality requires our learning to interpret the "classics" of a tradition.[55] Ricoeur understands these classics to be primarily narrative classics, generally religious in scope. This point opens the possibility of the Christian ethical classics being a major source for such a narrative tradition.

But in spite of this emphasis on the role in ethics of inherited communal practices and traditions, Ricoeur goes beyond the traditionalism of most forms of communitarianism. Ethical action at this stage deals only with communally patterned aspirations; we have not yet arrived at the arena of full morality. Why is it that our ethical aspirations toward the goods of life do not, in themselves, deal with the core of genuine moral maturity for persons? The answer seems to be this: according to Ricoeur, the goods of life conflict and thereby produce various forms of violence. As I indicated above, the field of ethics, in contrast to the arena of morality, is born out of our purposive search for the good. Morality itself, however, assumes and builds on our ethical and teleological aspirations, but it also goes beyond them.[56] Morality in the proper sense of the word is born out of the tragic conflict between the goods of life. According to this point of view, these

---

55. Hans-Georg Gadamer, *Truth and Method* (New York: Crossroad, 1982), p. 255.
56. Ricoeur, *Oneself as Another,* p. 205.

goods are premoral goods; they are morally relevant but not fully moral. Why? For one simple reason. Premoral goods can conflict with one another. We see it happen all the time. The good of education can conflict with the good of health; we can study too hard, stay up too late, drink too much coffee, and generally abuse ourselves in the name of getting an education — in the name of gaining the good of knowledge and the good of skills. Moreover, my good — my health, wealth, knowledge, affections, enjoyments, sexual pleasures, and so on — can conflict with the good of other people.

Morality mediates conflicts between goods and the persons seeking these goods.[57] Morality does this, Ricoeur believes, by employing tests about which of our moral maxims are universalizable. Such tests can be found in Kant's second formulation of the categorical imperative, "Act so that you treat humanity, whether in your own person or in that of another, always as an end and never as a means only."[58] Ricoeur calls Kant's principle the "deontological test" because, in contrast to the teleological concern to associate ethics with increasing the premoral goods of life, it identifies morality exclusively with justice and respect for persons as ends, without reference to these premoral goods. In the context of religions such as Judaism and Christianity, one finds similar tests in the Golden Rule. In Christianity, we find the principle of neighbor love — "You shall love your neighbor as yourself" (Matt. 22:39) — the principle which leads to the ethic of equal-regard that I get from Louis Janssens and use to fine-tune Niebuhr's theory of love and justice. These principles show solicitude and respect for both other and self, tell us to treat all persons as ends and never as means alone, and require us to recognize that in their humanity alone *all* individuals are deserving of just and fair access to the goods of life.[59] Actions pursuing goods that pass this test of universalization are moral actions in contrast to simply worthy ethical aspirations.

It is at the moment of this test that Kohlberg's model of moral development would be valued and find a place within Ricoeur's fuller hermeneutic theory of moral thought and action. As we noticed above, Kohlberg's thin view of moral thinking finds no place for ethics as the pursuit of the goods of life, no place for our pleasurable, self-actualizing, kin-altruistic, or attachment needs and aspirations. Ricoeur, by associating the field of ethics with the search for the goods of life, can find a place for these aspirations, even though he interprets them through the lens of the

---

57. Ricoeur, *Oneself as Another,* p. 207.
58. Kant, *Foundations of the Metaphysics of Morals,* p. 47.
59. Ricoeur, *Oneself as Another,* p. 206.

classic practices that order them. Furthermore, Kohlberg finds little place for tradition and the narrative classics that give broader meaning to our ethical strivings. But because Ricoeur can include Kantian, Kohlbergian-like critical tests within his more encompassing teleological and tradition-based narrative approach, he also can criticize all positions in philosophy (MacIntyre), moral theology (Hauerwas), or psychology that uncritically reduce morality to the virtues and narratives of a tradition. The practices of traditions, in his view, can be and must be at times critiqued. They must pass the test of universalization, neighbor love, and equal-regard.

In discussing the test of universalization, Ricoeur has already moved into his third step, the moment of *prescription.* But prescription for Ricoeur has several dimensions to it. First, Ricoeur has given us a synthesis of two great, and often thought to be conflicting, models of philosophical ethics. He has brought together Aristotle and Kant and done this by disciplining Aristotle's ethics of desire, habit, virtue, and community formation with the tests of Kant's morality of the categorical imperative and other similar principles of universalization. But this is still not enough to provide a full statement of the nature of moral reflection and action. There must be, according to Ricoeur, a moment of wisdom where the moral actor returns to the original concrete situation of moral action. The tests of our ethical strivings toward the goods of life accomplished by employing the universalization principle located within the categorical imperative, the Golden Rule, or neighbor love must now be fine-tuned to the actual constraints of specific situations and the concrete goods that are there at stake. Ordering and ranking these conflicting goods requires a judgment of practical wisdom. This is a matter of being wise. It requires taking seriously the situation in all of its complications and ambiguity. This is a turn to the *Sittlichkeit;* this is the point at which Ricoeur supplements Aristotle's teleology and Kant's deontology with the situationalism of Hegel. It is now, however, a situationalism guided by the narratives and virtues of a classic tradition and the tests of universalization, rather than some form of utilitarianism that generally guides situation ethics.[60] Although Niebuhr, as I have argued, never adequately formulated the principle of justice that makes up the deontological test, he was deeply committed to justice and was concerned to return to the reality of situations to determine what was possible within the concrete context that created the original conflict. This is why Niebuhr is often called a "Christian realist."[61] He was interested in

---

60. Ricoeur, *Oneself as Another,* p. 240.

61. Charles Kegley and Robert Bretall, *Reinhold Niebuhr: His Religious, Social, and Political*

the meaning of justice within the concrete value conflicts and power realities of actual situations — a point that is substantially the same as Ricoeur's moment of practical wisdom.

The critical hermeneutic perspective, explicit in Ricoeur and implicit in Niebuhr, points to a fuller and more adequate model of development toward mature moral reflection and action than can be found in either the teleological or deontological foundationalism of much of modern psychology. We should help children, young people, and adults understand that they are moral interpreters who receive or inherit traditions of moral practice. Parents, schools, and religious institutions should help them understand that the first step of a moral decision is an act of hermeneutical interpretation; it involves asking, what is the meaning of the deeply coded practices that they have inherited? They should learn to inquire into the proper way to interpret these practices. They should learn to ask, Do I understand these traditions of practice correctly? What are the images of the good life and the narratives that give them meaning? They should be taught to be sensitive about whether their practices and the goods they embody conflict within themselves or conflict with, and perhaps destroy, the practices and goods of others. They should then learn to exercise some version of the principle of universalization or equal-regard. Finally, they should learn how to return to the original situation to determine how their narratives and the principle of universalization help reorder within the constraints of that context the conflicting goods that engendered the original violence.

Moral deliberation in Ricoeur's model is inextricably related to understanding and interpretation by the moral self and, in fact, the moral self in dialogue with a community of moral selves. Something like this model of moral reflection and action should guide our social, cultural, and religious effort to develop moral persons. Something like this model should guide our human and social sciences in their research to grasp the more detailed conditions for moral development. In the chapters to come, I will show how this model can be more directly appropriated for relating contemporary moral psychology to the specific features of Christian ethics.

Thought (New York: Macmillan, 1956), p. 173. Niebuhr referred to his thought as Christian realism as well. See Reinhold Niebuhr, *Love and Justice* (Louisville, Ky.: Westminster John Knox, 1957), pp. 43, 44, 91.

The Illustration of Love

Much of what I have done in this chapter has been preparing to address the nature of Christian ethics by rehabilitating the category of tradition. It is hard to get Christian ethics a hearing in the contemporary world because it is difficult to get a hearing for tradition. In the coming chapters, we will listen more deeply to the Christian tradition itself, principally to its teaching about love. Much of the argument of this present chapter can be focused around the nature of Christian love and its related implications for justice. These concepts are at the center of Christian ethics. The propositions below, which will gradually unfold in the remaining chapters, should help the reader follow my line of thought.

First, modern moral psychology can help clarify the *teleological* foundations of love, that is, the strivings toward the goods of life that love seeks. The higher manifestations of love cannot be realized unless certain basic human needs for attachment, pleasure, and self-regard are met and patterned by intimate communities such as the family and larger communities of memory — authoritative communities such as churches, synagogues, mosques, and various other intergenerational voluntary organizations with an extended history and narrative. The hope is that these authoritative communities can themselves work together in some kind of ecumenical spirit. The fragmenting dynamics of the modernization process demand this. In order to support the idea of authoritative communities, I have presented Ricoeur in some detail and suggested how he provides some philosophical grounds for Niebuhr. Together they begin to develop both the philosophical and the theological basis of the idea of an authoritative community. Giving Niebuhr, and other Christian ethicists, some philosophical legs makes it possible to provide a more convincing case for the relevance of Christian ethics to moral psychology. It also helps show how Christian ethics can profit from a dialogue with moral psychology.

Second, the science of moral psychology helps us clarify that aspect of the Christian tradition which demonstrates that love for the neighbor, stranger, and even the enemy is built on an analogical generalization of the meeting of these basic teleological needs and their patterning into the "good" of regular practices.

Third, modern moral psychology can help clarify the conditions that give rise to the "deontological test" that is implicit in the Golden Rule and the Christian principle of neighbor love, and that is given philosophical account in Kant's categorical imperative. But moral psychology itself cannot provide an account of why these principles are moral principles. Nor can it provide and justify the grounds or beliefs about the status of humans that these principles assume. Only some form of religious faith — such as the Jewish and Christian belief in the status of all humans as children of God — can adequately provide and justify these grounds.

Fourth, modern moral psychology alone can provide no explanation or justification for those expressions of love that go beyond simple reciprocity, beyond a love predicated on the assumption that helping others also provides a return or advantage for the self or kin. Although Christian love recognizes a rightful place for reciprocal love (and indeed, even love as self-regard), it holds that the nature of God, the action of Jesus, and the status of all human beings require love as equal-regard for self and all others as the central goal of life. But this neighbor love requires self-sacrificial love as a necessary submoment to renew love as equal-regard. Even this interpretation of Christian love, which is not the only possible interpretation, is arrived at partially through the clarifications provided by the modern moral psychologies.

I now turn to an amplification of the ideas in this chapter and to a wider engagement with Christian theological ethics.

Chapter 3

Going Deeper: The Relation of Moral Education to Christian Ethics

A friend of mine once told me that anything worth doing once is worth doing twice. That is what will happen in this chapter. By reviewing the very important work of the University of Nijmegen Roman Catholic practical theologian Johannes (Hans) van der Ven, I will expand and go deeper with some of the points I made in Chapter 2. Van der Ven has written widely and made significant proposals not only about practical theology but in the areas of moral psychology and Christian ethics. He shares my interest in bringing practical theology, theological ethics, and moral theology into closer dialogue.

I believe that it is impossible to be practical in the sense of "applied" without sooner or later making clear the norms that guide one's practice. In short, it is very difficult to draw a clean line between the moral and the practical. So, for the purposes of this book, when I use the phrase "practical theology," I am including Christian ethics or moral theology with a genuine concern not only to articulate norms but also to transform lives and institutions, to get down to specifics — to get practical. Sometimes I will use the phrase "practical theological ethics" to describe what I am about.

Although van der Ven is both a practical theologian and a theological ethicist, he does not use my phrase "practical theological ethics." Nonetheless, he is helpful for my cause. I will view van der Ven mainly from the perspective of his outstanding book *Formation of the Moral Self.*[1] In this seminal text, he makes the claim that the common element in all forms of moral education is "moral communication."[2] This is a concept closely re-

---

1. Johannes van der Ven, *Formation of the Moral Self* (Grand Rapids: Eerdmans, 1998).
2. Van der Ven, *Formation of the Moral Self,* p. 30.

lated to the idea of "hermeneutic communication." But before we investigate these two ideas — before we even define them — we ought to take a peek at van der Ven's theory of the relation of religion and morality.

The Relation of Religion to Morality

The *Formation of the Moral Self* is about moral education. It is a massive analysis and critique of the entire field of moral education, probably the most complete and satisfying available in the contemporary secular or religious literature. It is also about the relation of religion to morality and the importance of the religious dimension of life to all moral education. This viewpoint is what moves his theory of moral education into the fields of practical and moral theology. His remarks on this issue are important and well worth pondering.

Van der Ven treats morality as a subtext within the wider and more encompassing narrative text of religion.[3] Religion incorporates, recontextualizes, and adds a narrative and ontological framework to a variety of nonreligious sources of morality. Once the moral subtext is incorporated into the religious narrative text, the moral subtext takes on new valences and meanings, but not in ways that cause it to completely lose its identity in the religious narrative. For instance, the Golden Rule has much the same formal logical structure whether found in Judaism, Islam, Confucianism, or Christianity. But Christianity bases the claim that we should treat others as we would have them treat us on the twofold premise that we are all made in the image of God and that, in addition, Christ died to redeem all of us. The Christian narrative adds these twists — these additional dynamic meanings — to the formal structure of the Golden Rule. These two beliefs — one coming from the narrative of creation and the other from the narrative of redemption — make us all equally worthy of respect before both God and each other. They make us all equally worthy of being treated as ends, as persons.

In the case of Christianity, moral insights from Plato, Aristotle, Greek and Roman Stoicism, and Roman law were absorbed and recontextualized by the various narrative structures of early Christianity. Since then, new nonreligious moral insights have constantly been absorbed, given new valences, and reframed by views of time and destiny found in the Christian vision of life. In one place, van der Ven says that "religion integrates, ori-

---

3. Van der Ven, *Formation of the Moral Self*, p. 13.

ents, and criticizes nonreligious morality."[4] Sometimes this means recontextualizing ordinary moral ideas into a larger whole provided by some religious narrative. Sometimes, as in the case of the Christian parables, it means "turning the world of moral common sense, habits, and conventions . . . upside down."[5] Van der Ven neatly summarizes the dialectical relation between religion and morality, especially when viewed from the perspective of the Christian religion, as containing three elements:

> First, it integrates external ideas, beliefs, values, and norms by relating them to the main Christian themes, that is, creation, alienation, liberation, and eschatological completion. . . . Second, in the course of this integration process, it orients these moral elements in a particular direction: hope of the new heaven and new earth, the kingdom of God, the new Jerusalem. Third, within this orientation process, religion carries out a moral critique of historical developments, assessing them in terms of how well or how badly they fit into the intrinsic values of nature and humanity as aimed at in God's creation.[6]

This view of the relation of religion and morality does not assume that religion itself is always the direct source of morality. Human experience and reason — and their distortion through power and pride — may be the source of much that goes into a society's religio-moral traditions. Van der Ven follows Paul Ricoeur's slight overstatement in *Oneself as Another*, where he wrote, "it must be asserted that, even on the ethical and moral plane, biblical faith adds nothing to the predicates 'good' and 'obligatory' as these are applied to action."[7] Nonetheless, according to Ricoeur and van der Ven, the recontextualizations of religious narratives contribute something extremely important. Van der Ven again quotes Ricoeur, this time saying, "Biblical *agape* belongs to an economy of the gift, possessing a metaethical character, which makes me say that there is no such thing as a Christian morality, except perhaps on the level of the history of *mentalités,* but a common morality . . . that biblical faith places in a new perspective, in which love is tied to the 'naming of God.'"[8] What Ricoeur and van der

---

4. Van der Ven, *Formation of the Moral Self,* p. 19.

5. Van der Ven, *Formation of the Moral Self,* p. 18.

6. Van der Ven, *Formation of the Moral Self,* p. 16.

7. Van der Ven, *Formation of the Moral Self,* p. 16, quoting Paul Ricoeur, *Oneself as Another* (Chicago: University of Chicago Press, 1992), p. 17.

8. Van der Ven, *Formation of the Moral Self,* p. 17, quoting Ricoeur, *Oneself as Another,* p. 25.

Ven really mean here is that our organismic experience (humanistic psychology, evolutionary psychology), inherited cultural practices, and capacity for reversible moral reason (Kohlberg) can contribute to, yet get further elaborated by, the narrative structure of the Christian story. But, as I will argue, this "new perspective" that comes from this story can make a very significant difference to the mundane ethic it illumines.

Van der Ven, Ricoeur, and Moral Education

Formation of the Moral Self extends this view of the necessarily dialectical relation between morality and religion and uses it to analyze the field of moral education, both secular and religious. The end result of this review is the following conclusion: *moral education cannot be complete without responsibly locating itself within the larger field of religious hermeneutics.* In fact, van der Ven argues that moral education should be a subspecies of religious hermeneutics or, at least, a subspecies of the hermeneutics of tradition. He bases his point of view, once again, on Ricoeur's hermeneutic understanding of ethics and morality. We have already had an introduction to Ricoeur's theory of ethics and morality. Now I want to examine how van der Ven uses Ricoeur.

Van der Ven employs Ricoeur's ethics to analyze and critique seven contemporary models of moral education. Two of these models — moral education as discipline and moral education as socialization — van der Ven calls "informal" approaches to the task of moral formation. They are informal because they occur in the natural interactions of shared communal life. The morality of discipline and the morality of socialization are taught when a family washes the dinner dishes together, when parents decide the children must join them for the evening meal, or when a teacher lines up his third-grade class for an orderly transition to the playground. No one is intentionally designing a moral program; it is just what the group does in its life together. These practices both provide a discipline — habits of everyday practice — and socialize the children into a common or shared way of behaving.

The five additional models are moral education as transmission, values clarification, moral development, emotional formation, and character education. Van der Ven calls them "formal" or intentional models of moral education.[9] They are a result of human planning and specific forms

9. Van der Ven, *Formation of the Moral Self,* p. 40.

of educational programming. They are more likely to occur in a public school, a church school, the Boy or Girl Scouts, or while taking lessons to learn the piano or guitar. His discussion of these various models culminates with a thorough review of character education. He writes, "I use the word *culminate* because education for character, in my view, is the highest objective of moral education."[10] In the next section of this chapter, I will illustrate his accomplishments by examining three of the seven models of moral education — values clarification, moral development, and the model which represents van der Ven's preferred perspective on moral education: education for character.

Van der Ven's bringing of the moral philosophy of Paul Ricoeur to the fields of moral psychology and education should not be seen as a radical step. As I have already noted, one reason for the power of the moral psychology of Lawrence Kohlberg was his self-conscious use of the tools and concepts of moral philosophy — specifically the moral philosophies of Plato and Kant — to establish the most adequate pre-empirical definition of morality upon which to base his empirical work.[11] *This, as I already have hinted, was also his weakness.* Although Kohlberg found empirical evidence supporting his theory of moral thinking, it is generally believed today that his model of morality was simply too thin from the beginning. Nonetheless, he understood the importance of the prior philosophical work needed to guide his empirical observations.

Van der Ven begins his analysis of the regnant models of moral education with a far richer philosophically developed theory of morality than can be found in Kohlberg. It is a moral philosophy that follows Ricoeur's belief that moral thought and action are processes of hermeneutic interpretation, reflection, and communication. Moral thinking and action develop for Ricoeur, as we have seen, along the following lines — lines that van der Ven follows rather closely. He affirms Ricoeur not only when the latter distinguishes between ethics and morality, but also when Ricoeur asserts the temporal priority of ethics over morality in the full circle of moral reflection. Ricoeur amplifies this distinction when he writes, "The present study will be confined to establishing the primacy of ethics over morality — that is, of the aim over the norm."[12] Van der Ven builds on Ricoeur when he asserts that the field of ethics springs from our desiring selves and from

---

10. Van der Ven, *Formation of the Moral Self,* p. 40.

11. Lawrence Kohlberg, *The Philosophy of Moral Development,* vol. 1 (San Francisco: Harper and Row, 1981), p. 22.

12. Ricoeur, *Oneself as Another,* p. 171.

our efforts to realize some good in our lives. But we discover the goods of life — the objects and things that will prove satisfying to our desires — not by directly examining our basic biological desires and wishes but in and through the cultural and communal practices into which we are socialized and disciplined. Van der Ven applauds Ricoeur for taking seriously all of our basic human tendencies all the way from the hardwired desire to connect, to Freud's libido, to humanistic psychology's actualization tendency, to evolutionary psychology's kin altruism (the desire to live on in our offspring or perhaps our siblings' offspring). They both agree that there are all kinds of desires that are brought to the field of ethics. Without solving the question of how many desires we humans have, Ricoeur and van der Ven think that this level of our motivations is ethically relevant.

I cannot emphasize enough, however, that they both hold that we do not experience our desires directly; very soon in life we know them indirectly through the practices that satisfy them. These practices, not the desires themselves, are the elementary goods of life. These practices crystallize the enduring goods, and the appropriate means to acquire them, that have proven satisfying to our desires. So far we hear in van der Ven and Ricoeur shades of Aristotle in the belief that ethics is primarily teleological — a search for the goods of life. We also hear shades of Alasdair MacIntyre and communitarianism in the belief that the goods of life are discovered through the inherited practices of a community and its traditions.[13] Both Ricoeur and van der Ven accept, up to a point, MacIntyre in his emphasis on the importance of traditions of practice for carrying the teleological goods of life.

This is why for both Ricoeur and van der Ven, tradition is the defining source of ethical action and reflection. For both, what Gadamer would call "effective history," our inherited traditions and customs working in our actual experience, provide the language and practices that define, guide, and give excellence to our desires and aspirations for the good.[14] Tradition and desire are not at odds in the minds of these three thinkers. Tradition, when rightly grasped, gives form and excellence to our desires.

But reflecting and acting on the inherited goods within a tradition of practice are for Ricoeur and van der Ven, in contrast to MacIntyre, just the beginning of ethics; they in no way exhaust the full meaning, or the entire field, of morality. Even this preliminary point, however, makes it possible

13. Alasdair MacIntyre, *After Virtue* (South Bend, Ind.: University of Notre Dame Press, 1981), p. 177.
14. Hans-Georg Gadamer, *Truth and Method* (New York: Crossroad, 1982), p. 267.

for van der Ven to show compelling contrasts between his views and those of several other theorists of moral education. For instance, this view complicates Freud's theory of desire and his view that the morality of the superego is formed by the repression of desire. That may be partially true, but it misses entirely another process relevant to the formation of the moral life. A tradition's communal practices that embody the goods of life are linguistically coded. This means that our desires are also encoded; we internalize from the beginning the linguistically patterned practices to which our desires become attached. It is not always and only the repression of desire that shapes the moral life; it is the guidance and patterning of desire into more classic objects and practices. This is the great insight into Freud, and correction of Freud, provided by Ricoeur's *Freud and Philosophy*, an insight that Ricoeur retained in his later moral philosophy. It is also adopted by van der Ven.[15] As we saw in Chapter 2, these desires are turned into human action by hierarchies of linguistic codes and practices that stretch all the way from simple means-end calculation to plans of life and overarching narratives that give unity and meaning to us in the midst of disappointments and conflicts.[16] All of these layers of linguisticality qualify and pattern our desires and practices at their very core and carry us toward more fully ethical action and, finally, to the threshold of morality.

But we must be reminded that ethical action at this first stage deals only with aspirations and evaluations; we have not yet arrived, in either Ricoeur's or van der Ven's view, at the arena of obligation — the sphere of morality as such. As we saw in Chapter 2, the initial aspirations and evaluations of the good do not, in themselves, deal with moral obligation — the genuine field of morality. The primary reason for this, according to both Ricoeur and van der Ven, is that the goods of life conflict. Morality is born out of the tragic, sometimes violent, conflict between the goods of life and between our various strivings for the good. Bill's desire for money in the bank (which helps him buy the goods of food and clothing or perhaps attract a wife) may conflict with Jim's desire for money in the bank (and his legitimate need for food, clothing, and so on). These goods can conflict because there may not be a job for both Jim and Bill and hence not enough money in the bank for at least one of them. We cannot fault either Bill or Jim for striving for these goods, but we can blame Bill if he tries to

---

15. Paul Ricoeur, *Freud and Philosophy* (New Haven, Conn.: Yale University Press, 1970), pp. 15-16, 395-405.

16. Paul Ricoeur, "The Teleological and Deontological Structures of Action: Aristotle and/or Kant?" in *Contemporary French Philosophy*, ed. A. Phillips Griffiths (Cambridge: Cambridge University Press, 1987), pp. 100-103.

solve the conflict and get the only job available by killing or disabling Jim. Morality mediates conflicts between goods and persons seeking goods.[17]

It does this by employing tests about which of our moral maxims can be generalized to fit a wide range of other conflicting situations. Such tests can be found in Kant's categorical imperative or the Golden Rule, principles that show solicitude and respect for both self and other, tell us to treat all persons as ends and never as means alone, and require us to recognize that in their humanity alone *all* individuals are deserving of just access to the goods of life.[18] Actions pursuing goods that pass this test of universalization (the deontological test) are moral actions. Resolutions to the conflict between Bill and Jim that could actually be universalized (that would respect each individual as an end but also help them actualize their respective needs and interests in the goods of life) might include these ideas: the two might share the job, or develop a system that could create another job (one for Bill, one for Jim), or a welfare system could be established that would give Jim an income until a job came along.

But finally, van der Ven's and Ricoeur's synthesis of Aristotle and Kant — their disciplining of Aristotle's ethics of desire, habit, virtue, and community formation with the deontological test of Kant's morality of the categorical imperative — is still not enough to provide a full statement of the nature of moral reflection and action. Two more dimensions are needed to give a full account of moral action. A close analysis will uncover, as Alasdair MacIntyre would point out, the explicit or implicit narratives or stories of life that surround both the teleological quest for the good and the deontological test. I will say much more throughout this book on the narrative (and narratives) surrounding these other dimensions of moral thinking, especially some of the unique features of the Christian narrative. And last, Van der Ven agrees with Ricoeur that there must be a moment of wisdom where the moral actor returns to the original concrete situation of action. The tests of more viable desires and practices accomplished by employing the categorical imperative's principle of universalization must now be fine-tuned to the actual constraints of specific situations and the concrete goods that are there at stake. Ordering and ranking these conflicting goods, within the constraints and possibilities of specific contexts, requires a judgment of *phronēsis* or practical wisdom in the more narrow sense of these terms. This is a matter of being wise. It requires taking the situation in all of its complications and ambiguity se-

17. Van der Ven, *Formation of the Moral Self,* p. 9; Ricoeur, *Oneself as Another,* p. 207.
18. Van der Ven, *Formation of the Moral Self,* p. 162; Ricoeur, *Oneself as Another,* p. 206.

riously. This is a turn to the *Sittlichkeit.* This is the point at which both van der Ven and Ricoeur supplement Aristotle's teleology, Kant's deontology, and MacIntyre's narrative dimension with the situationalism of Hegel.[19]

This is the fullness of a critical hermeneutical model of moral reflection. We humans as moral actors receive or inherit traditions of moral practice. The first part of a moral decision must be an act of hermeneutical interpretation: what is the meaning of the deeply coded practices and deeply coded experiences of the goods of life that I have inherited? How should I interpret them? Do I understand them correctly? And if my inherited practices and their goods conflict with one another or conflict with and perhaps destroy the goods of others, how do I respectively interpret and evaluate our shared or differing traditions? Moral deliberation is inextricably related to understanding and interpretation in the model of moral *praxis* proposed by Ricoeur and van der Ven. The key resources of Hans-Georg Gadamer's hermeneutic philosophy stand in the background of van der Ven's and Ricoeur's theory of moral education and communication. Together, these powerful perspectives on moral reflection provide us with a theory supporting the idea of authoritative communities. They also provide philosophical support for the theological frameworks of Niebuhr, Janssens, Aquinas, and others that I use in the pages of this book.

Critical Hermeneutics and the Models of Moral Education

Van der Ven puts to good use this critical hermeneutic model of moral reflection and action. He appreciatively critiques each of the seven models of moral education. In short, he finds a place for each of them in Ricoeur's comprehensive theory of moral deliberation, but he also demonstrates their respective weaknesses. I will illustrate his accomplishment with reference to three of these models — the values-clarification perspective, Kohlberg's theory of moral development, and van der Ven's preferred model, character education.

Critique of Values Clarification

Values clarification was mentioned briefly in Chapter 2. Now it is time to look at it more carefully. Values clarification was a model of moral edu-

---

19. Van der Ven, *Formation of the Moral Self,* p. 77; Ricoeur, *Oneself as Another,* p. 240.

cation designed to handle the issue of pluralism in modern differentiated societies. It was influenced by the humanistic psychology behind
Carl Rogers's theory of client-centered counseling. Values clarification is
a group process that encourages members to attend to their individual
positive and negative experiences of life events. It does not promote una-
nimity but, instead, tries to clarify through listening and reflection the
abiding experiential valuations that individuals bring to their moral decisions. *Prizing* one's experience, *choosing*, and *acting* within a context of
mutual understanding — these are the goals of values clarification.[20] Van
der Ven calls it a process of "experiential utilitarianism."[21] This is an interesting comment; values clarification encourages both attention to
one's immediate experience and the assessment of consequences — "taking all relevant consequences into account," as he puts it.[22] Utilitarianism is interested in consequences as well, although classically it was far
more interested in their rational calculation than the individual sense of
feeling good or fulfilled by them. In values clarification, this experiential
process must arise from within oneself. Van der Ven writes, "One of the
basic assumptions of humanistic psychology and education is that for
values to become one's own, they must emerge from one's own experience rather than being imposed from outside through socialization and
then internalized."[23]

The strength of the values-clarification approach to moral education
is that it elicits the experiential energies of the individual as part of the
moral-reflective process. It invites people to experience and reflect on
their teleological aspirations. Its weakness is its massive denial of the full
hermeneutical circle of this experiential and reflective process. Van der
Ven reconstructs values clarification in light of the framework of
Gadamer's and Ricoeur's hermeneutic understanding of moral reflection,
and redefines the three steps of choosing, prizing, and acting listed above.
He writes,

> In themselves, the three processes represent three important as-
> pects of what the clarification mode in moral education ought to
> be. However — and this applies to all three processes — it seems to
> me that they should apply not in a linear but in a circular sense. It
> would be even better to conceive of them as a spiral, in which each

20. Van der Ven, *Formation of the Moral Self,* p. 243.
21. Van der Ven, *Formation of the Moral Self,* p. 252.
22. Van der Ven, *Formation of the Moral Self,* p. 244.
23. Van der Ven, *Formation of the Moral Self,* p. 244.

process, carried out at successively higher — or deeper — levels, builds on what the other two processes have already led to.[24]

In effect, van der Ven is recommending that good values clarification should be seen as a full hermeneutic circle in Gadamer's understanding of that term.[25] It should begin with reflection on the moral practices and experiences of the individual-in-community, not just the experiences of the person conceived as an autonomous and isolated entity. This reflection focuses not only on one's raw experience, which is an inauthentic construct to begin with, but on experience conceived as a mixture of our own bodily valuations and their linguistic coding by the "effective history" that touches us from the past.[26] Hence, to understand experience, we must also follow it backward in history in an attempt to understand the source of the narratives and visions of the good life implicit in one's experienced practices. The hermeneutic nature of values clarification should conceive of the inner experience of the individual as really a dialogue between what George Herbert Mead called the "I" and the "me."[27] But the "me," when properly understood, is not just Mead's thin social me. It is the thick social-historical "me" that entails not only an internalization of the social gestures of one's immediate environment but also the effective history that shaped the values, culture, narratives, and visions of the social others that have shaped the "me." The experiencing and valuing self is really the "I" in dialogue with its "me": this is the self that one brings to the values-clarification process.[28]

Values clarification as typically practiced overvalues immediate experience and undervalues the interpretation and criticism of tradition. Van der Ven proposes revising values clarification into a full hermeneutics of tradition. This move also has immense implications for models of education in clinical pastoral education and for the general process of education for ministry, as one can see in van der Ven's important book *Education for Reflective Ministry*.[29] In other words, it has implications for the meaning of "hermeneutic communication," what van der Ven believes is the central

---

24. Van der Ven, *Formation of the Moral Self,* p. 256.

25. Gadamer, *Truth and Method,* pp. 235-36.

26. Gadamer, *Truth and Method,* pp. 305-6.

27. George Herbert Mead, *Mind, Self, and Society* (Chicago, Ill.: University of Chicago Press, 1934), pp. 4-5.

28. Van der Ven, *Formation of the Moral Self,* p. 258.

29. Johannes van der Van, *Education for Reflective Ministry* (Grand Rapids: Eerdmans, 1998).

function of ministry. Hermeneutic communication is closely associated with, if not identical to, what *Formation of the Moral Self* calls moral communication; it is communication about normative matters that takes into consideration the full critical hermeneutical circle.

Critique of Kohlberg's Structuralism

Although I already have touched on Kohlberg, it is useful to get van der Ven's commentary as well. Van der Ven finds a similar neglect of the role of tradition in Kohlberg's highly influential theories. He concentrates on Kohlberg's use of the words "conventional" and "postconventional" to distinguish between the middle two stages and the last two (and allegedly higher) stages of Kohlberg's six-stage theory of moral development.[30] Van der Ven perceptively observes that Kohlberg's belief that the postconventional is a later, and more inclusive, stage of moral development implies a devaluation of conventional stages of moral thinking — hence a devaluation of tradition that shapes conventionality. It suggests that the higher stages of moral development entail a transcendence, if not an alienation, from both the conventional and tradition. Kohlberg's sharp separation of conventional from postconventional morality raises the crucial issue of where ethics and morality begin. Van der Ven asks,

> Again, where does morality start? Does it begin only at stage 6, the last and highest stage, at which the individual's thinking is determined by universal principles of justice? Or does morality include stage 5, which relates to social contract principles and human rights? Or does it already start at the conventional level, including stage 3 and stage 4, or perhaps already at the preconventional level with stage 1 and stage 2? In short, what does "morality" mean in relation to "convention" and its derivatives "preconventional" and "postconventional"?[31]

Kohlberg's moral psychology invites a neglect of tradition and an uncritical preoccupation with modernity's tendency to unify differences through increasingly more abstract and universal commonalities — all at

---

30. For a full discussion of Kohlberg's six-stage theory (divided into the three broad stages of preconventional, conventional, and postconventional), see his *Philosophy of Moral Development*, vol. 1, pp. 97-190.

31. Van der Ven, *Formation of the Moral Self,* p. 224.

the expense of the full richness of the dialectic between the good and the right, tradition and critique.

To balance this tendency in Kohlberg, van der Ven uses Ricoeur's model of moral reflection to suggest a very important amendment to Kohlberg's theory of moral development. He proposes substituting the phrase "convention-critical" for "postconventional."[32] Both van der Ven and Ricoeur assume that important moral accomplishments occur at the preconventional and conventional stages of moral development. These are the stages in which a child's egocentricity is gradually overcome as the child is socialized into the wisdom of a tradition. This is when a child learns manners, learns that telling the truth is important, and learns that his or her peers have feelings and that parents do too. This is when the child learns to value the premoral goods of knowledge, health, punctuality, and economy of resources. When this process of socialization goes well, we all celebrate the moral accomplishments that it entails. But sometimes it does not go well. Furthermore, traditions have their own defects, misinterpretations, and ambivalences. Some traditions teach children to be honest with their parents but not necessarily to people outside the family. Some communities promote in their young the virtue of loyalty — generally a fine quality to have — and then use this to fight unjust wars.

In short, these social learnings should be both transmitted and criticized. The element of Kantian-like critique that Ricoeur believes should come into play on the goods and practices of specific traditions is analogous to what Kohlberg envisions as the postconventional stage of moral development. It is analogous to Janssens's concept of equal-regard that I use to rehabilitate Niebuhr's view of mutuality. But Kohlberg's postconventionality is different in that Ricoeur and van der Ven maintain a much stronger dialectical relation between the Kantian critique and the moral wisdom embedded in the practices, images of the good life, and narratives of a transmitted tradition. Hence, van der Ven argues for reconstructing Kohlberg's fifth and sixth stages of moral development and naming them "convention-critical" in place of "postconventional." He concludes his argument with the following words:

> There is no sudden discontinuity between these stages. In a structural sense the relation between them is characterized by overlap, in that the criticism that is present within conventional traditions in turn feeds the convention-critical perspective. Temporally, their re-

---

32. Van der Ven, *Formation of the Moral Self,* p. 227.

lation is marked by a gradualness of change from the conventional to the convention-critical stage, generally without any abrupt transition from one to the other.[33]

Notice the similarities between van der Ven's criticism of these two models of moral education — the values-clarification approach and the cognitive/moral development perspective. Both cut short the full hermeneutical circle that goes into moral reflection. Values clarification does this by arresting moral reflection in the alleged wisdom of raw experience itself; it does not recognize the thickness of experience and how traditions shape it, which would require a hermeneutic interpretation and critique of how traditions qualify experience. Kohlberg's moral development theory also short-circuits the full hermeneutic circle. It arrests moral thinking at the point of a historically uninformed capacity for universalization, guided only by assumptions about the rationality and personhood of other humans. Both are foundationalist perspectives; the values-clarification perspective grounds morality on the foundation of raw experience, and the cognitive/moral development perspective grounds it on the foundation of the human capacity for reversible rational thinking applied to the field of morality. Van der Ven and Ricoeur appreciate the teleological and value-driven character of human experiencing, as does the values-clarification approach. They also see the importance of moral generalization and critique, as does Kohlberg's moral development perspective. In contrast to these two approaches, however, van der Ven and Ricoeur understand how these anthropological grounds for morality are linguistically coded by traditions and require interpretation in light of the classics and monuments that have provided their normative and narrative context.

On the Nature of Character

Much more can be said about the rich position that van der Ven develops. But we should now turn to his interpretation of the nature of character in preparation for reviewing his perspective on moral psychology and the Christian message. This is where his empirical and hermeneutic maneuvers get used in his interpretation of the Christian faith. His specifically theological reflections are often terse and condensed but nonetheless highly insightful. And it is precisely these explicitly theological discus-

33. Van der Ven, *Formation of the Moral Self,* p. 233.

sions that we should encourage van der Ven to develop even more in the future.

The pinnacle of van der Ven's own theological position comes in the concluding chapter of *Formation of the Moral Self.* It deals with the processes and goals of moral education for character. Among the models of moral education he reviews, character education is clearly his preferred model. Character education, as van der Ven conceives it, should not be categorically distinguished from the other models that he examines (education for discipline, socialization, transmission, development, values clarification, and emotional formation). According to him, character education includes, completes, and yet critiques each of these. Education for character builds on the fundamental human elements of morality — desires, goods contained in classic practices learned in socialization, reason, and narrative.[34]

One of the most informative discussions in his review of character education is his analysis of human desires. First, there are "sense-desires," which refer to the desire for pleasure through the senses; such pleasures might include those resulting from viewing beautiful art, tasting fine wine, or touching the skin of one's beloved.[35] The concept of sense-desires is close to neuroscientist Antonio Damasio's view of emotions, as we will see in Chapter 8. Second, there are the "passional desires," which evaluate situations to determine whether they are favorable or not and whether or not we want them to continue. Passional desires are close to what Damasio will call feelings, and they have a more distinctively cognitive feature to them than sense-desires.[36] Finally, there are "rational desires," which motivate people "on the basis of judgments of good and evil."[37] Van der Ven follows Ricoeur, and before that Aristotle, in seeing education for moral character as building on all of these desires. In doing this, he includes in character education the experiential and affectional dimensions of both values clarification and psychoanalytically informed views that see moral education as the formation of the emotions.

Goods, as we have seen, are on a higher and more inclusive order than desires. There are extrinsic goods such as the actual objects that satisfy our sense and passional desires: beautiful objects, beautiful people, lovely sounds and tastes. And there are intrinsic external goods, such as friend-

---

34. Van der Ven, *Formation of the Moral Self,* pp. 346-54.
35. Van der Ven, *Formation of the Moral Self,* p. 346.
36. Van der Ven, *Formation of the Moral Self,* p. 347.
37. Van der Ven, *Formation of the Moral Self,* p. 348.

ship.[38] These are goods in themselves even though external. On the other hand, van der Ven follows Aristotle in classifying our specifically moral virtues, skills, habits, and character as intrinsic internal goods.[39] Virtues such as temperance, fortitude, justice, and wisdom are components of character and help us pursue the good morally, and they are therefore goods in themselves.

The virtue of wisdom is really our habits of practical reason and is motivated by the rational desires mentioned earlier. Our capacity to exercise wisdom, or practical reason, is of the very essence of character. It makes it possible for us to evaluate our sense-desires, passional desires, and life situations in light of historically embedded images of the good life — images of the good life that are also informed by cultural and religious narratives about the origins, directions, and destiny of life.[40] Van der Ven's theory of character, following Ricoeur, sees the central virtue of practical reason or wisdom as functioning within a narrative context. Character built around the capacity for practical reason assesses our human needs and tendencies, reviews situations for their dangers and possibilities, and is framed and balanced by inherited narratives. Yet it also critiques strivings, ideals, and narratives in the light of the principles of justice, universality, and reversibility, that is, the fair distribution of the goods of life. Furthermore, character as practical wisdom determines how its narratively and critically informed judgments can be actualized within the restraints of actual contexts. This is what is needed, according to van der Ven, to deliver the ideas of moral character and virtue out of the clutches of a static essentialism and toward a model that is open, situation sensitive, flexible, yet sufficiently abstract to handle a variety of different contexts and challenges.[41]

In light of modern studies into human development, virtues, and personality traits, van der Ven tries to reformulate the classic view of character — Plato's and Aristotle's view of character as substantial and static — into a far more interactional view. The theory of morality found in the American philosopher John Dewey suddenly becomes very important for van der Ven. He writes,

> What does "interaction" mean here? The term interaction simply refers to the fact that the human person as the bearer of character

38. Van der Ven, *Formation of the Moral Self,* p. 350.
39. Van der Ven, *Formation of the Moral Self,* p. 350.
40. Van der Ven, *Formation of the Moral Self,* p. 348.
41. Van der Ven, *Formation of the Moral Self,* pp. 342-44.

is intrinsically embedded in and constantly exchanging with the situation he/she is in. The human character is not something one has before entering into and finding oneself in a particular situation. It is rather the consequence with and within this situation. Character does not unfold from within the person in isolation, but is called out through interaction with others in the situation, and through the grappling with tasks and challenges that are part of that situation. . . . As Dewey understood, this seemingly simple idea of interaction has far-reaching implications, which resolve some of the objections that are made against Platonic and Aristotelian ethics for failing to take sufficiently into consideration the aspects of human character that characterize modern thinking on the subject: its interactive, dynamic, unique, and open-ended aspects.[42]

Van der Ven drives the point home even further when he tells us that "the theory known as character and personality trait theory has to be criticized for its assumption that traits are situations independent and cross-situationally stable."[43] Hence, van der Ven sees something like Dewey's interactional model in Ricoeur's theory of character. He sees both moral thinking and the development of character as shaped by desires and passions, embedded in communally patterned practices and virtues, guided by images of the good life (which are themselves embedded in religio-cultural narratives), critiqued by reason and the categorical imperative, and *finally fine-tuned and adapted to the contingencies of situations*. It is an *interactional* theory of character, and, insofar as the interpretive process involves dialogue with other people, it is also an *intersubjective* theory of character.

There is one thing wrong with this summary formulation that I have advanced. It omits the fact that the motivating passions and quests for the good are shaped in van der Ven's view by situations from the beginning even as they must also return to situations a second time (or indeed, time and time again) for the refinements of wisdom or practical reason. But this raises the question: Is van der Ven developing a theory of character that corresponds to the infamous claims of situation ethics?[44] Is there a shadowy and disguised Joseph Fletcher lurking in the wings of van der Ven's theory of moral education and character? Does, in this model, the character who can maximize the widest range of nonmoral or premoral goods in a situation for self and others pass muster as the truly good per-

---

42. Van der Ven, *Formation of the Moral Self,* pp. 353-55.

43. Van der Ven, *Formation of the Moral Self,* p. 355.

44. Joseph Fletcher, *Situation Ethics* (Philadelphia: Westminster, 1966).

son? Does teleology win out in van der Ven's model, and a rather situationally domesticated teleology at that?

The answer to this series of questions, I think, is "no." But what saves this position from becoming a new, fresher, and fancier kind of situation ethics? My answer is this. The role of narrative in van der Ven's view gives tradition a firm and restraining power over the situation-dictated calculation of the greatest overall satisfactions relevant to the context at hand. The principle of the greatest overall satisfaction is the typical principle of obligation in all classical "act" utilitarianism, which, after all, is what situation ethics is. Tradition itself, and the codes of intrinsic goods that it houses, becomes a kind of critique and restraint in van der Ven's model. Furthermore, narrative frames a richer interpretive background for practical reason to do its work than situation ethics provides, even when located within the context of theology, as it was with Fletcher. Finally, both tradition and the situation must, in van der Ven's view, pass through the deontological critique, which is a quite different logic than that provided by the situation-ethics principle of the greatest good for the largest number of people pertinent to the context in question.[45] But the full meaning of this cannot be understood until we say more about the importance of narrative in the shaping of character and practical reason.

Character and the Tragic

Van der Ven believes that Aristotle did not fully account for the conflict of goods. The tragic character of human life is found in the fact that goods of extrinsic and intrinsic values and the goods of various virtues can, in fact, conflict with one another. The conflicting goods of life present us with choices.[46] As we have seen, Ricoeur says the same thing but even more dramatically; morality and moral character are, for him, born out of "violence" — the need to confront and resolve the violence of conflicting goods.[47] Sophocles' *Antigone* illustrates the conflict of goods found in the moral situation of the genre of Greek tragedy. Antigone was dedicated to family and blood ties and demanded the respectful burial of her brother in spite of his acts against the state. Creon was dedicated to the good of the state and would not permit the honoring of one who had defiled it. Both fidelities were good, but they were in deadly conflict with one an-

---

45. William Frankena, *Ethics* (Englewood Cliffs, N.J.: Prentice-Hall, 1973), p. 36.
46. Van der Ven, *Formation of the Moral Self,* p. 361.
47. Ricoeur, *Oneself as Another,* pp. 249-55.

other without the presence of some larger vision, some greater story, that could put the two contending values into perspective.[48] Moral character contains a tragic dimension within it, and the best religio-cultural narrative is one that holds together and reconciles to some degree the tragic tensions of character. Van der Ven builds on various hints in Ricoeur to show how the Christian story informs character and addresses the tragic conflicts of human existence.

Character and the Parable of the Last Judgment

The central theological section of *Formation of the Moral Self* deals with van der Ven's interpretation of Matthew 25, the parable of the Last Judgment. The narrative depicts the Son of Man in the eschatological kingdom exercising the final judgment over who should inherit a place in that "kingdom prepared for you from the foundation of the world" (Matt. 25:34). Here Jesus divides the nations of the world before him into sheep and goats and places the sheep on his right hand and the goats on his left. Those on his right are received into the kingdom prepared by "my Father" and those on the left are cast into the eternal fire "prepared for the devil and his angels" (Matt. 25:41). Why are they so judged? Those on the right gained this reward for their acts of kindness and justice. Jesus says, "for I was hungry and you gave me food, I was thirsty and you gave me something to drink, I was a stranger and you welcomed me, I was naked and you gave me clothing, I was sick and you took care of me, I was in prison and you visited me" (Matt. 25:35-36).

The story tells us that those on his right hand were perplexed and asked, "Lord, when was it that we saw you hungry and gave you food, or thirsty and gave you something to drink? And when was it that we saw you a stranger and welcomed you, or naked and gave you clothing? And when was it that we saw you sick or in prison and visited you?" (Matt. 25:37-39) The reply from Jesus, now the risen Lord and Judge of all history, is stunning. He says, "Truly I tell you, just as you did it to one of the least of these who are members of my family, you did it to me" (Matt. 25:40). The story concludes by looking at the reverse situation. Those on his left did not do any of these things. They did not provide food and drink, did not give clothes to the naked, did not take in the stranger, did not visit the sick and imprisoned. It was not that they literally neglected to do these

---

48. For van der Ven's interpretation of *Antigone*, see *Formation of the Moral Self*, pp. 362-65; for Ricoeur's interpretation, see *Oneself as Another*, pp. 241-49.

things for Jesus. Rather, it was this: "just as you did not do it to one of the least of these, you did not do it to me" (Matt. 25:45).

Here is van der Ven's brief summary of this narrative.

> This text contains at least two layers, a moral and a religious one. The moral layer encourages the listener or reader to give food to the hungry, drink to the thirsty, clothes to the naked and to visit the sick and the imprisoned. The religious layer consists of Jesus' identification with the "least of mine," so that what is done to them is done to him.[49]

What is fascinating about this story is how religious narrative and moral universality reinforce each other. First, however, notice the teleological dimensions of the story. It assumes that all people pursue the elementary goods of life, in this case fairly basic desires for food, drink, clothing, and fellowship. In fact, the story assumes that these basic desires, when deprived, turn into needs and necessities. We cannot be human without food and drink. And we cannot be fully human without clothes and fellowship. There is a sense, in this story, that both religion and morality are about fulfilling these teleological goods and possibly many others not explicitly thematized in the narrative. It is true, as Ricoeur has reminded us, that we know these goods as good through our practices of actually eating and being nourished, of actually drinking and having the fluids of our body replaced, of having clothes and feeling protection from the elements, and of concretely enjoying the presence of loved ones and friends. When the goods are taken away from us, we treasure them even more. These elementary goods are not the only goods of life, but this story is insightful in that it shows how both religion and morality are about the fulfillment of the teleological goods of life.

The ingenious part of the narrative is the identification of Jesus with the suffering individuals of the world. He is they; they are he. And this seems to be true in some basic metaphysical sense. As the spirit of God dwells in all creatures, the spirit of Jesus does too, especially in the lives of suffering humans. Hence, all suffering affecting finite individuals also, according to the narrative, affects Jesus and is felt — indeed undergone and suffered — by him. But Jesus is not only the finite suffering individual, he is the Son of God and participates in the final judgment about who inherits eternal life. *Jesus is the ideal observer monitoring all deeds, the*

---

49. Van der Ven, *Formation of the Moral Self,* p. 366.

ideal recipient of all deeds, and the final judge of all deeds. The story of the Last Judgment is about a universal ethic of equal-regard which tells the Christian he has a generalized ethical obligation to meet the needs of all persons equally. But this is not an abstract Kantian ethic; it is an ethic reinforced by the drama of God's salvatory and judging work through Jesus, who both observes and receives the consequences of all acts. In passing, we should note that van der Ven's view of Christian love and justice is more strenuous than that of Niebuhr, who tends to swing back and forth between the impossible demands of self-sacrificial love and a view of finite love and justice that is closer to conditioned reciprocity. But Niebuhr has other things to offer, and I will return to them at a later point.

The drama of the Last Judgment, according to van der Ven, also addresses certain pervasive aporias of moral action — the conflict between care of self and care of others, the conflict between caring for close loved ones and the care of the stranger, and the conflict between care for immediate needs of the poor and their long-term institutional support.[50] The narrative of the Last Judgment does not resolve these paradoxes; in fact, its eschatological message says that moral action must keep these tensions open. Moral character and the narratives that shape it should not too easily settle the tension toward one or the other set of our obligations; in fact, it should work indefinitely into the future to attend to both sides of one's commitments until one finally faces Jesus at the Last Judgment.[51] Van der Ven sees the story as proclaiming that self-regard must be balanced with other-regard, care for intimates balanced with care for strangers, and short-term care for the poor with their long-term provision. Jesus is everywhere and in the end will, with God, judge all people and every act. We do not get off the hook.

A Critique of van der Ven

Van der Ven's exposition of character education, its relation to tragedy, and his use of the parable of the Last Judgment to illustrate the contributions of narrative to moral principles and virtues is challenging and very suggestive. Within a very few pages, he brings together and synthesizes an enormous number of insights from theology, moral psychology, and moral philosophy. One sees in this illustration all the elements of

---

50. Van der Ven, *Formation of the Moral Self,* p. 368.
51. Van der Ven, *Formation of the Moral Self,* pp. 368-78.

Ricoeur's critical hermeneutical model of moral formation — teleological strivings for the good life, critique performed by the principle of universalization now embedded in the person of Jesus as both sufferer and judge, the narrative eschatological framing of both teleology and deontology, and finally the ambiguity of returning to the situation to concretely hold together as best one can the aporias of the moral life. Certainly, as is the case with situation ethics, there is emphasis on the concrete context of action. But the logic of van der Ven's view of moral character is not a form of act utilitarianism. The moment of deontological critique and the narrative framing it function to guide reflection in the concrete situation quite differently than is the case with classic situation ethics.

But as is always the case in this finite world, his argument could be made even more convincing and complete. Nevertheless, this is a happy situation for the critic: I support the direction van der Ven is going. He both extends and enriches Ricoeur by bringing Ricoeur's work into the total field of moral education. *Formation of the Moral Self* also greatly enriches the hermeneutical model of an empirical practical theology that van der Ven has been developing over the last decades. It also helps us understand the moral dimensions of religious reflection in theology, ecclesiology, and ministerial reflection.

Van der Ven and the Christian Narrative

Two further moves, I believe, could strengthen the argument even more. One move would be to offer a richer discussion of the contributions of the Christian narrative to moral education. Space in this chapter permits only a few brief illustrative comments — comments that will be elaborated later in this book. For instance, there is no discussion by van der Ven of the way the metaphor of God the Creator, as Niebuhr calls it, contributes to moral education. Niebuhr could say that God the Creator makes all creation good in a basic premoral sense, and that that gives us an ontological right to view our various natural desires positively, to bring them consciously into the moral formation process rather than repressing them. Even Ricoeur has something to contribute here. The doctrine of creation, Ricoeur would argue, offers an economy or ontology of the "gift." It tells us that the premoral goods that we tend largely to assume — life itself, health, provisions, pleasure, beauty, children, friendships — are goods we receive freely out of the fullness of creation and out of the superabundance of God's gifts to us.[52] What this does is to bestow an ontological blessing on all our teleological strivings toward the good life. This is the unearned grace of creation which is continued in the unearned grace of salvation. This ontology of the gift of creation gives birth to a Christian humanism which only occasionally has been fully developed in the history of Christianity. The Christian theology of creation, which is in reality a theology of the gift of the goods of life, grants Christians an ontological right to enjoy the goods of life but only if they do so within the right moral and narrative framework — one that contains the deontological test and also understands the drama of the gift of creation, human fallibility, the Last Judgment, and redemption.

The reality of sin and the violence of competing goods require the deontological test, as Ricoeur and van der Ven fully acknowledge. But the presence of sin and violence also requires the grace and forgiveness of salvation, as Niebuhr, Ricoeur, and van der Ven all would insist. The narrative of the Last Judgment brilliantly illustrates the deontological critique and how, in fact, it is ensconced in the very structure of the Christian narrative. But van der Ven's rendition of the story does not show how the gifts of creation, salvatory grace, and forgiveness hold and renew us in the context of critique and judgment. Remember, van der Ven sees Christian character as a manifestation of practical reason shaped by the Christian narrative. He does a good job of helping us understand how Christ is both recipient and judge (something close to Niebuhr's God as Judge) of all human action and thereby supports the Christian's capacity for universal moral judgments.

But there is more in this narrative. How does the Christian story free practical reason from the bondage of sin? I contend that this is the role of grace and forgiveness. As I will point out at some length with the help of Niebuhr in Chapter 9, grace and forgiveness liberate us from the bondage of sin so that practical reason can function more freely — more fully and completely. Grace and forgiveness are also part of the transforming power of the Christian narrative. All of these themes I will discuss more in Chapter 9. It is not that van der Ven does not touch on these truths; rather, he does not touch on them enough, especially in the context of his work on moral formation.

---

52. Paul Ricoeur, *Figuring the Sacred* (Minneapolis: Fortress, 1995), pp. 99, 279.

Van der Ven and the Premoral Goods

There is another move that would help. This has to do with developing a fuller and more concrete discussion of the concept of premoral goods. Actually, van der Ven says much about this aspect of moral theory. Remember that he follows Ricoeur in viewing ethics, in contrast to morality, as dealing with human strivings for the premoral goods of life. There is a certain way, as we have seen, that the Protestant neo-Orthodox Niebuhr would agree with this and, as we will see later, the entire Thomistic and neo-Thomistic Catholic Christian tradition would as well. These premoral goods are ethically relevant. It should be remembered, however, that their pursuit is not fully moral until conflict between premoral goods is mediated by the deontological critique and by wise judgments about how they can be ordered justly in the original situation of the conflict. Furthermore, van der Ven's distinction between sense-desires, passions, and rational desires, which we reviewed above, is in fact a discussion of the premoral goods of life that are ethically relevant but not fully moral until they pass the deontological test and the judgments of wisdom. What more, then, is there to say about this aspect of life?

Quite a bit. Much of van der Ven's discussion of these premoral goods, all of which is quite useful and insightful, is still abstract. He becomes more concrete when he turns to illustrations, such as the reference in his discussion of sense-desires to beauty, art, tasting fine wine, and touching the beloved. What is noticeably absent in these references is any discussion of what evolutionary psychologists would call the premoral good of "kin altruism."[53] In fact, what is absent in his entire discussion, amazing in its comprehensiveness, is any reference to the powerful new moral theories of evolutionary psychology, the work of scientists and thinkers such as W. D. Hamilton, Robert Trivers, E. O. Wilson, Richard Alexander, Frans de Waal, Mary Midgley, and many others. These theorists claim to have discovered why mate selection and kin altruism are fundamental to human moral development. According to evolutionary psychology, several realities — that human infants are highly dependent, that infants carry 50 percent of the genetic material of their biological mother and father, and that parents generally see their own image in their children — constitute the naturalistic grounds for parental investment, care,

---

53. For an introductory definition of the concept of kin altruism and its distinction from reciprocal altruism, see Robert Wright, *The Moral Animal* (New York: Pantheon, 1994), pp. 189-209.

empathy, and mutual attachment and identification. Evolutionary psychologists argue that these are the "ultimate" general conditions, in contrast to the "proximate" conditions, that contribute to the emergence of affection and mutual sympathy between parent and child and thereby lead to the formation of conscience at the human level.

James Q. Wilson, as we have seen, argues that all of the basic virtues required for the moral life are in some sense derived from and stimulated by kin altruism.[54] But Wilson argues that kin altruism is also the source of moral virtues that extend to non-kin. He writes,

> What evolution has selected for over countless millennia is not simply a desire to reproduce one's genes in the next generation, or even to ensure that similar genes among one's kin get reproduced, but a particular psychological orientation that has as one of its effects a preference for kin but extends to nonkin as well.[55]

The moral virtues or sentiments that Wilson has in mind are sympathy, fairness, self-control, and duty. Each is somehow a derivative of the special investment humans have in their children. Sympathy springs from the sense that the child is mine and part me; hence I extend to the infant the feelings of empathy and sympathy I have for my own pains and pleasures.[56] The infant responds to this sympathy in kind and gradually learns to extend it to non-kin as well; the baby, and later the child, slowly discovers that even strangers are also thinking, feeling persons like her and like the members of her immediate family. But without first learning sympathy in the intimate context of the family, the infant will have difficulty learning to extend it to others.

Kin altruism is also the central source of the sentiment or virtue of fairness. Fairness is closely associated with sympathy; without feeling what others feel, we have little motivation to treat them fairly. Of course, fairness requires a bit of intelligence as well; it requires being able to generalize our feelings to others in order to imagine how they feel on the basis of a variety of clues.[57] If Wilson is correct about the origins of our sense of fairness, then kin altruism can be seen as contributing to our capacity to enact the deontological test. It must be nurtured by reason and culture, but that is the point; reason and culture can

---

54. James Q. Wilson, *The Moral Sense* (New York: Free Press, 1993), pp. 13, 15-23.
55. Wilson, *The Moral Sense*, p. 23.
56. Wilson, *The Moral Sense*, pp. 44-55.
57. Wilson, *The Moral Sense*, pp. 49-65.

build on the structures of kin altruism to become a more thoroughly moral capacity.

Self-control comes from the matrix of kin altruism as well; to be able to delay gratification we need to be able to sympathize with how our actions affect others, indeed will affect ourselves at some future time.[58] And, finally, a sense of duty springs from the mutual identifications inspired by kin altruism. Developing the sentiment or virtue of duty to others requires the stability provided by sympathy, fairness, and self-control.[59] Of course, all of these virtues can be developed in children by surrogates to biological parents. But this formation process may be much more difficult in those cases. Evolutionary psychology argues that even though these parental capacities and inclinations can be activated by non-biologically related infants and children, the parental potentials themselves are "retentions" of an evolutionary history building on the inclinations associated with kin altruism. And these inclinations to parental investment are never quite as strong with others as they are with one's own offspring. From the standpoint of Christian ethics, adoption should be predicated on the needs of the vulnerable or abandoned child. The self-fulfillment of the adopting parent is a relevant but secondary justification for adopting. Adoption is a heroic Christian act, somewhat parallel to the self-sacrificial moment in Christian love as equal-regard, but it is not to replace the finite but highly central good of parenthood based on kin altruism.[60]

One need not absolutize natural parenthood in the Christian life in order to give it a serious role in shaping the premoral goods and energies that go into good moral character and moral education. The natural energies, investments, sympathies, and identifications flowing from kin altruism are still relative goods and give rise to relative moralities. They are part of the basic desires of life that make up the teleological beginning of the field of ethics. Furthermore, they are always further interpreted, and need to be further interpreted, by various linguistic codes, patterns, practices, and traditions. In addition, they need to be supported and stabilized by cognitive judgments and powerful narrative frameworks, as they have most powerfully and explicitly, we will discover, in most of the Roman Catholic tradition of Christian theology. Kin altruism is a relative good,

58. Wilson, *The Moral Sense*, p. 90.

59. Wilson, *The Moral Sense*, pp. 101-10.

60. For my position on the role of adoption in Christian ethics, see my "Adoption and the Moral Significance of Kin Altruism," in *The Morality of Adoption: Social-Psychological, Theological, and Legal Perspectives,* ed. Timothy Jackson (Grand Rapids: Eerdmans, 2005).

as are all the premoral goods of life; it is morally relevant but not morally determinative. Kin altruism is something from which attachments grow and spread outward to non-kin. Kin altruism and the attachments that cling to it are the bridge between families and authoritative communities. In a time when family disruption is rampant, when children are more and more separated from natural parents by nonmarital births, divorce, poverty, artificial reproduction technology, and war, and when increasingly we are hearing of "no-parent children" who are being raised in foster homes or by assortments of less invested relatives or accidental acquaintances, Van der Ven should not ignore the relative contribution to moral formation of the premoral value of kin altruism.

My concluding points have been these: Van der Ven's important application of Ricoeur's "little ethics" to the field of moral education could be strengthened at two points. First, it could profit from a fuller development of the many ways the Christian narrative on creation and salvation (as interpreted by Niebuhr and others) can inform character built around practical reason. This is a theme I continue to develop throughout this book. Second, it could be strengthened by including a discussion of the importance of the premoral good of kin altruism to moral formation and character.[61] But these small suggestions should not obscure the power and importance of van der Ven's contributions to moral education, moral psychology, and Christian ethics.

---

61. In fairness, it should be noticed that quite recently, van der Ven has attended more fully to evolutionary psychology and cognitive science and hence is beginning to move in the direction I wished he had taken earlier. See his response to my article, and other articles, in the recent Festschrift titled *Hermeneutics and Empirical Research in Practical Theology: The Contribution of Empirical Theology by Johannes A. van der Ven,* ed. Chris A. M. Hermans and Mary E. Moore (Leiden: Brill, 2004), pp. 331-88.

Chapter 4

The Dialectic of Belonging
and Distanciation

D iscussing the relation between Christian ethics and modern moral
psychology requires addressing the relation of tradition and science. In doing this, I have from time to time mentioned the concept of
"distanciation." I want to talk more about this idea, but I also want to introduce a closely related concept, the idea of "diagnosis." The cultural
drive toward science must be seen as a drive toward distanciation from
tradition-laden knowledge. Instead of wanting to achieve distanciation
(or simply "distance," if you prefer), scientists often aspire to objectivity.
But the word "objectivity" implies philosophical foundationalism and ob-
scures the truth that, at best, science only attains varying degrees of distance or distanciation from the tradition-shaped beginnings of its knowing and understanding. When applied to human behavior, this drive
toward distanciation can be useful as a kind of diagnosis of the natural
regularities embedded in tradition. It is my argument, however, that the
drive toward the objective science of any aspect of human action, including a science of moral psychology, should be seen only as a kind of
submoment to the wisdom of traditions — a distanciating and diagnostic
submoment with immense potential for clarification, but a submoment
nonetheless. Science cannot function as a foundation upon which to erect
once again a moral edifice — or for that matter a moral psychology —
from scratch. These concepts will help us find the way between science
and tradition in both moral psychology and Christian ethics.

Practical Theological Ethics

The discipline that studies the ethical implications of the Christian tradition is referred to in Protestant quarters as theological ethics and in Roman Catholic circles as moral theology. Since I am a Protestant, I will generally use the term "theological ethics." But I add something that is not always done. I use the phrase "practical theological ethics." What is that? It is a combination of the two fields in which I have been working over the last twenty years — the discipline of theological ethics and the discipline of practical theology. I bring the two together because I am convinced that practical theology — generally associated with the disciplines that study the caring, preaching, worshiping, and teaching tasks of the church with real people in their actual lives — needs a stronger normative grounding in theological ethics. I am also convinced that theological ethics needs a stronger interest in describing the situations it addresses and more concern with what it actually takes to transform situations. Practical theology needs to be more normative and theological ethics needs to be more descriptive and transformative — hence the term "practical theological ethics."

The borderline between practical theology and theological ethics has become blurred because of the rise of what is commonly called "practical philosophy."[1] By practical philosophy, I mean the rather widespread trend in modern philosophies to give *phronēsis* or practical reason a renewed place of honor. According to Richard Bernstein, this movement toward the practical can be found in Wittgenstein's ordinary language analysis, Gadamer's philosophical hermeneutics, American pragmatism, Marxism, Habermas's discourse ethics, and Ricoeur's critical hermeneutics.[2] Ricoeur's critical hermeneutics is the main resource used in this book. More specifically, *phronēsis* as the practical attempt to establish and implement the norms of action is being viewed by many as providing the contextual framework for both *theōria* (theoretical reason) and *technē* (technical reason).

To understand the contributions of practical philosophy to the reformulation of both practical theology and theological ethics, it is useful to bring to mind once again what Ricoeur calls in *Oneself as Another* the

---

1. Ricoeur refers to the complex set of studies as "practical philosophy." See his *Oneself as Another* (Chicago: University of Chicago, 1992), p. 19.

2. For careful characterizations of these philosophical perspectives as types of practical philosophy, see Richard Bernstein's *Praxis and Action* (Philadelphia: University of Pennsylvania Press, 1971), *The Reconstruction of Social and Political Theory* (Philadelphia: University of Pennsylvania Press, 1978), and *Beyond Objectivism and Relativism* (Philadelphia: University of Pennsylvania Press, 1983).

"three-step rhythm" of any hermeneutics of the self and its actions, that is, the steps of describing, narrating, and prescribing.[3] This is one of the many happy formulas that Ricoeur provides to unify the complex texture of his thought and guide us through his many methodological detours. It should be understood in light of his other famous and useful formulas, such as the early rule in *Freedom and Nature* that "the voluntary is by reason of the involuntary while the involuntary is for the voluntary."[4]

These two formulas together help us understand the dialectic between the teleological quest for the good and the deontological test of justice. They also help us understand why description is so important for ethical reflection; it is through description that we first grasp the practices that encode the goods of life. These practices, however, still may need interpretation and critique at the more properly moral level. To understand this threefold movement even more fully, one should interpret it in close relation to Ricoeur's other famous formula that defines morality "as aiming at the 'good life' with and for others, in just institutions."[5] It is this threefold rhythm understood in close relation to these other formulas that opens for Ricoeur an understanding of the self in relation to its world. It is the rhythm of describing, narrating, and prescribing that reveals the nature of the self as a practical thinker, both within the context of philosophy and, as I will claim, within the context of practical theology and normative Christian ethics, or practical theological ethics. This formula also reveals the special role of narrative in linking the self as describer with the self as prescriber. This insight is important for practical theological ethics, and it also is important for moral psychology. The moral self is in a constant rhythm of describing, narrating, and prescribing.

From Hermeneutics to Critical Hermeneutics

This parallel between Ricoeur's three-step hermeneutics of the self and the methods of the new practical Christian ethics is no accident. Gadamer and Ricoeur are chief sources for the methodologies of the new practical theology and ethics.[6] In many ways, however, Ricoeur is more important

3. Ricoeur, *Oneself as Another,* p. 20.

4. Paul Ricoeur, *Freedom and Nature* (Evanston, Ill.: Northwestern University Press, 1966), p. xv.

5. Ricoeur, *Oneself as Another,* p. 172.

6. Johannes van der Ven, *Entwurf einer Empirischen Theologie* (Kampen: Weinhim, 1990), *Ecclesiology in Context* (Grand Rapids: Eerdmans, 1996), *Formation of the Moral Self* (Grand

for this movement than Gadamer. This is because Ricoeur finds a place in human understanding for both ideology critique and the distanciating methods of science in ways that elude Gadamer. Using Ricoeur, rather than Gadamer alone, makes it possible for practical theological ethics to become both a hermeneutical and a critical discipline. It also equips it to use the social sciences in its descriptive moment and in all succeeding steps without losing its unique identity as a religiously grounded form of *phronēsis*. The concept of distanciation is also crucial for refining the pre-empirical theory of the self that is needed for moral psychology.

In the following paragraphs, I will amplify this statement by showing briefly where Gadamer and Ricoeur agree, where they diverge on the role of empirical scientific method in moral reflection, and some differences these points make for practical theological ethics. I also will discuss certain ambiguities in Ricoeur's view of the role of distanciation in the understanding process and what this concept means for the descriptive and prescriptive tasks of both the moral self and practical theological ethics.

Among the many observations I will make, my central claim is this: As Ricoeur's thought has developed, there has been at least one important loss. There has been a blurring of the meaning of his important concept of diagnosis. This concept, closely related to the idea of distanciation, was crucial in the early Ricoeur for showing how the objectifying attitudes of science can contribute to an understanding of the experiencing self. I will argue that Ricoeur's significant contribution to ethics can be heightened if the concept of diagnosis is revived and used to clarify the teleological goods assumed in both his deontological test and the task of "practical wisdom." In what follows, I will attempt to clarify this admittedly dense formulation.

Gadamer and Ricoeur

There are important parallels between Gadamer and Ricoeur, and Ricoeur would be the first to acknowledge the impact of Gadamer on his thought, in spite of their important differences. I draw attention to their similarities and differences in order to unpack the concept of diagnosis and also the meaning of Ricoeur's injunction to describe, narrate, and prescribe.

First, before we can grasp the idea of diagnosis, we must comprehend

---

Rapids: Eerdmans, 1998); Gerben Heitink, *Practical Theology* (Grand Rapids: Eerdmans, 1999); Friedrich Schweitzer, *Die Religion des Kindes: Zur Problemgeschichte einer religions-pädagogischen Grundfrage* (Gütersloh, Germany: Gütersloher Verlaghaus Gerd Mohn, 1992).

what it means to describe. Both Gadamer and Ricoeur believe that human understanding is primarily a historically situated dialogue or conversation exhibiting the features of question and answer.[7] To describe is first to understand the situated dialogue in which one is already embedded — the dialogue that also already makes up the self. Hence, description, even social-science description, is not primarily an objective process of standing outside one's historically located dialogue. Rather, it is first a matter of accounting for what already has shaped us in the unfolding situation we are attempting to describe. Both Gadamer and Ricoeur believe that the prejudgments or prejudices, shaped by our cultural inheritance from the past and therefore implicit in our questions, are crucial for the understanding process.[8] They are shaped by the continuing presence in our experience of the "effective histories" of the past, especially the classic texts and monuments that have shaped our civilization.[9] These prejudgments must be brought to light as referents in relation to which we understand new experience.

For example, let's assume I want to understand and influence the contemporary debate over the family raging in American society and, increasingly, throughout the world. Gadamer and Ricoeur would say that, rather than jumping out of my historical skin and going directly to the objective social-science study of families, I and all Americans, as individuals and as a collective, should start with our own effective experience, that is, with our own pre-understandings of families as they have been shaped by levels upon levels of history. Some of this effective history has been formed by classic ideas and images of family that have stood the test of time, but some of these images also have been distorted or unable to cope with changing circumstances. Starting with the effective history of most Americans — especially the dominant Protestant and Catholic majorities who also had so much influence in shaping the official legal and cultural ethos of families in both the United States and most Western nations — we would need to work backward. We would need to understand how Jewish creation stories and legal traditions shaped early Christianity, how early Christian reworkings later interacted with Aristotelian philosophy and Roman law in the formation of Catholic canon law in the tenth and eleventh centuries,

7. Paul Ricoeur, *Hermeneutics and the Human Sciences* (Cambridge: Cambridge University Press, 1981), p. 62; Hans-Georg Gadamer, *Truth and Method* (New York: Crossroad, 1982), pp. 330-31.

8. Ricoeur, *Hermeneutics and the Human Sciences*, pp. 66-67, 76-78; Gadamer, *Truth and Method*, pp. 238-40.

9. Ricoeur, *Hermeneutics and the Human Sciences*, pp. 73-76; Gadamer, *Truth and Method*, pp. 267-74.

how much of this was passed on to the Protestant Reformation, and how both Lutheran and Calvinist countries shaped a new culture and law of families that radiated outward to most Protestant countries in Europe and to the United States. We would need to understand how Roman Catholic canon law traditions continued to shape Catholic countries and even some of the southern states of the United States. This is the classic tradition that has shaped our family ideals, making the value of mutual consent the essence of marriage, gradually outlawing polygamy and emphasizing monogamy, and requiring fathers to be accountable for their children.

Now there are indeed tensions in that tradition, especially over the status of women and the way this tradition both critiques and copes with modernization, especially work and family tensions. The idea of distanciation and diagnosis, as we will see, would say that the social sciences can clarify and help rework some of the elements of this tradition, and this is to the good. But social sciences would not be able to reinvent our family traditions or create them anew from scratch. This is the meaning of an anti-foundationalist approach that builds in a place for science, as does Ricoeur, in contrast to a foundationalist approach that would start with science, forget tradition, and try to build a fresh and new family ethic on supposedly neutral empirical knowledge.[10]

Gadamer's idea of the classic and Ricoeur's idea of narrative constitute the link between description and prescription. Gadamer speaks more about classics than narratives; Ricoeur writes about both but ends by suggesting that classics really come in the form of narratives. The point for both men is this: when we describe something, the normative horizon of our effective histories (composed of classics and narratives) rightly casts a fringe of meaning over the object of description. But the same is true, rightly and necessarily, for the self's act of prescription. Our practical actions and strategies are shaped, although not necessarily totally dictated, by our individual and cultural narrative backgrounds.

But Gadamer and Ricoeur see the process of understanding, including understanding the classics or narratives that help shape our selfhood, as a *practical or applicational process* through and through. Our practical situations and questions shape our construal of the normative horizon of

---

10. For a more systematic review of the history of the Western traditions of family and marriage and the complex interaction between religion, law, and naturalistic judgments, see John Witte, *From Sacrament to Contract: Marriage, Religion, and Law in the Western Tradition* (Louisville: Westminster John Knox, 1997), and Don Browning, *Marriage and Modernization: How Globalization Threatens Marriage and What to Do about It* (Grand Rapids: Eerdmans, 2003), pp. 55-76.

our effective histories just as these horizons in turn shape our description of situations. Gadamer wrote, and Ricoeur would affirm, the following words that invoke the authority of Aristotle:

> We, too, determined that application is neither a subsequent nor a merely occasional part of the phenomenon of understanding, but co-determines it as a whole from the beginning.[11]

A concern with application or relevance is not something we tack on at the end of the understanding process. Interests in application, what to do and how to do it, shape understanding from the beginning.

In an earlier paragraph, you may have noticed me say that our classics or central narratives shape *but do not necessarily totally determine* our prescriptive and strategic actions. This qualification, I believe, is more in accordance with the sensibilities of Ricoeur than with those of Gadamer. Ricoeur steers a delicate course between the respect for tradition found in Gadamer and appreciation for the critique of tradition found in the Frankfurt school and the thought of the German social theorist Jürgen Habermas. As we have seen, Ricoeur eschews foundationalism (the attempt to base knowledge and ethics on objective science, sense data, or transcendental phenomenology) whether in scientific epistemology or in ethics. Foundationalism in its various guises has an alienating disregard for tradition, the histories that have formed us and to which, therefore, we *already belong.* In one essay he writes, "History precedes me and my reflection: I belong to history before I belong to myself."[12]

The Role of Distanciation

On the other hand, Ricoeur readily acknowledges the place for what he calls cognitive distanciation in both epistemology and practical ethics. But he views whatever cognitive distanciation is possible as a submoment within a more basic background of historical belonging and understanding. Hence, rather than celebrating either the hyper-distanciating pretensions of objective science or an uncritical embeddedness in tradition, Ricoeur asks, "Would it not be appropriate . . . to reformulate the question in such a way that a certain dialectic between the experience of belonging and alienating distanciation becomes the mainspring, the key to

11. Gadamer, *Truth and Method,* p. 289.
12. Ricoeur, *Hermeneutics and the Human Sciences,* p. 68.

the inner life, of hermeneutics?"[13] Hence, for Ricoeur, truth (which he identifies with hermeneutic understanding) and scientific method are not viewed, as they are for Gadamer, as a matter of either/or. He sees truth and scientific method not as "a disjunction" but rather as "a dialectical process."[14]

This interlude opens us to the central theme of this chapter — the potential role of distanciation (and the related idea of diagnosis) in describing, narrating, and prescribing, the three moments of self-understanding that I have said are so important for the contemporary field of practical theological ethics. In short, there is for Ricoeur a subordinate role for the explanatory interests of distanciation in each of these three moments. This, finally, is why Ricoeur more than Gadamer has been so useful for the struggle of Christian ethics to control its use of the social sciences in all its various submoments, but especially its descriptive and prescriptive ones.

The Three Moments Again

Obviously, there is a parallel between describing, narrating, and prescribing, and Ricoeur's account of normative action as moving from ethics, through narrative, to the deontological test and wisdom. The reader should now recall the outlines of Ricoeur's moral philosophy laid out in Chapters 2 and 3. My task in this chapter is to show how the concepts of diagnosis and distanciation have a role in analyzing and criticizing confusions about conflicting goods in the first and last moments of Ricoeur's threefold view of moral reflection — the first moment that he calls ethics and the third moment of the deontological test and practical wisdom.

Let us recall Ricoeur's formula for the moral life as "aiming at the 'good life' with and for others, in just institutions." This formula reminds us that Ricoeur sees moral reflection as beginning with the teleological quest for the good life and the various discrete goods that make up this life. We should recall that Ricoeur teaches that these goods are first of all discovered indirectly through our inherited and multidimensional social practices. Practices as viewed by Ricoeur are multi-layered or thick; they consist of many different dimensions — the push and pull of

13. Ricoeur, *Hermeneutics and the Human Sciences*, p. 90.
14. Ricoeur, *Hermeneutics and the Human Sciences*, p. 93.

our basic desires, goal-oriented instrumental actions, more encompassing rules of the game, ideals of the good life, and finally integrating narratives about life that subordinate and contextualize the earlier mentioned dimensions.[15] To *describe* the goods we desire and think we need (the first step in a moral hermeneutics of the self) is to describe or interpret them within the full thickness of the history and tradition of social practices that have encoded them.

The dominant narratives that surround our practices and their embedded goods provide the self, in its exercise of *phronēsis,* with a plot that gives some unity to the discordant goods we experience. This narrative, if it is a strong one, also provides a home within which the self can experiment with solutions to the tensions of life.[16] Telling stories is an act of *phronēsis;* it is a way of rehearsing the meaning and consequences of various possible plots for one's life. In Ricoeur's view, the interpretation and retrieval of the narrative or narratives that inform our practical actions is a primary task for moral reflection. This is why acting morally, as we have seen, entails first *description* and then *narration.* Description in its fullest expression is about describing our ethical practices — the various ways we pursue the goods of life. Narration, on the other hand, is about retelling the stories that we use to make sense of the various levels and conflicts in our ethical practices.

The third moment of prescription, as we have seen, is actually divided by Ricoeur into two parts — the so-called deontological test (a variation on Kant's *Moralität*) and the test of practical wisdom (a variation on Hegel's *Sittlichkeit*).[17] But for Ricoeur, the deontological moment does not by itself constitute a sufficient test. One must return to the original ethical situation (the *Sittlichkeit*) to determine what this abstract test means for the pursuit of the original conflicting goods first described in the ethical moment of moral understanding.[18] This is why description in moral philosophy, just as in practical theological ethics, is not a trivial aspect of the reflective task. Without describing the original practices and their encoded yet conflicting goods, there is no adequate way to return to that situation and fulfill the test of wisdom. Description is essential for the exercise of wisdom.

15. Ricoeur, *Oneself as Another,* pp. 153-63; Ricoeur, "Teleological and Deontological Structures of Action: Aristotle and/or Kant?" in *Contemporary French Philosophy,* ed. A. Phillips Griffiths (Cambridge: Cambridge University Press, 1987), pp. 99-103.

16. Ricoeur, *Oneself as Another,* p. 164.

17. Ricoeur, *Oneself as Another,* pp. 250-63.

18. Ricoeur, *Oneself as Another,* pp. 241, 250-55.

A Modest Critique

Ricoeur's model of moral reflection is highly suggestive, but it is not without problems. He overlooks the difficulties that emerge in both the descriptive and prescriptive moments of moral understanding. In the descriptive moment, our task is to describe the conflict of goods that emerges in our ethical or teleological pursuits. But can we always describe adequately? And the prescriptive moment, on the other hand, is concluded by wisdom returning to the original ethical situation of conflicting goods, but this time not just to describe but to weigh the clashing goods that first emerged there and to place them in a hierarchy. The test of universalization, even when formulated to include premoral or teleological goods, is too abstract to provide any prioritization of conflicting concrete goods in specific contexts. But does Ricoeur provide a method that goes beyond description and actually helps us make judgments that rank conflicting goods, as required for wisdom?

Ricoeur is aware of this problem and has invoked Alan Donagan's theory of fundamental human goods to refine his own reformulation of the Golden Rule. Taking his cue from Donagan, Ricoeur recently has rendered the Golden Rule to read, "Act so that the optative goods to which your practice aims conform with the normative goods entailed by the Golden Rule."[19] But what are these optative or fundamental goods, and how does Ricoeur derive them? They are certainly more than Kant's empirical desires ruled by the hypothetical imperative. Fundamental or optative goods for Ricoeur doubtless include but are more concrete than Rawls's social goods of liberty, opportunity, and wealth or Rawls's natural goods of health and intelligence.[20] In one place, Ricoeur refers to these fundamental goods as "interests" that we must respect in our solicitude for the other's pursuit of the good life.[21]

Ricoeur does give hints as to how one might evaluate and prioritize conflicting goods. Clearly, the hermeneutic retrieval of a tradition would be the first source, because traditions themselves are carriers of hierarchies of goods. For instance, most religious traditions value pleasure — even sexual pleasure. This is especially true of Judaism and Islam. But even then, sexual pleasure is subordinate to the good of family and marital stability. Most traditions value bodily health and material wealth but

---

19. Ricoeur, "Teleological and Deontological Structures of Action," p. 18.

20. John Rawls, *A Theory of Justice* (Cambridge: Harvard University Press, 1971), p. 62.

21. Ricoeur, "Teleological and Deontological Structures of Action," p. 110.

also try to restrain these goods from destroying the good of sociality. As far back as Ricoeur's *Freud and Philosophy*, when his turn to hermeneutic philosophy was well in place, he argued that knowledge of our desires and needs is always mediated through language and the traditions that give us our linguistic systems.[22] Although Ricoeur gives us little discussion of precisely how teleological goods are prioritized for specific situations, we must assume that he believes that the traditions ensconced in our classic narratives carry indices and scales of fundamental or generic goods that have reliably satisfied basic human desires and needs through the ages.

The Path of Diagnosis and Distance

Ricoeur does open an additional yet subordinate procedure for the discovery and evaluation of the optative goods to be pursued in our ethical practices. It is subordinate in that it refines and clarifies the ambiguities of tradition; it does not discard tradition and start anew. This is the path of "diagnosis." This concept is closely associated with the two concepts of explanation and distanciation, two ideas more fully developed in Ricoeur's later thought. The concept of diagnosis is prominent in earlier works such as *Freedom and Nature* and *Freud and Philosophy*.

Ricoeur's concept of diagnosis entails the following elements. Diagnosis is designed to uncover the involuntary yet pervasive regularities of the human will. It functions analogously to the process of diagnosis in medicine where the doctor first approaches the body of the patient through the selfhood of the patient, seeing the embodied consciousness of the ailing person as the first line of inquiry for gaining insight into the states, needs, and symptoms of the body.[23] The patient tells the doctor what he is experiencing — his aches and pains, fevers and chills, dizziness and faintness. But then, just as the doctor uses her medical instruments to supplement, corroborate, or qualify the conscious and intentional reports of the patient, Ricoeur in these early works used scientific psychology, psychoanalysis, and biology in correlation with his phenomenological descriptions of the patient's intentional reports to discern enduring regularities and needs. As he wrote in *Freedom and Nature*, "This is why our method will be most receptive with respect to scientific psychology, even though it will make only

---

22. Paul Ricoeur, *Freud and Philosophy* (New Haven: Yale University Press, 1970), pp. 15-16, 395-405.
23. Ricoeur, *Freedom and Nature*, pp. 12-13.

diagnostic use of it."[24] He could have included in this sentence the disciplines of biology and psychoanalysis as well.

The diagnostic use of these distanciating disciplines offers two sets of learning: (1) the clarification of opaque aspects of our involuntary needs that escape the full lucidity of consciousness, and (2) the recovery of structures of intentionality that are assumed, but often ignored or unthematized, by so-called objective studies of our motivations and needs.[25] With regard to the first point, the field of biology known as genetics may clarify aspects of my experienced body — my susceptibility to asthma, my astigmatism, or my signs of health — that are too obscure for the cogito fully to discern. But the significance of the biological analysis rests in what my genetic heritage *means to me*, that is, in how this diagnosis helps clarify and is finally assimiliated by my embodied cogito (my self).

With regard to the second point, Ricoeur is pointing to the subtle ways scientific analysis of human behavior entails countless unrecognized assumptions about the intentions of the self, which science's aspirations to objectivity tend to disregard, overlook, or actively suppress. To summarize, *Ricoeur's concept of diagnosis allows us to correlate what we know about our fundamental needs and goods through the route of a hermeneutics of self and its traditions with what we can learn about them through a diagnostic use of the distanciating explanations of the scientific disciplines.*

Take the following example. Assume that I have been following the classic and health-giving spiritual practices of my tradition, but that I recently have become depressed. I go to the doctor. Before giving me a battery of medical tests, the doctor talks to me. She asks *me* how I feel and what I have been doing. She asks about *my* practices — physical exercise, sleep, work, love life, sexual life, prayer life, relaxation habits, and a bit about my history (my family, its history, its illnesses, and so on). In effect, she is asking about *my interpretation* of my medical history. She learns that I have been a big coffee drinker but recently quit cold turkey. She tells me that there is scientific evidence that too rapid withdrawal from caffeine can create depression.[26] She hypothesizes that I have a choice — either reduce coffee slowly or wait for the depression to subside, which it probably will. She also tells me that it is a mild depression, not a clinical one. Finally, being a good and well-informed doctor, she adds that I should keep up

---

24. Ricoeur, *Freedom and Nature*, p. 13.

25. Ricoeur, *Freedom and Nature*, pp. 12-13, 87-88.

26. Anthony Komaroff, *Harvard Medical School Family Health Guide* (New York: Simon and Schuster, 1999), p. 48.

with my spiritual practices and probably get more exercise. In short, she confirms some of my tradition of practices and suggests I avail myself of other classic practices that I have been ignoring. She uses both diagnosis and scientific distanciation to help explain my state. But she does not disrupt or disregard my intentionality and selfhood. In fact, she informs *me* in all my concreteness of her distanciated and explanatory insights and makes them available to *me* in my embodied selfhood. She tells me of needs that I have and to some extent already know but do not fully grasp.

This rather trivial example points to a healthy use of science in our efforts to exercise judgments about the goods of life. I will give other examples as the book progresses, especially around the use of the concept of kin altruism in clarifying the Christian understanding of love. The moral task is to order conflicting goods, *but part of this work is first of all to discover what the relevant goods actually are.* The dialectical relation between tradition and distanciation can help clarify the question of goods if that information is used diagnostically. But science can only clarify the goods that tradition has come to know in the first place. Science is meaningful only in dialectical relation to the wisdom of tradition.

This kind of thinking is quite evident in the early phases of Ricoeur's work on the philosophy of the will. It becomes more implicit and less obvious in his later work on morality. A more energetic use of the concept of diagnosis in his mature moral philosophy would have given Ricoeur ways to make more fine-tuned evaluations of conflicting goods in the moment of wisdom. For some reason, the idea of diagnosis is not well developed in his *Oneself as Another,* the scene of his definitive moral statement. It is, I confess, only implicit in his recent dialogue with neuroscientist Jean-Pierre Changeux in *What Makes Us Think?*[27] Moreover, as important as it would be for Ricoeur to use his concepts of diagnosis and distanciation more forcefully in this moral theory, even then it would not give us a totally reliable systematic index of basic human needs or capabilities. Using these conceptual tools would not give us a catalogue of needs and capabilities of the kind assumed by twentieth-century documents on human rights or found in Martha Nussbaum's powerful list of the human capabilities that ground her theory of human rights.[28] Although Ricoeur has at times expressed skepticism about the normative use of the category of

27. Jean-Pierre Changeux and Paul Ricoeur, *What Makes Us Think?* (Princeton, N.J.: Princeton University Press, 2000), p. 129.

28. Martha Nussbaum, "Non-Relative Virtues: An Aristotelian Approach," in *The Quality of Life,* ed. Martha C. Nussbaum and Amarta Sen (Oxford: Clarendon, 1993), pp. 263-65.

needs because of his perception of their cultural relativity, in *Oneself as Another* and *The Just* he invokes the concept of "capacity," a somewhat analogous concept.[29] Ricoeur tells us that our self-esteem, partially mediated through the regard of others, is precisely esteem for our basic capacities.

But what are these capacities? Ricoeur's language of capacity is primarily about "being-able-to-do" and being able to impute one's actions to oneself — in other words, to own one's personal narrative.[30] But does not the question of capacities also open the issue of underlying regularities of human needs and basic capabilities that must be satisfied, exercised, and prioritized if we are to live well with others in just institutions? And in order to apply the test of practical wisdom, don't we need a more differentiated and articulate language of these needs, capacities, and capabilities than Ricoeur presently provides? In other words, don't we need a language of *premoral needs and goods?*

I believe that such a language is needed and that Ricoeur himself hints at the necessity of it. Whatever progress Ricoeur might make on this issue, he would doubtless turn first to the long route of hermeneutics — identifying needs, capacities, and capabilities from the perspective of traditions of interpretation and using the distanciating features of scientific diagnosis and explanation in only a secondary way. His list of needs and capacities, as a consequence, would be more heuristic and tentative — used more as a stimulant to dialogue than as a measuring rod for determining the adequacy of our various societies and cultures. In the end, these refined insights would not constitute definitive resolutions of conflicting goods. They would, however, help test our convictions and move them from being naive beliefs to more critically tested attestations.

In recent years, Ricoeur's early concept of diagnosis has tended to merge into his theory of explanation in his famous dialectic of understanding-explanation-understanding. The idea of explanation in his later thought has been associated closely with the structural analysis of texts, a perspective that he claims is meaningful only when placed within a text's wider semantic and narrative frameworks.[31] Hence, the hermeneutic realism and naturalism of his early thought — for instance, *Freud and Philosophy* — seems less visible in his later writings. Retrieving the concept of di-

29. Ricoeur, *Oneself as Another,* p. 181, and *The Just* (Chicago: University of Chicago Press, 2000), p. xvi.

30. Paul Ricoeur, "Reply to Ted Klein" and "Reply to Peter Kemp," in *The Philosophy of Paul Ricoeur,* ed. Lewis Hahn (Chicago: Open Court, 1995), pp. 367, 397.

31. Paul Ricoeur, *Interpretation Theory* (Fort Worth, Tex.: Texas Christian University, 1976), pp. 80-86.

agnosis within his hermeneutics of human goods would enable him to develop firmer indices of human needs and capacities and the fundamental human goods required to support them. This could happen, I believe, without losing the cultural sensitivity of his hermeneutic beginning point. This modest amendment would strengthen Ricoeur's critical hermeneutics and its important contributions to moral psychology, moral philosophy, and the new practical theological ethics.

Understanding and Distance in the Social Psychology of Youth and Adolescents

I want to illustrate the dialectic of understanding and distance by discussing the social-psychology of youth and adolescents in the outstanding new work of Christian Smith. Smith teaches sociology of religion at the University of North Carolina, but his work contains a great deal of psychology as well, which is why I am able to use him in a book on moral psychology. In a variety of articles and books and now in his recent, well-received *Soul Searching: The Religious and Spiritual Lives of American Teenagers*, Smith presents an approach to understanding the relation of religion to American adolescents that illustrates what I have been saying about the dialectical relation of understanding and distance, explanation, and diagnosis.

Smith tries to demonstrate the consequences of religion to the life of teenagers. Is it, on the whole, good or bad for them — at least the ones who are influenced by religious institutions? In asking, and trying to answer, that question, Smith makes a number of important and valid methodological assumptions. First of all, he starts with religion as a normative moral and narrative tradition. In doing this, he reflects a kind of hermeneutic beginning point not unlike what we have found in Ricoeur, even though Ricoeur, as such, is not invoked by Smith. In fact, he indicates that his methodological and philosophical godfathers are sociologists such as Robert Bellah, Amitai Etzioni, and Robert Wuthnow as well as philosophers such as Charles Taylor and Alasdair MacIntyre.[32] All of them, according to Smith, take seriously

> the idea of substantive cultural traditions grounded upon and promoting particular normative ideas of what is good and bad, right and wrong, higher and lower, worthy and unworthy, just and unjust,

---

32. Christian Smith, "Theorizing Religious Effects among American Adolescents," *Journal for the Scientific Study of Religion* 42, no. 1 (2003): 20.

and so on, which orient human consciousness and motivate human action. Importantly, these distinctions of judgment and valuation with moral order are understood as not established by people's own desires, decisions, or preferences, but instead are believed to exist apart from and above them, providing standards by which human desires, decisions, and preferences can themselves be judged.[33]

Notice that he is assuming a world in which "judgments and valuations" are not established by people's own "desires" but by inherited norms that "exist apart from and above" these desires and preferences even though they connect with them, channel them, and point them in truly satisfying directions. This is similar to Ricoeur's view of the thickness of inherited human practices that are also qualified and conditioned by ideals of the good life, narratives about the purpose of life, and critical tests that handle the conflict of premoral goods. So, in short, Smith and Ricoeur are in the same ballpark, with similar views about the thickness of human praxis.

But as a sociologist, Smith also asks what the consequences for youth well-being are of the inherited practices, norms, and narratives of the Christian faith, especially as they are mediated by Christian communities — something close to what *Hardwired* has called "authoritative communities." In fact, Smith was one of the experts on youth who helped to write and then sign the *Hardwired to Connect* report. Although Smith does not use the phrase "authoritative communities," in many ways that is precisely what he is writing about. I will not burden the reader with facts from his numerous statistical tables showing the consequences of youth participation in such communities. Smith and his team did thirty-minute telephone interviews with one parent and fifty-minute interviews with one teen in 3,290 households, with in-depth, face-to-face follow-up interviews with 269 adolescents in forty-five states.[34] It is the largest survey of adolescent religious behavior that has ever been done in the United States.

Smith summarizes some of his findings with a note of irony. He writes,

> Although many teens cannot see it or are not able to articulate it, according to the findings . . . , the differences between more religious and less religious teenagers in the United States are actually significant and consistent across every outcome measure exam-

33. Smith, "Theorizing Religious Effects," p. 20.
34. Christian Smith with Melinda Lundquist Denton, *Soul Searching: The Religious and Spiritual Lives of American Teenagers* (Oxford: Oxford University Press, 2005), pp. 6, 32.

ined: risk behaviors, quality of family and adult relationships, moral reasoning and behavior, community participation, media consumption, sexual activity, and emotional well-being. [Religiously active] teenagers are in fact quite different from religiously disengaged teens in a host of ways.[35]

Smith divides the teens he surveyed into types — devoted teens (8 percent of American youth), the regulars (27 percent of American youth), the sporadics (17 percent), and the disengaged (12 percent).[36] When balanced by the demographic variables of gender, age, race, region of residence, parental marital status, parental education, and family income, devoted and regular teens

> are much less likely to smoke cigarettes regularly, drink alcohol weekly or more often, get drunk every few weeks or more often. More religiously involved teens are also more likely to not drink alcohol and not smoke marijuana. By comparison, it is the least religiously active teens who smoke marijuana the most. Among those attending school, the more religiously active teens are much less likely to cut classes in school, to cut a lot of classes when they do cut, and to be expelled from school. They also tend not to earn poor grades in school. Finally, the more religiously involved teens are much less likely to be said by their parents to be rebellious or to have a bad temper. . . . The most religiously involved American teens appear to watch less television during the week and on the weekends and are much less likely to watch R-rated movies.[37]

So it goes, on and on. And throughout the book, table upon table, statistic upon statistic, bears out these generalizations.

In fact, Smith develops his own theory of action with many dimensions that seem close to Ricoeur's theory of praxis as well as to the five dimensions I have pulled from Ricoeur. But Smith develops a simpler three-dimensional model. He lists "moral order, learned competencies, and social and organizational ties."[38] But when he begins to talk about these three aspects of religious practice, they sound surprisingly like the fuller theory I have been developing in this book. Take moral order: here is how

35. Smith and Denton, *Soul Searching*, pp. 218-19.

36. Smith and Denton, *Soul Searching*, p. 220.

37. Smith and Denton, *Soul Searching*, p. 222.

38. Smith and Denton, *Soul Searching*, p. 240; Smith, "Theorizing Religious Effects," p. 19.

he describes it and what it does for young people. "American religions promote specific cultural moral directives of self-control and personal virtue
grounded in the authority of long historical traditions and narratives into
which members are inducted, such that youth may internalize these moral
orders and use them to guide their life choices and moral commitments."[39]
Notice his reference to the "authority of long historical traditions"; this
long history is part of what *Hardwired* believes gives authoritative communities their depth and plausibility. Notice too the reference to "narratives."
A tradition is not just a batch of rules and general principles; such injunc-
tions and guidelines are surrounded by narrative expressions telling us
about the meaning of life in which these more explicit moral conventions
function. The overarching narratives are important, but so are the specific
moral practices, rules, and virtues. Smith's illustrations are instructive:

> For example, different religious traditions teach their young adher-
> ents moral commitments, such as tithing from one's income for
> the church, synagogue, and the common good; seeking reconcilia-
> tion instead of vengeance; treating one's body as the temple of the
> Holy Spirit; honoring one's parents and elders; avoiding self-
> indulgent gluttony and sexual promiscuity; respecting the dignity
> of others because they are made in the image of God; faithfully
> fasting during Ramadan; acting in honesty and fairness even at a
> cost to oneself; practicing Zakat, the giving of alms to the poor as
> Allah commands, the Four Noble Truths, the Eightfold Path, the
> Five Precepts, and so on.[40]

But in discussing the moral and narrative aspect of a tradition and
what it does to consolidate more specific moral rules, principles, and virtues, Smith mentions something that this book has not emphasized
enough — the role of *religious experience*. In differentiating the first of his
three dimensions of religious praxis — moral order — he makes another
important generalization that summarizes his research: "American religions provide the organizational contexts and cultural substance, foster-
ing in youth spiritual experiences that may help to solidify their moral
commitments and constructive life practices."[41] Religions do not only socialize youth into inherited rules, virtues, principles, and narratives, they
wrap these many elements into religious experiences. Smith says it this

39. Smith and Denton, *Soul Searching*, p. 241.
40. Smith and Denton, *Soul Searching*, p. 241.
41. Smith and Denton, *Soul Searching*, p. 242.

way: "Religious youth are facilitated in this process by personal Spiritual experiences that often legitimate and reinforce their religious moral order."[42] Smith, however, is not just talking about religious experiences that drop from the sky or mystical experiences that seem totally disconnected from everyday life. True to his sociological point of view, and true to the hermeneutic views of this book, he sees spiritual experiences within the context of what Gadamer and Ricoeur would call "effective experience" — a tradition that both shapes and interacts with contemporary social contexts. He writes, "From a sociological perspective, religious experiences tend not to float down from the sky as autonomous or self-generating encounters. Rather, sociologists are attuned to how spiritual experiences often arise from the immediate or distant contexts of religious traditions and organizations."[43]

But religious youth do better in school, develop more social skills, and avoid risky sexual, drug, media, and eating habits because the traditions are mediated by organizations. A tradition's practices are mediated by institutions which function within the context of other institutions, many of which are not explicitly religious and some of which actually undermine religious traditions, such as many modernizing and commercial social institutional processes in America today. Space does not allow me to follow Smith in detail on these institutional mediating factors. But understanding him on this issue helps illustrate how explanation, distanciation, and diagnosis function in a social-science perspective that also takes tradition seriously, as Smith does. For instance, Smith subdivides the dimension of moral order into the three subdimensions of moral directive, spiritual experiences, and role models. We already have touched on most of these. He differentiates learned competencies into community and leadership skills, coping skills, and cultural capital (additional contacts and practical knowledge beyond family and friends). Finally, he differentiates social and organizational ties into social capital, network closure (safe groups that separate youth from unsafe groups), and extra-community links (community, national, and even international contacts beyond the specific confessing community).[44]

Smith's *Soul Searching* collects data on religious youth in all of these categories and then weaves these data into a coherent, multidimensional theory of religious practices that helps *explain* why religious youth do

42. Smith and Denton, *Soul Searching,* p. 242.
43. Smith and Denton, *Soul Searching,* p. 242.
44. Smith and Denton, *Soul Searching,* pp. 243-51.

better. He invokes a number of social-science measures for youth well-being, health, and social success. He uses these indices to get *distance* from the immediacy of the language and institutional experiences of the youth. He uses these measures as a way of stepping back and analyzing the "factors," "conditions," and "social mechanisms" (favorite words of social scientists) that diagnose why religions do good, why they help young people attain commonly held social measures of the good life. *But we must beware.*

Why? Why should we be cautious of these measures, these indices, these criteria of the good that tell us that religion is in some ways working for teens? First, Smith reminds us that these measures do not exhaust what these religious traditions are about, or at least these measures are not what religious traditions are about exclusively and without remainder. These traditions are not out to make us successful Americans, successful entrepreneurs, or even successful students and scholars. They are about realizing the goods of life in view of inevitable conflict of goods, finitude, and guilt in ways that make human community possible. These social-science measures are simply indices of commonly held values in American life shaped by a mélange of traditions, the health sciences, and experience. Furthermore, they are primarily sociological in nature. In spite of the fact that Smith participated in and signed the *Hardwired* report, he does not discuss directly the need to connect and the importance of kin altruism as diagnostic indices of the human good mediated by religious traditions — two of the most central factors I have talked about in the previous chapters. The nearest he comes to this is in his discussion of the importance of role models mediated by a tradition, the importance of warm, accepting, and admirable persons in communities of faith with whom teens can connect and whom they can aspire to be like.[45] Furthermore, *Smith says nothing about the importance of critique — the importance of the deontological test — that traditions sometimes provide but finally must use to review and refine their own practices.* Nonetheless, Smith's argument is close to the one that I am developing in these pages and helps us gain a much more concrete view of what my argument means for the actual life of children and adolescents in American society. In Smith, social science functions as diagnosis; it does not function as philosophical foundationalism would have it.

Before leaving Smith, I want to mention two other themes found in his work that I will return to later in the book. These have to do with what his work implies for how religious youth learn to handle the pressures and temptations of market forms of modernization which celebrate the values

---

45. Smith and Denton, *Soul Searching,* p. 243.

of competition, individualism, and consumerism. Authoritative religious traditions help youth resist these pressures and guide them through these many distractions. But, on the other hand, Smith has evidence that these pressures do have a way of diluting what adolescents actually understand about their traditions. For the most part, American adolescents identify with the religion of their parents. They are not big religious and social rebels. They are, for the most part, religiously conventional. And although about 50 percent of American youth are not particularly religious, about 50 percent are, and they are the ones who look very much like their parents; they are also the ones who, for the most part, are doing relatively well in American society when viewed against all the measures Smith uses.

But, in the end, these same youth do not understand their religions very well. They are not articulate about the central beliefs of their conventional religiosity.[46] They benefit from their religion and its implicit moral wisdom, but they don't understand it well. In fact, they often distort it. Smith says that although some form of Christianity is the dominant religion of religious youth in the United States, Christianity tends to turn out in their minds as a form of moralistic therapeutic deism. This is a rather impersonal view that relegates God to the gentle task of granting warmth and blessings for a relatively moral life.[47] The doctrinal substance of the religions informing even relatively religious teens for the most part escapes them. Nonetheless, moralistic therapeutic deism is not a separate religion. It is one that runs through the official and institutionally embodied American religions and feeds on them. As Smith says, "It cannot sustain its own integral, independent life; rather, it must attach itself like an incubus to established historical religious traditions, feed on their doctrines and sensibilities, and [expand] by mutating their theological substance to resemble its own distinctive image."[48]

Conclusion

I have spent time unpacking the concepts of diagnosis and distanciation because of the way in which they clarify the contributions of the social sciences, especially certain forms of psychology, to practical moral philosophy and theology. The modern moral psychologies are riddled with a

---

46. Smith and Denton, *Soul Searching*, p. 167.
47. Smith and Denton, *Soul Searching*, pp. 165-70.
48. Smith and Denton, *Soul Searching*, p. 166.

host of psychological and psychobiological concepts designed to explain the raw motivations and regularities that people bring to their moral lives. We already have seen the concept of libido in Freud, the drive for self-actualization in the humanistic psychologies, kin altruism in evolutionary psychology, and the need to connect or attach taken from psychoanalytic object-relations theory and neuroscience. I am not concerned to discuss the scientific validity of these various concepts; I am assuming that they help us account for some aspects of moral behavior but sometimes overlook other dimensions.

I am more concerned to locate the logic of their contribution to ethics, granting that they have some sort of validity for accounting for certain kinds of behaviors. I am also interested in asking the question, where do we begin both in understanding the moral life and in doing reflective ethics? *Do we begin with these basic explanatory concepts from so-called scientific psychology and build up our ethics from them, as some of these moral psychologies seem to suggest? Or are the concepts to be used diagnostically in relation to beginning with our inherited traditions?* For those of us who are Christians, the latter option would mean beginning with our Christianity and its impact on our history and culture.

It is the argument of this book that we should use these concepts from contemporary moral psychology diagnostically. We should use them when the traditions, because of their complexity or because of histories of mistaken interpretations, seem unclear about the range of motivations and human regularities we bring to our moral development. Only after we have first tried to critically interpret our inherited traditions, determining what they have learned and achieved, can these concepts, and whatever scientific supports they can muster, be used to clarify remaining conflicts and ambivalences in what has come to us from the past. As we have seen, this is how Reinhold Niebuhr used Freud and Darwin to enrich his theological anthropology for understanding more profoundly how human sexuality relates to the formation of our basic human attachments — insights significantly developed by Bowlby, his followers, and the authors of *Hardwired.* Niebuhr used these insights diagnostically in dialectical relation to insights he already had gained from the Christian tradition.

In the chapters that immediately follow, I will try to illustrate the diagnostic value of two of the more recent and commanding moral-psychological traditions — evolutionary psychology and the psychoanalytic ego-psychology of Erik Erikson. I will show the deft way Erikson brought early smatterings of these traditions together with a remarkable capacity to understand and interpret traditions.

Chapter 5

Attachment, Love, and Moral Development

In this chapter and the next, I turn to the subject of love. I will review many different kinds of love, including Christian love. In fact, I will look at the tensions within Christianity about the nature of love and the relation of Christian love to other kinds of love. I will examine ways religion and science can cooperate in defining the ideals and conditions of a theory of love needed to guide human development. The capacity to love is often thought to be a goal of moral development. But what is love and what does science, particularly the emerging field of evolutionary psychology, have to offer to our understanding of love and, indeed, our understanding of Christian love?

Two ideas will organize what I want to say. First, a fruitful dialogue between science and religion on the nature of love should proceed within Ricoeur's "critical hermeneutical" perspective on both of these fields. Second, when this happens, science will have a clearer picture of some of the ideals of human love that it should clarify and serve but cannot itself invent, create, or adequately describe; these ideals come from our inherited traditions and are the result of many centuries of critical dialogue about the meaning of the classics on love of these traditions. On the other hand, such a dialogue will provide religion with a more critical grasp of its own ideals and a clearer understanding of *some*, although not all, of the conditions needed to approximate these ideals.

As I have pointed out more than once, a simple foundationalist approach to any subject is never adequate. The question of love illustrates this even more decisively. Foundationalism, as philosopher Richard Bernstein defines it, sets aside the possible truths of all aspects of a culture's traditions — be they philosophical, religious, or cultural — and assumes that all scientific and moral truth will be discovered and gradually assembled on the basis of sure and certain beginning points.[1] A foundationalist would say that sooner or later we can discover what love really is and do so independently of the long history of defining the various forms of human love. Hans-Georg Gadamer, Paul Ricoeur, Richard Rorty, and Bernstein himself have exposed the potential cultural nihilism of a thoroughgoing foundationalism.[2] It assumes that the wisdom of traditions would be delegitimized until science in some utopian future finally finishes rebuilding our edifices of cognitive and moral knowledge. This position implies that parents will have to wait before having any really reliable knowledge of what to say about love to their offspring and to themselves. It assumes that the meaning of marital love, love for neighbor, love for the stranger, love for the enemy, and love between friends will never be clear or sufficiently certain until science reinvestigates and redefines these areas of human life all over again. This view also assumes that someday science finally will find a way to bridge the chasm between *is* and *ought* — the facts of life and our normative ideals — that most modern philosophers believe exists, at least in some fashion. This, they hope, will help ground the socialization of the young and our ideals of maturity on more solid foundations.

But, in reaction to foundationalism, much of continental philosophical hermeneutics and British ordinary language analysis goes too far in another direction toward a particular brand of nonfoundationalism. Many critics, and I count myself among them, believe that these antifoundationalist philosophical perspectives go too far in uncritically accepting tradition and over-crediting it with truth and authority. Such a position tends to rule out science in discussing such matters as the meaning of love.

Ricoeur's critical hermeneutics is a better solution for understanding the proper relation between objectivity and historically mediated visions, narratives, and norms.[3] As we saw in the last chapter, Ricoeur goes a long way in agreeing with Gadamer: traditions are storehouses of wisdom — moral, religious, and even cognitive. He concurs that we cannot become oriented to any problematic contemporary moral or social issue — even the

1. Richard Bernstein, *Beyond Objectivism and Relativism: Science, Hermeneutics, and Praxis* (Philadelphia: University of Pennsylvania Press, 1983), pp. 1-34.
2. Hans-Georg Gadamer, *Truth and Method* (New York: Crossroad, 1982); Paul Ricoeur, *Hermeneutics and the Human Sciences* (Cambridge: Cambridge University Press, 1981); Richard Rorty, *Philosophy and the Mirror of Nature* (Princeton, N.J.: Princeton University Press, 1979).
3. Ricoeur, *Hermeneutics and the Human Sciences,* pp. 88-95.

question of the nature of love — without reviewing the history of the traditions that have formed our cultural thinking about that issue. This history — even the history of love — is already in us; it is part of what Gadamer called our "effective history," even if we are totally unaware of it.[4]

But critical hermeneutics does not simply stay with history and tradition; it finds a place as well for the diagnostic, distanciating, and explanatory interests of science as a subordinate moment. Ricoeur holds a highly appreciative but nonfoundationalist view of science. He holds that science, especially the social or human sciences, can and should aspire only to various degrees of cognitive "distanciation" from the inherited traditions that form and shape all persons — even scientific inquirers. The remarkable thing about *Hardwired to Connect* is that it intuitively recognizes this truth — something quite rare for a statement shaped by so many natural scientists and psychiatrists. It believes in the importance for children and youth of communities of tradition. The important work of Christian Smith, as we saw in the last chapter, does the same. I do, too. And in this chapter and the next, I try to illustrate this by showing how tradition houses or contains our basic understandings of love — a central concept for socialization. I also show how our traditions' views of love can profit from the refinements of science and moral psychology.

Love and the Traditions

Insofar as science and religion talk with each other about love, their discourse will be primarily philosophical — that is, a step or two removed from either the immediacy of religious confession or more focused exercises in scientific observation and experimentation. Furthermore, it should be clear from the beginning that we cannot become oriented to this discussion without starting first with the philosophical and religious traditions that have shaped our ideals and languages of love — hence the importance of the interpretive or hermeneutical beginning point.

A short history of our languages of love is in order. I present one not to be comprehensive but to illustrate the importance of beginning with our social inheritance — as Wittgenstein, his followers R. S. Peters and Peter Winch, and the continental hermeneutic philosophers would all urge us to do.[5] We first learn that our various languages of love have been in

---

4. Gadamer, *Truth and Method,* pp. 267-74.

5. Ludwig Wittgenstein, *Philosophical Investigations* (Oxford: Blackwell, 1953); R. S. Peters,

conflict. It is a conflict, however, that the distanciated perspectives of science may help clarify, although probably not completely resolve.

Take the terms *agapā, erōs,* and *caritas.* They all can be translated into English as "love," but historically they have had quite different meanings. *Agapē* is the Greek word for love as it was often used in the Christian Scriptures, especially the letters of Paul. In the language of much of Protestant theology, as Anders Nygren taught in his magisterial *Agape and Eros,* it has been defined as self-sacrificial activity on behalf of others, made possible by God's grace and with no thought for the good returned to oneself.[6] Nygren tells us that *agapē* is "spontaneous and unmotivated," "indifferent" to the value of the object of love, "creative" in that it creates "value" in the other, and initiated by God, meaning it flows first from God and then through the faithful and outward to others.[7]

Even some influential secular models of love, such as the one associated with the moral philosophy of Immanuel Kant, reflect the values of this classic Protestant model.[8] They share the idea that love should not be predicated on the value of the loved or on some thought of return. Nygren believes that *erōs* and *agapē* are completely separate and disconnected. *Erōs* reaches upward for the good and true; *agapē* flows downward in generosity and superabundance to the lower and the more needy. Furthermore, *erōs* has generally been seen as more egocentric; the lover is viewed as attempting to elevate or increase his good through the love of a higher or better being, be it God or another person.

Finally, *caritas* is the Latin translation of the New Testament word for love rendered in Greek as *agapē.* The concept of *caritas,* however, has been interpreted in Roman Catholic circles to contain more elements of self-fulfillment *(erōs)* and mutuality than do Protestant Reformation interpretations of Christian love. This view of love opens more space for a balance between other-regard and self-regard. Even this short discussion raises sev-

---

The Concept of Motivation (London: Routledge and Kegan Paul, 1958); Peter Winch, *The Idea of a Social Science and Its Relation to Philosophy* (London: Routledge and Kegan Paul, 1958).

6. Anders Nygren, *Agape and Eros* (Philadelphia: Westminster, 1953), pp. 41-48. For a typology of Christian views of love that clusters several Protestant thinkers from Luther to Bonhoeffer, Barth, and Bultmann toward strong self-sacrificial views of love, see Garth L. Hallett, *Christian Neighbor-Love: An Assessment of Six Rival Versions* (Washington, D.C.: Georgetown University Press, 1989).

7. Nygren, *Agape and Eros,* pp. 175-81.

8. Ronald Green, "Kant on Christian Love," in *The Love Commandments,* ed. Edmund N. Santurri and William Werpehowski (Washington, D.C.: Georgetown University Press, 1992), pp. 261-80.

eral questions. Which of these classic models should guide the direction or goals of human development and the socialization of children into adulthood within the Christian community? Do the claims of the Christian tradition have any validity for the wider non-Christian community, either in part or in whole? Which model of love should we bring to our human relations — our friendships, marriages, family obligations, and community service? What conditions for love would science discover, depending on which of these three models guided the empirical search? Furthermore, what are the implications of science — especially the concepts of kin and reciprocal altruism — for mediating between these conflicting classic views?

But the plot thickens when additional terms are introduced. Roman Catholic *caritas* models of love combined Aristotelian models of love as friendship *(philia)* with the love motifs of the New Testament. Aristotle discussed three kinds of friendship — friendships of pleasure, friendships of utility, and friendships of virtue.[9] Aristotle valued each of these kinds of friendship but believed that some were more expressive of the uniqueness of human nature than others. For instance, he valued yet subordinated friendships of utility and friendships of pleasure to the higher good of friendships of virtue. Friendships of virtue were friendships in which intellectual and moral equals valued one another for their intrinsic deliberative and moral qualities. Thomas Aquinas, the great medieval Roman Catholic Aristotelian, built his concept of Christian love in large part around Aristotle's model of friendships of virtue. This provided a stable place in Thomas's view of Christian love for elements of individual striving, fulfillment, and mutuality — features of love often absent, as I indicated above, from classic Protestant models.

The Catholic association of Christian love with mutual friendship seems justified. We must remember that the Golden Rule ("In everything do to others as you would have them do to you; for this is the law and the prophets"[10]) and neighbor love ("You shall love your neighbor as yourself"[11]) make self-regard and one's natural concern for one's own good in some sense a measure or guide to other-regard. These ancient principles find an equal place for both love of other and love of self and are nicely summarized, as I will argue more extensively below, in the concept of love as equal-regard.

The Thomistic view of Christian love, of course, does not eliminate

9. Aristotle, *Nichomachean Ethics,* in *Basic Writings of Aristotle* (New York: Random House, 1941), bk. VIII, iii.

10. Matthew 7:12.

11. Matthew 19:19.

the role of self-sacrifice; sacrificial love within Thomism, however, is not so much an end in itself as it is a matter of being, with the grace of God, steadfast and active in working to restore broken relationships to love as mutuality or, as Gene Outka and Louis Janssens call it, love as equal-regard.[12] In its emphasis on steadfastness and the effort needed to renew and restore broken relationships, love as equal-regard has many of the features of the Hebrew Scriptures' covenantal view of love as *hesed*.

To speak of *hesed* requires us to introduce one final word for love that we find in the various Western religious and philosophical traditions — the idea of love as *storgē* or parental love. Steadfastness is a characteristic of both *hesed* and *storgē*. But *storgē* adds an element of deep and preferential investment by parents in the children who are in some sense a part of themselves. It is noteworthy to observe how the metaphor of the parent-child relation has been used time and again — as Stephen Post and John Miller have reminded us — to symbolize the very heart and nature of God.[13] When this happens, God is depicted not only as steadfast but as moved by the misfortunes and delighted by the well-being of God's children.

From a psychological perspective, it could be suggested that Jewish, Islamic, and Christian views of God are projections of kin altruism (as I will define it below) into the very nature of God. In much of the Abrahamic tradition (the three faiths that establish their origins with reference to the biblical Abraham), there is developed the additional idea that not only is God like a good and invested parent but that God is also this kind of parent to all persons, making no fundamental ontological preferences among them. To take seriously the parental analogy when applied to God also suggests that love, by both humans and the divine, entails elements of investment, attachment, need, gratification, and joy — the kind of need, joy, and gratification that most natural parents have in the life and fortunes of their own children. This suggests that when the parental analogy is applied to either human or divine love, it is quite different than the idea of strong *agapē* or extreme self-sacrificial love. In fact, strong agapic models of love would find the elements of parental gratifi-

12. It is my opinion that Roman Catholic moral theologian Louis Janssens states adequately the Thomistic understanding of the relation of self-sacrificial love and equal-regard. See his "Norms and Priorities of a Love Ethics," *Louvain Studies* 6 (spring 1977): 207-38. For a significant Protestant statement of love as equal-regard, see Gene Outka, *Agape: An Ethical Analysis* (New Haven: Yale University Press, 1972), pp. 36-42.

13. Stephen Post, *Spheres of Love: Toward a New Ethics of the Family* (Dallas: Southern Methodist University Press, 1994), pp. 60-63; John Miller, *Biblical Faith and Fathering* (New York: Paulist, 1998).

cation and joy unacceptable as elements of ideal love. Extreme agapic views seem to find offensive the idea that either human parents or God base their love in part on the joy they get out of it.

Evolutionary Psychology and Tensions between Traditional Models of Love

My excuse for presenting this brief history of different models of love in Christian ethics is to make the following point: *various contemporary forces, including the insights of evolutionary psychology, are working to shift Christian models of love away from the historic Protestant strong agapic view toward the synthesis of Aristotelianism and New Testament Christianity that is found in a variety of Roman Catholic formulations.* I make this report not as a Roman Catholic, but as a liberal Protestant observer of the contemporary theological discussion. Hence, love as mutuality or equal-regard, with "openness to self-sacrifice"[14] serving as a transitional ethic designed to restore love as equal-regard, is an emerging dominant model of love in contemporary theological ethics. It can be found in much of feminist theology,[15] some newer Protestant voices,[16] and a variety of neo-Thomistic Catholic sources.[17] The pressure to reinterpret the tradition in this direction comes from several sources: new insights into the tradition itself,[18] new perspectives from the psychotherapeutic disciplines,[19] changing gender roles in society, ideology critiques of extreme self-sacrificial models of

14. I will discuss Timothy Jackson's concept of "openness" to self-sacrifice in more detail later in this chapter. See his *The Priority of Love* (Princeton, N.J.: Princeton University Press, 2003), p. 10.

15. For representative feminist theological statements, see Christine Gudorf, "Parenting, Mutual Love, and Sacrifice," in *Women's Consciousness, Women's Conscience: A Reader in Feminist Ethics,* ed. Barbara Andolsen, Christine Gudorf, and Mary Pellauer (New York: Harper and Row, 1985), pp. 175-91; Barbara Andolsen, "*Agape* in Feminist Ethics," *Journal of Religious Ethics* 9 (spring 1981): 69-81.

16. In addition to Outka's *Agape: An Ethical Analysis,* see also Stephen Post, *A Theory of Agape: On the Meaning of Christian Love* (Lewisburg, Pa.: Bucknell University Press, 1990).

17. Louis Janssens's "Norms and Priorities of a Love Ethics" is the best representative of neo-Thomistic perspectives on love as equal-regard.

18. Victor Furnish, "Neighbor Love in the New Testament," *Journal of Religious Ethics* 10 (fall 1982): 227; Luise Schottroff, "Non-Violence and the Love of One's Enemies," in *Essays on the Love Commandment,* ed. Reginald Fuller (Philadelphia: Fortress, 1978).

19. For an ethical analysis of the modern psychotherapies and how they emphasize, often with excess, an ethic of self-actualization, see Don Browning, *Religious Thought and the Modern Psychologies* (Minneapolis: Fortress, 1987, rev. ed. 2004).

love by feminists and minorities,[20] and evolutionary psychology. Allow me to concentrate on the contributions of evolutionary psychology.

The concepts of kin altruism, inclusive fitness, and reciprocal altruism are beginning to influence theological-ethical views of love. The ground-breaking work of biologists William Hamilton, George Williams, and Robert Trivers on these concepts has not gone unnoticed in theological debates about love.[21] The biological evidence for kin altruism and inclusive fitness have led some theological ethicists to research the tradition for similar insights assumed by, and sometimes embedded in, Christian concepts of love.

What is meant by the concepts of kin altruism and inclusive fitness? These concepts advance the idea that genetic parents will under certain conditions sacrifice for their offspring, that nature has selected for parental care, and that other genetically related family members (brothers and sisters, uncles and aunts, nephews and nieces) are more likely to sacrifice for one another than are non-kin. Kin altruism springs from the deep tendency of parents to consciously and unconsciously strive to extend their lives by working for the survival and flourishing of those with whom they are closely related.

The Roman Catholic scholar Stephen Pope has found naturalistic observations in the thought of Aristotle and Thomas Aquinas that have interesting similarities to the findings of evolutionary psychology; they both understood the role of kin preference in mammalian relations and also human love. I have contributed to this research as well.[22] Thomas Aquinas, for instance, had his own theories of kin preference but without, of course, the benefits of modern genetic theory. He also had insights into the role that the long period of human infantile dependence has played throughout history in bonding male and female into families. He correctly observed that, in mammalian species where infants rapidly learn to feed and take care of themselves, mothers and their procreating male con-

---

20. See the feminist critiques of self-sacrificial love listed above, especially Andolsen's "Agape in Feminist Ethics."

21. W. D. Hamilton, "The Genetic Evolution of Social Behavior II," *Journal of Theoretical Biology* 7 (1964): 17-52; George Williams, *Adaptation and Natural Selection* (Princeton, N.J.: Princeton University Press, 1966; Robert Trivers, "Parental Investment and Sexual Selection," in *Sexual Selection and the Descent of Man,* ed. B. Campbell (Chicago: Aldine, 1920).

22. Don Browning, "Biology, Ethics, and Narrative in Christian Family Theory," in *Decline and Renewal of Marriage in America,* ed. David Popenoe, Jean Bethke Elshtain, and David Blankenhorn (Lanham, Md.: Rowman and Littlefield, 1996), pp. 119-56, and *Marriage and Modernization* (Grand Rapids: Eerdmans, 2003).

sorts do not bond. Male-female long-term bonding, he believed, was a consequence of human infant dependency — a popular concept in the new evolutionary psychology as well. Listen to this remarkable quote from the "Supplement" of the *Summa Theologica.*

> Yet nature does not incline thereto in the same way in all animals; since there are animals whose offspring are able to seek food immediately after birth, or are sufficiently fed by their mother; and in these there is no tie between parents, although for a short time, there is a certain tie, as may be seen in certain birds. In man, however, since the child needs the parents' care for a long time, there is a very great tie between male and female, to which ties even the generic nature inclines.[23]

But, according to Thomas, the human male generally only joins, or at least stays for a long time with, the mother-infant dyad to take care of the offspring when he recognizes, or has some reason to assume, that the infant is his — is an extension of his life, his being. Aquinas realized that there was natural conflict in the tendencies of human males. On the one hand, males tend to want intercourse with as many females as possible. He writes in the *Summa Contra Gentiles* that human males naturally desire "to indulge at will in the pleasure of copulation, even as in the pleasure of eating." On the other hand, males tend to "resist another's intercourse with their consort."[24] Aquinas believed, as does the field of evolutionary psychology today, that the human male tends to invest in and care more easily for the child if he thinks that the child is actually his and not the offspring of some other male. "Man naturally desires to be assured of his offspring: and this assurance would be altogether nullified in the case of promiscuous copulation."[25] Aquinas understood the tendency in human males to take care of themselves and to care for that which they recognize as part of themselves. He acknowledged the role, in creating paternal investment, of a father's recognition that a child is his (contains his "substance," as Aquinas would say). This tendency, of course, applied equally to the mother, but Aquinas realized that fathers were more uncertain than mothers that the child was theirs.

---

23. Thomas Aquinas, *Summa Theologica,* III, "Supplement" (New York: Benziger Brothers, 1948), q. 41, a. 1.

24. Thomas Aquinas, *Summa Contra Gentiles,* bk. 3, pt. 2 (London: Burns, Oates, and Washbourne, 1928), p. 112.

25. Aquinas, *Summa Contra Gentiles,* p. 118.

Furthermore, Aquinas grasped the additional role of "mutual assistance" between mother and father (or what evolutionary psychologists would call reciprocal altruism) in creating family and community solidarity.[26] Aquinas was also aware, as was Aristotle before him, that love as kin preference could, under certain conditions, spread *analogically* to relationships outside of families; because we first learn to care and love in our family of origin, we gradually under certain conditions develop the capacity to share this love with others in nonfamilial relations.

Stephen Pope, in his *The Evolution of Altruism and the Order of Love* and other writings, has done more than any other moral theologian to demonstrate how Aquinas's pre-Darwinian observations on what we today call kin altruism were integrated into his view of Christian love.[27] Pope, whom I will discuss more in the next chapter, helps us see how Thomas's insights gave rise to a theory of love that saw the developmental importance of kin preference, strong parental investment and attachment, and the dialectical relation between self-regard and other-regard, and how these early formative influences, with the right communal and symbolic reinforcements, can be analogically extended to include non-kin neighbors, strangers, enemies, and God. Pope argues for a reconstruction and extension of Catholic naturalism in light of insights from evolutionary psychology.

Since self-regard and other-regard are more dialectically related in both Christian Thomism and contemporary theories of kin and reciprocal altruism, new reconstructions of Christian love using these sources would give rise to a theory of love with the following features. It would place higher value on self-regard, understand how early experiences of bonding and attachment prepare for adult capacities for sympathy, give more emphasis to mutuality and equal-regard, and interpret self-sacrificial love (and associated Christian symbols of the cross) as functioning to renew mutual love rather than constituting an end in itself. Something like this model of love is serving increasingly to guide theories of human development in certain contemporary Roman Catholic and Protestant circles. It has much to offer secular models of moral development as well.

---

26. For evidence of these generalizations, see Thomas Aquinas, *Summa Theologica,* III, "Supplement," qq. 41-42; Aquinas, *Summa Contra Gentiles,* III, ii, chaps. 121-27; discussions of these texts in Don Browning, Bonnie Miller-McLemore, Pamela Couture, Bernie Lyon, and Robert Franklin, *From Culture Wars to Common Ground: Religion and the American Family Debate* (Louisville: Westminster/John Knox, 1997), pp. 113-24; and extensive writings of Stephen Pope, especially his *The Evolution of Altruism and the Ordering of Love* (Washington, D.C.: Georgetown University Press, 1994).

27. Pope, *Evolution of Altruism,* pp. 128-48.

A New Voice for Strong *Agapē*

In spite of the intellectual pressures pushing us to reclaim an understanding of Christian love as equal-regard that also builds on the natural affections of kin altruism, new expressions of strong *agapē* have recently emerged. And they are sophisticated voices as well. One of the most articulate can be found in the writings of Emory University theological ethicist Timothy Jackson. In two important books, *Love Disconsoled* and *The Priority of Love,* Jackson has resisted the trends from theological feminists and the social sciences to build into the ideal of Christian love a stronger role for natural attachments, biological investments, and self-regard. Jackson sees Christian love pretty much working from the top down. He writes,

> God is love (1 John 4:8), and we are dependent on God's gracious self-revelation for a rudimentary understanding of and participation in this Goodness. Since God is the Creator of all that is, God's loving nature cannot be totally alien to — much less contradictory of — creatures, especially those made in the divine Image. But to seek to ground an account of agapic love in the rhythms of the material universe or the recesses of the human heart is to travel down the now dead-end of immanence. . . . Natural processes are too arbitrary and amoral to be the chief inspiration for virtue, and human instincts are too frail and fallible.[28]

Agapē, according to Jackson, comes from the "holiness of God."[29] It cannot be reduced to almsgiving or formalized philanthropy. Its object is not only human life but all of life, from animal life all the way to plants and other living things. All of these participate in God's creative good and are therefore objects of *agapē.* Jackson makes the following points about his view of *agapē:*

> I defend a position I call "strong *agape.*" Let me elaborate on both words in the quoted phrase. When viewed interpersonally, as the conversion of human relations wrought by the grace of God, *agape* involves three basic features: 1) unconditional willing of good for

---

28. Jackson, *The Priority of Love,* p. 8. Jackson's other important work on this subject is *Love Disconsoled: Meditations on Christian Charity* (Cambridge: Cambridge University Press, 1999).

29. Jackson, *Priority of Love,* p. xiv.

the other, 2) equal regard for the well-being of the other, and 3) passionate service open to self-sacrifice for the sake of the other. Lest the first two features seem to refer only to internal dispositions, the third puts an explicit premium on a particular action: bearing one another's burdens (cf. Gal. 6:2). The "strong," in turn, implies that agapic love is a metavalue, that virtue without which one has no substantive access to other goods, either moral or nonmoral.[30]

Jackson acknowledges that there is an appropriate place for self-love in Christian love, but the accent is very different than it is in the Catholic tradition of *caritas*. He writes, "Self-love is compatible with or even part of *agape*, broadly construed, but proper self-love comes only through self-transcendence. Self-realization comes, that is, via interpersonal service that does not look first to personal gain."[31]

Jackson argues for the priority of love interpreted as strong *agapē*. But the emphasis on priority does not mean that there are not other important virtues or habits in the Christian life. For instance, justice is important, and although it is distinguishable from love as *agapē*, it is still love's regard for and passionate service to all persons that is the presupposition for the virtue of justice.[32] Freedom and prudence — the highly valued virtues of modernity and democracy — are also, in Jackson's view of things, important virtues for the Christian life, but still gain their appropriate meaning in relation to love as a supernaturally granted capacity for love as *agapē*.[33]

How do I respond to Jackson's forceful new statement in defense of an understanding of Christian love that can be found in Luther and his modern champions Anders Nygren, Barth, and Bultmann? How should we evaluate his in-your-face rejection of the pressures of not only the modern psychotherapeutic psychologies but theological feminism, the neo-Thomism of Janssens, the implications of modern attachment theory and evolutionary psychology, and *Hardwired*'s claims for the importance of our very natural needs for connectivity — needs that must be met before higher capacities for love, commitment, and service to others can be formed?

Our differences are both less and more than one might think at first glance, especially since I have explicitly rejected the strong agapic point of view. Our differences are less when it is observed that neither Jackson nor

---

30. Jackson, *Priority of Love*, p. 10.
31. Jackson, *Priority of Love*, p. 11.
32. Jackson, *Priority of Love*, p. 8.
33. Jackson, *Priority of Love*, p. 6.

I are foundationalists. I believe that Jackson's arguments against grounding Christian love in the rhythms of nature is really a reluctance to use nature — even our need for attachment and the role of kin altruism in meeting this need — as a source for *deriving* Christian love. Here I agree: the dynamics of attachment and kin altruism will not by themselves provide humans with the capacity to treat the distant other — especially the stranger — with equal-regard, nor will they alone give us the capacity for going the second mile when our love is resisted and outright rejected. But this is not my argument, not my reason for using attachment theory and kin altruism in relation to Christian love. In fact, the reader should remember that I begin with tradition — the history of revelation as mediated by tradition — and use the distanciated insights of attachment theory and evolutionary psychology *diagnostically*. As Christians, we learn to regard the other (whether offspring or stranger) as an end and never as a means because our tradition reveals that all humans are children of God and made in God's image. We learn to go the second mile because our tradition has revealed to us the model of Christ and grants us the grace and resolve to endure in our efforts to be reconciled with our neighbor. Nonetheless, God also works through the affections of family attachments and kin altruism as preparations while we learn that the stranger and enemy too, in the eyes of God, are our brother, sister, mother, and father.

From my perspective, Jackson neglects to develop a fully articulated theology of both creation and salvation. Jackson believes that because God created all the world, all objects in the world are worthy participants in God's goodness and therefore deserving of God's love. On this, Jackson is right. But Jackson fails to see the various ways God *works through* created nature. Nature is not quite as chaotic and undependable as Jackson believes. Insights from the psychology of attachment, from evolutionary psychology's understanding of the motivations of kin altruism, and from the studies of naturalist Frans de Waal on the capacity for natural sympathy in chimpanzees and bonobos all suggest that God may be working through nature just as God works through revelation. To suggest that our natural tendency toward self-regard, our natural needs for attachment, or our natural investments in our children are antithetical to God's agapic love and grace is to limit one's view of the workings of God. It may be more consistent with the Christian tradition to believe that God works in two directions and that the findings of the social and psychological sciences help us gain diagnostic insights into the working of God in nature.

There is another point of tension between Jackson's strong agapic view of Christian love and the *caritas* view of love as equal-regard that I am developing in this volume. At first glance, it might appear that Jackson is building a much more robust place for the self-sacrificial moment of love than I do or than does Janssens, upon whom I rely so heavily for much of my point of view. I sometimes say that self-sacrifice is not the goal of Christian love; it is a requirement of Christian love when the realities of finitude, error, and sin disrupt community (disrupt love as equal-regard) and extra effort is needed to endure, go the second mile, and do all that is possible to restore community, equal-regard, and mutuality. In this sense, I have called the self-sacrificial moment of love a *transitional ethic;* it is not the goal of Christian ethic, but something we have to go through — something we have to suffer and endure, sometimes indefinitely — to realize the strenuous ethic of equal-regard and mutuality. I know, even through personal communication, that Jackson objects to the idea of self-sacrificial love as transitional.

Yet, his position is not too different from the one I have presented, and to the degree that this is true, his efforts to revise the strong *agapē* point of view result in a view of *agapē* not quite as extreme or complete as the classic formulations put forth by Nygren and others. Jackson does not quite say that the ideal of Christian love is perpetual and constant self-sacrifice for the good of the other. He says, instead, that Christian love entails an "openness" to self-sacrifice, not a constant and steady state of self-sacrifice. In using the word "openness," he tacitly acknowledges the complaint from feminists and minorities that the ethic of the cross — the ethic of sacrificial love — can be used to exploit the powerless by idealizing a sacrificial servanthood that makes them vulnerable to exploitation and manipulation. The idea of openness to self-sacrifice suggests that Christian love must be willing, under certain circumstances, to reach out in love even at great cost to the self. But Jackson does not tell us what these circumstances might be. He does not give us guidelines for when the openness to self-sacrificial love should be translated to actionable and actual self-sacrifice for the good of the other.

The self-sacrifice of the cross required by the love ethic of equal-regard is the self-sacrifice (the work) required to reinstate a relationship — both interpersonal and social, both intersubjective and political — to equal-regard and mutuality once again. I call this a transitional ethic even though it could be, in reality, both long-term and even enduring unto death. I call it transitional only to communicate that the suffering itself is not the goal of the action; the goal is the restoration of community to mutuality and equal-regard — the marks of the kingdom of God and the blessed community.

The Metaphysics of Love

I must admit: I can be somewhat sympathetic with Jackson's skepticism about the moral significance of nature and the disciplines that study it, such as evolutionary biology and psychology. There is little doubt that much of this literature has problems from the perspective of Christian ethics. This emerging congruence or dialectic between the evolutionary perspective and Christian ethics on the nature of love should not blind us to important tensions between them. For instance, the philosophical naturalism that undergirds research guided by evolutionary theory is understandable and to be expected. Stephen Pope, in his forthcoming *Evolution and Christian Ethics,* makes an important distinction between methodological reductionism, epistemological reductionism, and ontological or metaphysical reductionism. Pope believes that the Christian ethicist should be willing to grant scientists and moral psychologists the right to exercise a degree of methodological reductionism as long as they do not inflate this maneuver into the broader and more dogmatic claims of epistemological and ontological reductionism. Pope helpfully distinguishes between the different reductionisms when he writes,

> Ontological reductionism is not required, either in practice or by logic, by scientific method. Evolutionary ontological reductionists share with the "creationists" a tendency not to separate properly scientific from philosophical claims. . . . there is a difference between trying to use science to explain as much about the phenomena as possible (methodological reductionism) and assuming that science alone has the ability fully to explain all phenomena (epistemological reductionism). There is also an important difference between employing science to discover whatever can be known about the material world (methodological reductionism), and assuming that the material world alone is real (ontological reductionism). Methodological reductionism does not require the further metaphysical commitment to the belief that the only things that exist are to be found in the natural or material world.[34]

When methodological reductionism and naturalism harden into a systematic worldview that excludes or denigrates all visions of life that provide for some sense of transcendence, this must be a concern to Christian ethics. No matter how far Aristotelian-Thomistic models of Christian

---

34. Stephen Pope, *Human Evolution and Christian Ethics* (manuscript), chap. 1, p. 22.

love go in acknowledging the naturalistic realities of kin and reciprocal altruism (and they do go far in this direction), love within this philosophical and theological tradition finally grounds itself on the sacred status of human personhood, the belief that all good (and all specific goods) come from God, and the confidence that the ultimate meaning and direction of all finite loves is toward the overarching love for and enjoyment of God. Thomas Aquinas begins with the reality of human desire, as does Ricoeur, but carries this forward to the full acknowledgement of the ultimate desire for union and community with God.

This has implications for the balance of kin altruism with wider and deeper realities. For instance, Thomas wrote that humans love their children for two mutually reinforcing reasons: first, because they are extensions of their own substance, and second, because they mirror the goodness of God.[35] Of course, the second reason was seen by Thomas as the more weighty — indeed, so significant that it was believed to command all humans to love even those children who are not their own.[36] Why should Christians love all children, even those not their own? Because all children — indeed, all humans — are first of all children of the one God who is author of both creation and salvation. But, even more important, for Aquinas the second reason for loving one's children built on and extended the first. The two worlds of biological functionality (the first reason) and the divine createdness of all children (the second reason) coexisted in Aquinas's pre-Darwinist thought. Although these alternative worldviews are not easily reconciled, must evolutionary psychology and Christian ethics compete today with the idea that one or the other must eventually vanquish its alleged enemy?

Recent amendments to evolutionary psychology have softened the opposition between these alternative visions, but they have not dissolved the conflict altogether. For instance, there is the recent emphasis, summarized by James Q. Wilson, on natural selection as functioning to create a variety of secondary mechanisms, such as our positive response to the smile of an infant, even if it is not our own flesh and blood — a hypothesis that helps us understand the motivation to adopt.[37] This insight suggests that rather than working simply to select the products of our genes as such, natural selection has worked to create more generalizable responsive inclinations. This has loosened evolutionary psychology from what some

35. Aquinas, *Summa Theologica*, II, ii, q. 26, a. 3.
36. Aquinas, *Summa Theologica*, II, ii, q. 26, a. 3.
37. James Q. Wilson, *The Moral Sense* (New York: Free Press, 1993), p. 127.

critics call the tyranny of the reproductive paradigm, thought by some to be a fault of early sociobiology. This advance makes it easier for theology to reconcile evolutionary models of love with more expansive theological models that do not center entirely on reproductive love as such.

A second example comes from the work of Frans de Waal in the field of primate psychology. In his observation of chimpanzees, he has found evidence not only of reciprocal altruism but also of cognitive mechanisms of remembrance and anticipation and, hence, what he calls "cognitive empathy." Not only humans but primates remember kind acts done to them and anticipate the possible good consequences of helpful acts they may do to others, even those beyond their kin. With these advanced cognitive capacities in mind, we can begin to understand how an ethic of reciprocity can sometimes take the long-term rather than the short-term view of reward and satisfaction.[38] This makes reciprocal altruism sometimes look almost, but still not exactly, like self-sacrificial love or *agapē* as theologians might define it.

But long-term reciprocal altruism and Christian sacrificial love are still not quite the same. The practical theological ethicist, even one influenced by Thomistic sensibilities, finally must ground both love as equal-regard and love as self-sacrificial gifts to the other on the Christian's belief in the infinite value of the other and on the sense that some acts of self-sacrifice are both willed and *empowered* by the grace of God. This is true even though self-sacrifice as such need not be seen as the central goal of Christian love. Recognizing the divine image and divine good in all humans is always the central motivating factor in Christian understandings of love; all love informed by rational calculations is always secondary, although it need not be entirely absent. This holds even if a Christian perspective also recognizes in a subordinate way the importance of the more egocentric elements of kin and reciprocal altruism. Hence, Christian love as strenuous mutuality or equal-regard should never be reduced to a logic of reciprocity. This is true no matter how complicated and nuanced reciprocity theory becomes. It is also true no matter how important reciprocity is in a secondary way for parties who first treat each other as ends, and never as means only, as must be the case for a Christian love ethic of equal-regard.

Third, more adequate metaphysical frameworks are now developing that can be brought to the field of evolutionary psychology to help save it

---

38. Frans de Waal, *Good Natured: The Origin of Right and Wrong in Humans and Other Animals* (Cambridge, Mass.: Harvard University Press, 1996), p. 135.

from its tendency to allow methodological reductionism to deteriorate into epistemological or ontological reductionism. Pope uses the theories of emergent complexity to help understand, even from the perspective of naturalism, how human cognitive capacities arise that help us transcend motivations that primarily contribute to our own inclusive fitness through offspring and relatives. Emergent complexity can help account for how humans sometimes become genuinely committed to the well-being of unrelated others who offer no immediate advantage.

He refers to the thought of neurophysicist John Eccles, physicist Paul Davies, theologian and physicist Ian Barbour, and scientist and theologian Arthur Peacocke to build his case. Pope relays Davies's belief that the "new science of complexity examines ways in which physical systems have an intrinsic tendency to move spontaneously from less to more complex and/or more organized states."[39] An example of this can be found when one heats a pan of water. The heat seems to produce a convection flow that assumes the shape of a hexagon. Davies and Pope see this as a "spontaneous leap into higher levels of organization."[40] Davies holds that life itself emerged when the universe gained enough complexity and organization to move from inorganic matter to rudimentary forms of life.[41] Pope extends Davies's argument by saying, "Life is not a sheer accident but rather the product of the same kind of innate tendency of less organized physical states to move to higher and more complex levels of organization."[42] This perspective leads us to entertain the possibility that evolution has given rise to human consciousness and intelligence, capacities that allow us to be interpreters of our effective experience and the traditions behind it. The theory of emergent complexity provides us with a model for understanding how humans can be not only hermeneutic interpreters but, in accordance with the major model informing this book, critical hermeneutic interpreters. This helps us understand how our natural inclinations toward kin altruism can be extended to others outside our kin when we come to understand and believe the Christian narrative that tells us that all others are related to us because of our common status as God's children. The world of evolutionary theory and the world of critical hermeneutics may be more compatible than one might first think.

39. Pope, *Evolution and Christian Ethics,* chap. 1, p. 33.

40. Pope, *Evolution and Christian Ethics,* p. 33.

41. Paul Davies, "Is the Universe Absurd?" in *Science and Theology: The New Consonance,* ed. Ted Peters (Boulder, Colo.: Westview, 1998), chap. 6.

42. Pope, *Evolution and Christian Ethics,* chap. 1, p. 34.

Conclusion

Evolutionary psychology can make immense contributions to understanding some of the conditions for the emergence of love as mutuality and equal-regard. The importance of kin altruism, the mechanisms of mutual attachment in both parent and child, the rise of empathy as the child develops the capacity to feel and know the needs of the other in analogy to how she comes to feel and know her own needs, the gradual extension of these dynamics to non-kin through belief in the symbolic representation of all humanity's kinship in God, and, finally, the development of more abstract capacities of cognitive empathy for persons we do not even know — these are elements that are essential for development of a love ethic of equal-regard and mutuality.

Stated in this way, such an evolutionarily informed equal-regard ethic would be continuous with Christian love, but not identical to it. *What makes love as mutuality and equal-regard uniquely Christian is the special way Christians ground their appreciation for the role of sacrificial love.* They do so on the belief that both self and other are made in the image of God and that in *renewing* mutuality through sacrificial steadfastness, the Christian is somehow reliving the sacrificial gift of Christ's own life — itself thought to be the final key to the nature of God. This narrative or story, when rightly presented, absorbs and recontextualizes the more naturalistic view of the rise of mutuality.

The conflicting worldviews of evolutionary psychology and Christian theology should be relativized. The dogmatic naturalism and ontological reductionism that sometimes grip the field of evolutionary psychology also should be relaxed. On the other hand, the phobia against material explanations in some quarters of theology should become less adamant. More metaphysical humility should characterize both Christian ethics and evolutionary psychology. This should happen in order to create a public philosophy that can guide the socialization processes of society as well as the communities of memory that *Hardwired to Connect* describes with such force.

Evolutionary psychology should realize that on the grounds of its discipline alone, it can neither confirm nor deny any particular worldview, even its own heuristic naturalism. Hence, at the margins of human thought, evolutionary psychology as a science should be charitably agnostic on metaphysical issues. Something analogous should be the case with Christian ethics. It should rid itself of its disdain for naturalistic explanations and instead try to recontextualize the insights of naturalism into a broader view of reality that permits elements of transcendence in both creation and redemption.

Both perspectives — evolutionary psychology and Christian ethics — should focus on the common ground between them. They should do this with an eye toward developing a more rational and public ethic that can interrelate both secular and religious perspectives for the guidance of parental love, formal religious education, public education, and the wider enculturation processes of society.

Chapter 6

Altruism, Feminism, and Family
in Christian Love

I n the last chapter, I discussed further the idea of kin altruism, a central concept in the new evolutionary psychology. This concept illumines the process of moral development. At least, many moral psychologists think it does. Kin altruism helps explain parental involvement with
and attachment to one's children. Theoretically, it helps explain why children, in response to the parental investment, become attached to their
parents and gradually identify with their moral values. According to our
full model of moral development derived from Ricoeur, evolutionary psychology helps account for the development of highly important
premoral affections and attachments, and then, later, the development
of what Freud called the superego or Kohlberg called conventional morality. But according to Ricoeur, kin altruism would not explain the
higher aspirational dimensions of morality carried by our religio-
cultural visions, which are imparted by communities of memory to their
followers and their wider cultures. Nor would it explain how our teleological wants and attachments pass the deontological test. Nonetheless,
evolutionary psychology throws light on an important part of what goes
into our moral growth.

But the claims associated with kin altruism raise important questions
about its relation to Christian love. I addressed some of these questions in
the last chapter, but there is more to say. In this chapter, I investigate
more deeply and advance more systematically certain arguments about
the mediating role of families between love of kin and love of the distant
neighbor. In addition, I will engage certain feminist theological views of
love in light of this dialogue between kin altruism and Christian views of
love.

The Context of the Question

At first glance, evolutionary psychology gives rise to a more or less pervasively egoistic view of the entire field of love. Love of children, spouse, friends, neighbor, country, and church appear as various complications and organizations of self-interest. Such views of altruism place it in striking contrast to most definitions of Christian love, especially more classically Protestant views with their tendency toward strong agapism.

There are several possible implications which follow from this tension. One might point to the eventual cultural demise, precipitated by the prestige of evolutionary biology, of any normative hold that the idea of Christian love has on the imaginations of people in Western societies. Indeed, the word may be getting around — "just give up on Christian sacrificial love." Some evolutionary psychologists are saying that, in fact, sacrificial love "just doesn't — just can't — really exist." Hence, this message implies, quit punishing yourself by trying to live by an ethic of self-giving love. The outcome of this might be the possible use of evolutionary psychology to justify more explicitly egoistic behavior, somewhat along the lines influenced by social Darwinism in the late nineteenth and early twentieth centuries.[1]

As important as this cultural trend might be, I want to investigate a more subtle concern. Evolutionary psychological views of altruism emphasize the importance of genetic, blood, or family relations as mediators between self-love and love for distant neighbors, strangers, and, perhaps, even enemies. Peter Singer, Mary Midgley, and others build on this idea and argue that we learn to love our distant neighbors by analogically generalizing outward — through kin and reciprocal altruism — the affections and identifications we achieve with our mothers, fathers, brothers, and sisters. Does this process of generalizing kin altruism outward to others bring this form of love into contact with Christian love?

The Future of Altruism and the Decline of Families

If there is truth in this theory, two threats to social solidarity are possible. In fact, they may be developing before our very eyes in modern societies. First, commentators such as David Popenoe, Christopher Lasch, and

---

1. Carl Degler, *In Search of Human Nature* (Oxford: Oxford University Press, 1991), pp. 10-16.

Brigitte and Peter Berger have argued that families in all Western industrial societies are in decline.[2] The growing rate of out-of-wedlock births[3] and divorce,[4] the high cost of divorce to children,[5] the feminization of poverty, the growing poverty among the children of single mothers,[6] the resultant feminization of kinship,[7] the declining role of fathers in families,[8] and the declining belief in the importance of families are visible in every Western industrial society. Mary Ann Glendon, the distinguished Harvard Law School professor and an authority on comparative family law, wonders whether families in industrial societies are now strong enough to stimulate the extension of our natural affections to larger spheres of citizenship and social solidarity. She refers to the research of Alice and Peter Rossi, the sociological team from the University of Massachusetts, that shows a "strong correlation between the sense of obligation people report that they feel for their kinfolk and their sense of obligation to a wider community and society at large."[9] If the two are correlated, the decline of families in Western societies would suggest a corresponding decline in an expansive and sympathetic citizenship.

Second, extreme self-sacrificial formulations of the Christian concept

2. David Popenoe, *Disturbing the Nest* (New York: A. de Gruyter, 1988); Brigitte and Peter Berger, *The War over the Family* (New York: Doubleday, 1984); Christopher Lasch, *Haven in a Heartless World: The Family Besieged* (New York: Basic, 1977).

3. Out-of-wedlock births have risen in the United States from 5 percent of all births in 1960 to approximately 34 percent today. In the black community, 66 percent of all children are born out of wedlock.

4. The divorce rate in the United States went up to nearly 50 percent of all new marriages in the 1970s, but has decreased a few points in recent years, partially as a result of the increase in cohabitation.

5. There is a growing literature in the United States about the high cost of divorce to children — financially, emotionally, and through a weakened capacity to form meaningful marital unions in the future. See Judith Wallerstein and Sandra Blakeslee, *Second Chances: Men, Women and Children a Decade After Divorce* (New York: Ticknor and Fields, 1989); Andrew Cherlin and Frank Furstenburg, *Divided Families: What Happens to Children When Parents Part* (Cambridge: Harvard University Press, 1991); and Paul Amato and Alan Booth, *A Generation at Risk* (Cambridge, Mass.: Harvard University Press, 1997).

6. For the ground-breaking discussion of this issue, see Lenore Weitzman, *The Divorce Revolution: The Unexpected Social and Economic Consequences for Women and Children in America* (New York: Free Press, 1985).

7. Reported in Judith Stacey, *Brave New Families: Stories of Domestic Upheaval in Late Twentieth Century America* (New York: Basic, 1990), p. 268.

8. David Popenoe, *Life without Father* (New York: Free Press, 1996).

9. Mary Ann Glendon, "Virtue, Families, and Citizenship," in *The Meaning of the Family in a Free Society*, ed. W. Lawson Taitte (Austin: University of Texas Press, 1991), p. 67.

of love may themselves unwittingly work against the spread of kin and re-ciprocal altruism to the wider community. Formulations of Christian love which exclude all self-regarding motives, as certain extreme self-sacrificial models are thought to do, may fail to harness the natural forces fueling kin, reciprocal, and group altruism, and therefore fail to extend them to wider circles. Hence, in the name of an expansive, other-regarding, and self-emptying love, strong agapic formulations of Christian love may par-adoxically diminish wider identifications and social solidarity by ignoring and thereby undercutting its natural springs. To say it differently, overly strong agapic views of Christian love may undermine processes of em-pathic identification with strangers and the needy by failing to recognize that *God may work from two directions* — from below through the natural processes of attachment and kin altruism (sometimes called the grace communicated through God's good creation) and from above through tradition-mediated witness to God's supernatural revelation and call to love all persons, even those who resist our love, strike back, and bring harm to us.

Sympathy, Families, and the Grounds of Social Solidarity

These two issues point to a great debate that has echoed throughout Western philosophical and religious history. This debate began with Aris-totle's criticism of Plato's position in *The Republic* on the relation of the family to public empathy and justice. In order for the philosopher kings of Plato's ideal republic to have empathy for the entire state rather than just their own flesh and blood, Plato suggested couples mate but then have their children taken away and raised by the state. His purpose was to create conditions under which children and parents would not know one another.[10] Plato believed that this would push the philosopher kings to extend their sympathetic and altruistic feelings to all the children of the state, not just their own. Since the philosopher kings would have no way of knowing which specific children were their own, they would tend to hold all children in common and "thus more than others have a commu-nity of pain and pleasure."[11]

Aristotle in his *Politics* did not respond kindly to Plato's thought ex-periment in *The Republic*. Aristotle believed that sympathy for the wider

---

10. Plato, *The Republic,* ed. Alan Bloom (New York: Basic, 1968), bk. V, pp. 461-65.
11. Plato, *The Republic,* bk. V, para. 464a.

community spreads outward from particular, embodied, and special family relations. He believed that what is everyone's responsibility easily becomes no one's responsibility. Plato had hoped for a community in which everyone would say "mine" and "not mine" at the same time about both the community's children and about all material possessions.[12] Aristotle believed "that what is common to the greatest number has the least care bestowed upon it" and that parents who are biologically attached to their children and who see themselves in their children are far more inclined to care for them than are exchangeable caretakers in some common pool of adults and children.[13] He believed that children who see themselves in their parents are also likely to be more responsive to adult guidance and direction.

The issue between Plato and Aristotle can be stated as follows: does sympathetic and altruistic behavior spread to the wider community through our natural family affections, as Aristotle thought, or is it achieved through the suppression of our natural familial affections, as Plato is portrayed as believing? In passages such as Matthew 10:37 ("Whoever loves father or mother more than me is not worthy of me"), Jesus is often interpreted as making a point similar to that of Plato in the *Republic* — to serve the transcendent aims of the kingdom of God one must suppress one's natural familial affections. Thomas Aquinas, however, clearly follows Aristotle on this matter. Jesus, he tells us, "commanded us to hate, in our kindred, not their kinship, but only the fact of their being an obstacle between us and God."[14] Aquinas's point, moreover, is even more positive than this. He tells us that we are positively commanded to love our own and to see this as an asset for the love of God. According to Aquinas, learning to love the members of our family should help us learn to be more loving in general, and this love can become the seeds for deepening both our love for God and our love for all our neighbors. But to extend these rudimentary natural tendencies to the more inclusive love of God and neighbor entails, as I have claimed, a process of learning and spiritual transformation. These natural inclinations do not contain the resources for their own highest completion.

In light of these preliminary considerations, let me state the two theses that will guide this chapter. First, I will reaffirm what I have already ar-

12. Plato, *The Republic*, bk. V, para. 462c.

13. Aristotle, *Politics*, in *The Basic Works of Aristotle*, ed. Richard McKeon (New York: Random House, 1914), bk. 1, chap. 2.

14. Thomas Aquinas, *Summa Theologica*, II, ii, Q. 26, art. 7 (London: R & T Washbourne, 1917).

gued — that, although kin altruism and Christian love should be distinguished, it is proper to see them as complementary and mutually enriching. Second, I will argue that the family is an important mediating institution between our natural affections and Christian love; as such, the family is important for the development of Christian love but, at the same time, must be transcended in certain respects for Christian love to find its fullest expression. *Kin altruism is thus an important but finite and relative good for achieving higher forms of love.* The reader should be very clear about my argument here. I am not making kin altruism — the inclination of biologically related people to become attached and invested in one another — into an absolute or idolatrous value. I am not saying that one's salvation depends upon being raised by those who begot you. Nor am I saying that all adopted children and stepchildren are doomed to less care and investment from their parents. But I am saying that kin altruism is an important and central, albeit finite, value relevant to the increase of moral capacity; it should be protected and built upon by higher-order values and transformations, both within Christianity and in the outside secular society. I will also argue that altruism as understood in evolutionary psychology is useful but limited in helping us understand how natural familial affections get transformed to apply to wider nonfamilial circles and thereby approach the expansiveness of Christian love.

The Return of the *Caritas* Model of Christian Love

To further this discussion about the role of family affections in generalizing love, I want to get more detailed about the historic debates on Christian views of love. This also will help us find the bridge between family affections and contemporary Christian feminist views of love. Garth Hallett in his *Christian Neighbor-Love* identifies six ways in which Christian love as *agapē* has been interpreted in the history of the church. There is Christian love as (1) self-preference, (2) parity, (3) other-preference, (4) self-subordination, (5) self-forgetfulness, and (6) self-denial.[15] These definitions move from more egoistic and self-regarding definitions (self-preference and parity) to more other-regarding and self-sacrificial definitions (other-preference, self-subordination, self-forgetfulness, and self-denial). Hallett identifies examples of all of these in both early and modern Christianity, Catholicism and

---

15. Garth L. Hallett, *Christian Neighbor-Love: An Assessment of Six Rival Versions* (Washington, D.C.: Georgetown University Press, 1989), pp. 2-10.

Protestantism. There has been, however, a tendency, as I already have hinted, for certain classic Protestant definitions of Christian love to gravitate toward the last two definitions, toward some form of love as self-forgetfulness or self-denial. Catholic models have, as I have already argued, found more of a place for elements of the first two definitions; that is, they have found more of a place for self-regard. Catholic models have tended to define *agapē* in the direction of *caritas,* which, in turn, balances self-regard and other-regard.

It is safe to say, I believe, that recently some Protestant theologians have defined Christian love more as *caritas* and have downplayed earlier classic Protestant definitions built around strong models of self-sacrifice or self-denial. There are various social and cultural reasons for these shifts. Feminists and minorities want to modify extreme self-sacrificial models of Christian love in view of the many ways these models historically have been exploited to justify the suffering, subordination, and chronic injustice done toward women, black people, and other disadvantaged groups. Humanistic-psychological and sociobiological perspectives on altruism constitute an additional cultural source that challenges Christian definitions of love to include elements of self-regard.

Certain Protestant definitions of Christian love such as Anders Nygren's are portrayed as de-emphasizing a place for natural self-regard. Nygren, we should recall, sharply distinguished *agapē* from both *erōs* and *caritas.* He defined *agapē* as spontaneous and unmotivated, as indifferent to the value of the object of love, as creative of value in those objects where little value exists, and as empowered by God rather than brought about by *erōs* or human desires, needs, and strivings, no matter how broadly they might be defined.[16] Nygren would have opposed Ricoeur's association of ethics with our desire for the good life and our general teleological aspirations. Or, at least, he would see these dimensions of life as having little to do with Christian love.

Nygren tells us that "caritas is not simply another name for agape."[17] *Erōs,* he asserts, represents the love that strives for a higher value, and it contrasts strongly with *agapē.* According to Nygren, *caritas* as a synthesis of Greek *erōs* and New Testament *agapē* has more to do with the egocentricity of *erōs* than with the self-giving qualities of *agapē.* The *caritas* doctrine, he believes, communicates inadequately the self-sacrificial themes of Jesus, Paul, and John. He holds that the founders of the

16. Nygren, *Agape and Eros* (Philadelphia: Westminster, 1953), pp. 75-80.
17. Nygren, *Agape and Eros,* p. 55.

Protestant Reformation, especially Luther, uncovered the true meaning of *agapē* as spontaneous, creative, downward-reaching, and impartial Christian love. Although Ricoeur had many Protestant sensibilities, Nygren would say that his teleological ethic is in tension with the classic Protestant suspicion of *erōs*. The newer formulation of strong *agapē* by Jackson would regard Ricoeur's teleological starting point for ethics in much the same way.

As we saw in the last chapter, it is precisely this strong definition of *agapē*, with its radical disjunction between *agapē* and *erōs*, that is now being tempered, even in Protestant theological circles. The emerging cultural implications of evolutionary definitions of altruism further mellow these extreme formulations of *agapē*. Emil Brunner and Rudolf Bultmann are both associated in the theological literature with variations of the strong agapic formulations.[18] Reinhold Niebuhr tried to state a less dichotomous relation between *agapē* and *erōs*. He ended, however, in defining *agapē* as self-sacrificial love and calling it the norm of the Christian life even though it was an "impossible possibility" in a world marked by finitude and sin.[19]

Theological Feminism and the Rejection of Strong *Agapē*

Several feminist theologians have rejected all strong self-sacrificial formulations of *agapē* and have criticized Niebuhr's more moderate views. Christine Gudorf, Judith Vaughan, and Judith Plaskow have each criticized Niebuhr's modification of strong *agapē*.[20] The feminist critique of strong *agapē* ends in redefining Christian love toward *caritas*. It does this by characterizing the norm of love as mutuality — a balance or equilibrium between the claims and concerns of the self and the other.[21] These critiques

18. Reinhold Niebuhr associates Bultmann with this position in his *The Nature and Destiny of Man*, 2 vols. (New York: Charles Scribner's Sons, 1941-1943), vol. 2, pp. 84-85; Hallett associates Brunner and Bultmann with strong *agapē* in his *Christian Neighbor-Love*, pp. 5-6.

19. Niebuhr, *The Nature and Destiny of Man*, vol. 2, pp. 82-85.

20. Christine Gudorf, "Parenting, Mutual Love, and Sacrifice," in *Women's Consciousness, Women's Conscience: A Reader in Feminist Ethics*, ed. Barbara Andolsen, Christine Gudorf, and Mary Pellauer (New York: Harper and Row, 1985); Judith Vaughan, *Sociality, Ethics and Social Change: A Critical Appraisal of Reinhold Niebuhr's Ethics in the Light of Rosemary Ruether's Works* (New York: University Press of America, 1983); Judith Plaskow, *Sin and Grace: Woman's Experience and the Theologies of Reinhold Niebuhr and Paul Tillich* (Lanham, Md.: University Press of America, 1980).

21. Some of the same attempts to make sociobiology less reductive that have been developed in Mary Midgley, *Beast and Man: The Roots of Human Nature* (Ithaca, N.Y.: Cornell

aspire to bring *erōs* into a redefined understanding of Christian love that emphasizes rigorous mutuality and equal-regard in place of self-sacrifice and self-denial. Christian love requires taking the other as seriously as the self but also demanding that the other respect you equally as well. This clearly moves Christian love closer to Catholic *caritas* models. But the Christian feminist concern with *erōs* is more typically modern and liberal in its limited interest in the category of nature and its primary concern with autonomy and self-actualization — an autonomy and self-actualization that have been suppressed by patriarchal institutions and by calls to endure this oppression through self-sacrifice and suffering.

From the standpoint of evolutionary psychology, however, most theological feminists rely on a thin view of *erōs* — a very thin theory of desire and need. Although the feminist rejection of strong *agapē* reintroduces *erōs* and brings Christian love closer to *caritas,* the leading authors of this movement are fearful of making use, however limited, of evolutionary psychological or sociobiological formulations of altruism. This hesitation probably stems from their fear that Christian theology would become entrapped once again in a static and rigid biologism of the kind that Aquinas is thought to have inherited from Aristotle and transmitted to the scholastic theology of the nineteenth century.

Feminist theological resistance to the insights of biological perspectives on altruism is understandable, but regrettable. It recently has been echoed by even feminist natural-law moral theologians such as Jean Porter in her impressive *Nature as Reason: A Thomistic Theory of Natural Law.*[22] Although her approach to natural law in Christian ethics is very similar to the position of Stephen Pope, after taking an initial step toward evolutionary psychology in her earlier writing[23] she has now taken another step away from it. Strangely, she seems to be more comfortable with the descriptive psychobiology of the medieval scholastics than with the more

---

University Press, 1978), and Peter Singer *(The Expanding Circle: Ethics and Sociobiology* [New York: Farrar, Straus, and Giroux, 1981]) have also been developed in George Pugh, *The Biological Origins of Human Values* (New York: Basic, 1977). All three of these perspectives repudiate the idea that moral values are hardwired into the human organism and that biology can tell us directly what our moral values should be. All three believe that biology can inform us about some of our premoral needs and "central tendencies," to use Midgley's phrase, which culture and free moral reflection must try to stay within. William James anticipated this argument in his article titled "Remarks on Spencer's Definition of Mind as Correspondence," *Collected Essays and Reviews* (New York: Russell and Russell, 1920), pp. 43-68.

22. Jean Porter, *Nature as Reason: A Thomistic Theory of the Natural Law* (Grand Rapids: Eerdmans, 2005), pp. 105-6.

23. Jean Porter, *Natural and Divine Law* (Grand Rapids: Eerdmans, 1999), pp. 217-18.

refined and explanatory power of the evolutionary psychobiology of the present. Hence, for one reason or another, several feminist theologians have overlooked how evolutionary psychological perspectives on altruism can balance the excesses of both strong *agapē* and a *caritas* model that allows *erōs* to be narrowed to either self-actualization or a freer form of the erotic. Furthermore, the thicker understanding of desire found in evolutionary psychology can add essential insights into the nature of *erōs* in the form of kin altruism and the role of families in shaping Christian love — insights which some Christian feminists tend to overlook, probably out of fear of being trapped by conventional constraints in the name of family obligations that Western societies have often prescribed for women.

Kin Altruism, Family, and Christian Love: Their Proper Order

We have reviewed some recent reactions to extreme agapism and the beginnings of a shift toward *caritas* models of love, especially under the impact of theological feminism. Biological perspectives on altruism have contributed a note of realism to this trend. It promises to go beyond finding a place in Christian love for *erōs* defined as autonomy and self-concern to provide insight into the natural springs of parental investment and infant attachment that all genuinely other-regarding love must necessarily build upon even if it must also be expanded and transformed. More specifically, modern evolutionary-psychological views on the origin of altruism offer to Christian ethics an updated biology to replace the metaphysical biology that Aquinas and nineteenth-century Roman Catholic scholasticism are said to have inherited. This is especially true for those forms of evolutionary psychology which have been reformulated with the thought of such philosophers as William James, Mary Midgley, and George Pugh, and even with some of the insights, although certainly not all, of the controversial Peter Singer.

To make this point, I turn again to Stephen Pope's efforts to find a balanced perspective on the relation of kin altruism to Christian love. A more careful review of his argument will help us see why feminists should have less fear of evolutionary psychology and more confidence that they can use it without being trapped in its frequent reductionism. Pope is concerned to balance the tendency of recent Roman Catholic ethics, best illustrated in the thought of Rahner, to adopt a personalism disconnected from nature and biology. He understands the problems with a Thomistic metaphysical biology. He also believes, however, that it is incomplete to settle on a philosophical personalism, of the kind found in Pope John Paul II, that is uninformed by a philosophically reconstructed evolutionary psychology.[24] Stephen Pope wants both; he wants a personalism of the human subject that also incorporates a naturalism — "an archeology," to use a phrase from Paul Ricoeur[25] — of the kind provided by evolutionary psychology. He proposes a flexible evolutionary psychology of the kind projected by Mary Midgley in her *Beast and Man*. Such a view avoids the rigid determinism of the early E. O. Wilson.[26] It holds that humans have "genetically influenced behavioral predispositions" which constitute a basic system of *premoral* valuations that more properly moral judgments must respect, stay within, and give some hierarchical organization to.[27] Central to these valuations are the processes of kin and reciprocal altruism; although these predispositions do not determine the nature of the *moral good* in the full sense of that term, insight into their preferences helps clarify and refine what Aquinas called "the order of charity."[28] Although Pope does not put his position in the language of Ricoeur, they both, in effect, agree that morality begins with the teleology of desire — with the premoral strivings of humans to realize the goods of life. But they also would agree that this beginning point is not itself fully moral. More is required if the desire for the good is to pass the test of the truly moral. Or to say it differently still, they both hold that there is a difference between the premoral and the moral good.

Pope follows Aquinas in the belief that God's creative activity and moral governance are expressed through the ordering of natural appetite. Or to say it more in the language of Niebuhr, God as Creator and God as Governor are both seen in and through our natural appetites, an insight that I thought Jackson in his return to strong *agapē* overlooked. Because of the centrality of kin selection among our appetites, Pope argues that parental love is the natural core of all love. He further argues, with the support of Aristotle, Aquinas, and contemporary evolutionary psychology, that parents' love of their children is associated in part with self-

24. Stephen Pope, "The Order of Love and Recent Catholic Ethics: A Constructive Proposal," *Theological Studies* 52 (1991): 257-62.

25. For Paul Ricoeur on archeology, see his *Freud and Philosophy* (New Haven: Yale University Press, 1970), pp. 459-93.

26. Edward O. Wilson, *On Human Nature* (Cambridge, Mass.: Harvard University Press, 1978), pp. 71-77.

27. Pope, "The Order of Love," p. 266.

28. Aquinas, *Summa Theologica* II, ii, Q. 26, a. 1.

love.[29] Evolutionary psychology finds in the field of modern genetics reasons for the special love relation between parents and their children that Aquinas found in the pre-scientific descriptive biology of Aristotle.

Pope believes that some of Aquinas's distinctions in the "order of charity" can be suggestive for contemporary discussions. For instance, Aquinas asks "Whether a man ought, out of charity, to love his children more than his father?" Aquinas answers that we should love them differently. A man should *honor* his father as his "creative principle" or source and as being for this reason nearer to God. At the same time, a man should love his children more in the sense of *caring* for them. Aquinas writes, "a man loves more that which is more closely connected with him, in which way a man's children are more lovable to him than his father, as the Philosopher states."[30] Pope's point is more methodological than substantive. He is saying that as Aquinas used Aristotle's biology in Christian ethics, so Christian theologians today can use a philosophically reconstructed evolutionary psychology to clarify the natural archeology of Christian love.[31]

In addition, Pope argues that Aquinas's biology and modern evolutionary psychology share, in spite of their many disagreements, at least some common affirmations. One of these is the view that more expansive forms of altruism for the wider community (reciprocal and group altruism) grow out of early parent-child investments and attachments. This is a point that Mary Ann Glendon, with the help of sociologists Alice and Peter Rossi, made on strictly sociological grounds, as I pointed out above. Pope writes that there are good biological grounds for "affirming that relatively stable and secure bonds of love within the family create the emotional basis for a later extension of love to persons outside the family and that the quality of these early bonds continues powerfully to inform subsequent adult affectional bonds."[32] Mary Midgley says something similar:

> The development of sociability proceeds in any case largely by this extension to other adults of behavior first developed between parents and young — grooming, mouth contact, embracing, protective and submissive gestures, giving food. In fact, wider sociality in its original essence simply is the power of adults to treat one another mutually, as honorary parents and children.[33]

29. Pope, "The Order of Love," p. 264.
30. Aquinas, *Summa Theologica* II, ii, Q. 26, a. 9.
31. Pope, "The Order of Love," p. 265.
32. Pope, "The Order of Love," p. 276.
33. Midgley, *Beast and Man*, p. 136.

The controversial Peter Singer contains some wisdom, at least, on this same point: he too finds the origins of mature forms of philosophical ethics in infant and child responses to parental investments. The title of one of his books, *The Expanding Circle: Ethics and Sociobiology,* expresses this point of view. Universal moral systems are not based on suppressing family attachments; such comprehensive moral perspectives evolve from the elaboration and expansion of family affections to wider nonfamilial circles.[34]

Pope, Midgley, and Singer are less rigid in their formulation of the relation of kin selection to altruism than the early E. O. Wilson or Richard Dawkins.[35] All three repudiate the narrow egoism of the "selfish gene" hypothesis. Pope believes that we cannot accept Dawkins's view of humans as mere "survival machines — robot vehicles blindly programmed to preserve the selfish molecules known as genes."[36] Pope represents this view well when he argues that the "error of such fatalism lies not in its uninhibited recognition of biological causality, but in taking it to be a quasi-exclusive causal factor that minimizes the force of a multitude of other causal factors (personal, cultural, economic, and so on)."[37] In taking this stand, these authors agree with the early position of William James voiced in the context of his critique of Herbert Spencer's narrow emphasis on survival as the sole motivation of human behavior. James, in his great article "Remarks on Spencer's Definition of Mind as Correspondence," acknowledged the existence of the biological interest to survive. He believed, however, that many other biologically grounded interests express themselves in "various forms of play, the thrilling intimations of art, the delights of philosophic contemplation, the rest of religious emotion, the joy of moral self-approbation."[38] James called these "brain born" human potentials in contrast to environmentally conditioned and hence learned capacities. James thought that these mental capacities probably just popped out, so too speak, of the strange workings of what evolutionary theorists call "free variation." These capacities and interests are retained by natural selection because, in certain unintentional and indirect ways, they also contribute to adaptation and survival, even though that is not their pri-

---

34. Singer, *The Expanding Circle,* pp. 27-36.

35. E. O. Wilson, *Sociobiology: The New Synthesis* (Cambridge: Harvard University Press, 1975); Richard Dawkins, *The Selfish Gene* (Oxford: Oxford University Press, 1976).

36. Dawkins, *The Selfish Gene,* p. ix.

37. Pope, "The Order of Love," p. 273.

38. William James, "Remarks on Spencer's Definition of Mind as Correspondence," *Collected Essays and Reviews* (New York: Russell and Russell, 1920 [essay originally published in 1878]), p. 52.

mary purpose. Although the theory of emergent complexity, which I reviewed in Chapter 5, does not evoke James's theory of our brain-born interests in art, play, and religious wonder, the outlines of the theory almost beg for a belief that there are such latent capacities that complexity itself activates into existence. Mary Midgley, in tune with James, also underscores the multiplicity of human biological motivations and interests; the selfish-gene motivation is simply one of many. "Self-preservation is not only a strong general motive with us," she writes, "it is also a positive duty. What it cannot be is our only motive or our only duty."[39]

What are the implications of this discussion for Christian love? I have already claimed that evolutionary psychological views of altruism question the intelligibility of extreme agapic understandings of Christian love and argue for reclaiming dimensions of *caritas* understandings. Basically, I have used evolutionary views of altruism not to claim an identity between Christian love and altruism, but rather to inject a note of realism into both classical Protestant formulations of strong agapism and recent Christian feminists' reliance on a thin understanding of *erōs* as autonomy and self-actualization. In effect, I have used evolutionary psychology in the way Owen Flanagan in his recent *Varieties of Moral Psychology: Ethics and Psychological Realism* suggests that moral psychology can be used to test normative ethics. Flanagan, whom I will discuss more deeply in Chapter 8, argues that the empirical discipline of moral psychology can help assess which philosophical and theological moral theories are psychologically feasible or possible, that is, which are consistent within the framework of psychological possibilities, tendencies, and limits. He calls it the Principle of Minimum Psychological Realism.[40] This idea is close to what Ricoeur means by his concepts of explanation, distance, and diagnosis; such epistemological maneuvers help Ricoeur find empirical regularities that also provide an element of realism.

I have used evolutionary psychology to claim that when measured by Flanagan's realism or some constraints uncovered by a diagnostic use of Ricoeur's distanciating and explanatory moment, extreme *agapē* not only appears implausible, it is positively self-defeating. Its suppression or neglect of family attachments deprives it of the affectional and attachment energies on which all more expansive and self-giving expressions of love must build, even if these energies must also be transformed. Furthermore,

---

39. Midgley, *Beast and Man*, p. 123.

40. Owen Flanagan, *Varieties of Moral Personality: Ethics and Psychological Realism* (Cambridge: Harvard University Press, 1991), p. 32.

I argue for a thicker or denser understanding of *erōs* than can be found in the idea of autonomy or the humanistic-psychology concept of self-actualization present in most feminist *caritas* or mutuality models of love. Evolutionary-psychological perspectives argue for a view of *erōs* built around parental love as kin altruism and its derivatives of reciprocal and group altruism. But this still leaves open the question, *how can erōs as kin altruism be expanded and generalized to individuals outside of immediate family and kin? Further, how can this concept be formulated to find a place for understandings of the Christian concept of the "cross" and the stronger notes of self-sacrifice that it historically has implied?*

One answer — a classic one — is the Christian concept of grace. The claim might be advanced that grace builds on yet expands kin altruism to wider social circles. In fact, at the heart of Nygren's characterization of the debate between strong *agapē* and *caritas* is the issue of whether God's grace builds on natural human affections, in some kind of synthesis between *agapē* and *erōs*, or whether grace bypasses them in a miraculous transformation of the will.[41] I argue for the first position. Before rushing to this conclusion, we should examine how various philosophical appropriations of evolutionary psychology's view of altruism have tried to explain how kin and reciprocal altruism are expanded to nonfamilial circles.

Christian Love and the Expansion of Family Altruism

Although Stephen Pope finds a place for sociobiology and evolutionary psychology in a reconstructed theory of natural law, he does not believe that biology alone can provide a complete ethic. Nor was this the belief of Aquinas. Pope follows Thomas Aquinas, in contrast to Catholicism's contemporary fascination with existentialism and personalism, in holding that attention to the innate predispositions of human biology, as important as they are, does not completely override historical and cultural considerations in concrete moral decision-making.[42] Furthermore, however important parental love is in the order of charity, it does not exhaust the meaning of Christian love. If parental love and attachment theory point to the naturalistic wellsprings of all love, how is this basic source amplified and generalized outward to nonfamilial others?

Philosophers such as Mary Midgley and Peter Singer have emphasized

41. Nygren, *Agape and Eros,* p. 92.
42. Pope, "The Order of Love," p. 265.

the role of reason in expanding the circle of kin and reciprocal altruism. Singer believes the capacity for reason is a spontaneous evolutionary emergent, something close to the view of William James. It entails not only the capacity for memory but the ability to generalize and to build anticipatory models for predicting the future. Contemporary cognitive neuroscience locates the capacity in the prefrontal lobes of the brain even though it also asserts that reason never works entirely independently of the premoral impulses of the limbic system and the middle brain, a point well established by the brilliant research and writings of Antonio Damasio.[43] What Ricoeur would call morality in contrast to mere ethics comes from the distinctively human capacity to guide biological altruism with the human capacity for reason. Singer writes, "Ethics starts when social animals are prompted by their genes to help, and to refrain from injuring selected other animals. On this base we must now superimpose the capacity to reason."[44] Singer builds his case about the generalizing capacities of reason by referring to the work of Lawrence Kohlberg. He could have used Ricoeur since he attends more to our teleological inclinations than does Kohlberg. In fact, Singer explicitly distinguishes himself from strictly Kantian-Kohlbergian theories of generalization because they tend to divorce themselves from all affections and attachments, including the affections of kin altruism.

Singer agrees with the point that I have been making — that ethics emerges when reason applies the affections between parents and children to others outside the family.[45] Mary Midgley argues that reason plays a similar role in ordering our biological predispositions. From her perspective, instinct and reason are not incompatible, as cognitive neuroscience is more and more telling us is the case. She would agree with William James that reason is informed by the premoral valuations of some of our social instincts. But it is precisely because humans have many contradictory instinctual tendencies and competing premoral valuations that they must use reason to guide, weigh, and generalize their more efficacious passions.[46] And, of course, this position would not necessarily preclude rea-

---

43. Antonio Damasio, *Descartes' Error: Emotion, Reason, and the Human Brain* (New York: G. P. Putnam's Sons, 1994), p. 53.

44. Singer, *The Expanding Circle*, p. 91.

45. Singer, *The Expanding Circle*, pp. 27-36.

46. Midgley, *Beast and Man*, pp. 72-82, 165-76. For James's understanding of the relation between instinct and reason, see William James, *Principles of Psychology*, vol. 2 (New York: Dover, 1950), pp. 323-72, 383-441, 486-593. See also Don Browning, *Pluralism and Personality: William James and Some Contemporary Cultures of Psychology* (Lewisburg, Pa.: Bucknell University Press, 1980), pp. 156-77.

son guided by Ricoeur's reformulation of the Golden Rule, his deonto-logical test.

In addition to the generalizing capacities for reason, both Singer and Midgley invoke culture and tradition as sources for the extension of bio-logical altruism. Singer believes that reason itself contributes to and builds on culture. Here he is getting very close to Ricoeur's understanding of the role of tradition in its capacity to retain, recall, and apply useful forms of practices, habits, and concrete rules. Reason gradually builds a stable culture of practical rules which encourage and guide altruistic be-havior beyond the boundaries of kin groups.[47] This suggests a gene-culture coevolutionary theory of the kind associated with the later work of E. O. Wilson and Ralph Burhoe.[48] Ricoeur's concept of "practices" and their various inherited rules and logics about reliable goods and moral ways to pursue them communicates much the same thing.

Singer and Midgley are right to a degree; reason doubtless plays a role in expanding our biological altruism. But the Christian tradition with its doctrine of sin has always been impressed with the instability and cor-ruptness of moral reason. Reinhold Niebuhr expressed it well when he ob-served that the self may use reason to conceive abstractly a universal moral point of view — but the self, because of its anxiety and sin, often uses reason in *concrete action* to rationalize the self's partial and self-serving purposes.[49] As a result, reason often fails to balance the natural af-fection for self and kin with the needs of individuals and families who are outside of the immediate range of intimate kin and reciprocal altruisms.

In face of this reality, the Christian tradition has conveyed a narrative that emphasizes a divine grace that overcomes sin's tendency to convert ordinate and ethically efficacious self and kin regard into inordinate and idolatrous love of both. I suggest, however, that theologians take seriously the evidence of evolutionary psychology and develop a theory that con-ceives of grace as building on and extending *erōs* — the natural affections of kin altruism — rather than viewing grace as working solely to trans-form the will, as is implied by Nygren's conception of extreme *agapē*.[50]

47. Singer, *The Expanding Circle*, pp. 156-66.

48. Pope, "The Order of Love," p. 272; Charles Lumsden and E. O. Wilson, *Genes, Culture, and the Mind: The Coevolutionary Process* (Cambridge: Harvard University Press, 1981); Ralph Burhoe, "Religion's Role in Human Evolution: The Missing Link between Ape-Man's Selfish Genes and Civilized Altruism," *Zygon: Journal of Religion and Science* 14 (June, 1979): 135-62.

49. Niebuhr, *The Nature and Destiny of Man*, vol. I, pp. 284-85.

50. Nygren, *Agape and Eros*, pp. 216-17, 223.

Altruism, the Cross, and Sacrificial Love

I conclude this chapter by developing a more systematic theory of Christian love, one that finds within it a place for both evolutionarily conceived altruism and elements of self-sacrifice represented by the Christian symbol of the cross. Louis Janssens's concept of *ordo caritatis* may provide a model.[51] Janssens was a Roman Catholic moral theologian who believed that the self-sacrificial love symbolized by the cross is derived from an understanding of Christian love as equal-regard. Self-sacrificial love is not an end in itself of the Christian life, according to Janssens. It is a transitional ethic in the service of reinstating equal-regard between both kin and non-kin relations.

The meaning of Christian love, for Janssens, can be found in the second half of the love commandment: "you shall love your neighbor as yourself." It is, of course, a slightly different formulation of the Golden Rule. A variation of the principle of neighbor love is found eight times in the New Testament (Matt. 19:19; 22:39; Mark 12:31, 33; Luke 10:27; Rom. 13:8; Gal. 5:14; James 2:8). Both Jesus and Paul use it as the hermeneutic key to the interpretation of the Jewish law. Janssens interprets neighbor love as equal-regard in order to make it consistent with the Catholic tradition's view of love as *caritas* — a love that balances self-regard and other-regard. He combines formal features of Gene Outka's neo-Kantian view of love as equal-regard with certain material theories about basic human premoral goods (the *ordo bonorum*) that equal-regard organizes and promotes.[52]

Janssens has a mixed deontological view of the Golden Rule and neighbor love similar to Ricoeur's. It is a formulation of Christian love that promotes the teleological good but also passes the deontological test. At the formal level, love as equal-regard requires that we should love the other (and in principle all others since we are each made in the image of God) with the same seriousness with which we naturally love ourselves. But the reverse is also true. We are entitled to love ourselves with the same seriousness that we are commanded to love the other. As we already have seen, Christian love, according to Janssens, is a rigorous form of equal-regard or mutuality. Neither self-love (ethical egoism) nor self-denying other-love (extreme *agapē*) is allowed to gain the upper hand in Janssens's formulation of Christian love. It is because of this rigorous balance be-

---

51. Louis Janssens, "Norms and Priorities of a Love Ethics," *Louvain Studies* 6 (spring 1977): 216-30.

52. Janssens, "Norms and Priorities of a Love Ethics," pp. 207-16.

tween self-concern and love of the other that Janssens's formulation has proved attractive to Christian feminists and minorities. It gives them grounds for a constrained self-affirmation while at the same time resisting the domination of others who might appeal to Christian self-sacrifice to encourage exploited persons to endure their sufferings. Such a formulation of Christian love constitutes the moral grounds for the nonviolent resistance of a Martin Luther King Jr., or a Gandhi. It requires love of the other, but it also demands pressing the other — even finally transforming the other — until the other respects you, your gender, your color, or your social class just as you respect and regard the other. The ethic of equal-regard is simultaneously an interpersonal ethic and an ethic that can guide wider social-systemic institutional arrangements.

In this view, self-sacrifice in the more extreme forms is derived from love as equal-regard. I already have said a few things about Janssens's view of sacrificial love and the cross. But now I must say more. Janssens writes, "In short, self-sacrifice is not the quintessence of love, since it can only happen in a world in which conflict and sin occur."[53] In a world of finitude and sin, equal-regard is difficult to achieve or even to approximate. Self-sacrificial love, as we have seen, should refer to the extra effort required to reinstate relations of equal-regard and mutuality. This is a love that both meets human need and actualizes the good while also passing the deontological test. Love as self-sacrifice, according to Janssens's reading of Scripture and tradition, is not an end in itself; it is a transitional ethic — an ethic we should be "open" to, to use the language of Timothy Jackson — which enacts the deontological test in an effort to realize the mutual good of self and other.

I want to conclude these reflections by considering how evolutionary-psychological perspectives on altruism can enrich Janssens's interpretation of Christian love. Janssens's theory of self-regard needs to be enlarged by the evolutionary psychological theory of kin and reciprocal altruism. Because of the genes we share with kin, we tend to share our self-regard with our offspring from the beginning. To balance self-regard rigorously with other-regard, as the ethic of equal-regard demands, Christian love would require us to balance our kin and reciprocal altruism with genuine concern for people beyond our families. The Christian doctrine of love as equal-regard asks us, at least in principle, to treat nonfamily groups with as much regard as our own loved ones. At the same time, according to this ethic, we would be *both permitted and required to love our kin and those with*

53. Janssens, "Norms and Priorities of a Love Ethics," p. 228.

whom we have more reciprocal relations. In fact, if one takes evolutionary psychology seriously, loving the remote other depends on the analogical extension of kin relations to this other, enabled by reason, grace, and the theological belief that all humans are created in the image of God and are children of God. There will be various degrees of conflict between these orders of love. *But Christian love, as interpreted in this chapter, does not call us to solve that conflict by denying the importance of the premoral goods of kin altruism. It more likely requires us to bring our kin affections to the deontological test, recognizing that the obligation we have to care for our own family is an obligation we must have to both respect and support other families in caring for their loved ones as well.* It also requires that when such balance between our family obligations and those of others does not exist, we must work hard, even sacrifice, to make it possible for all families to discharge their kin attachments and altruisms.

Love for the remote other entails — as Aristotle, Aquinas, and Pope argue — building on, not repressing, natural kin affections. Reason, culture, and the communities of memory celebrated in *Hardwired to Connect* are required to extend these basic affections beyond natural intimate circles. Christians will insist, however, that the grace of God must also further transform and extend our affections and our reason in order for the outer reaches of self-sacrificial love to be achieved. Altruism and Christian love are distinguishable, but evolutionary psychology can help clarify the natural foundations of love that the grace of God, along with reason and culture, extends.

Chapter 7

Generativity, Ethics, and Hermeneutics:
Revisiting Erik Erikson

F ew American scholars have made more of a contribution to our understanding of children and youth than did the psychoanalyst Erik Erikson (1902-1994). Furthermore, he seemed to understand the role of communities of memory in forming the identity of youth. He even had important things to say about the role of religion in forming identity.

Erikson has been dead for several years, but he has not been forgotten. I once wrote a book on Erikson titled *Generative Man*.[1] The book analyzed in detail Erikson's central ideal for mature adulthood — his concept of *generativity*. The mature person, either male or female, was for Erikson a generative person — not the self-actualized person, not the self-fulfilled person, but the generative person. Ever since writing that book, I have believed that Erikson's concept of generativity was more than a psychological construct defining adult maturity. I have been convinced that it was instead a mixed concept that artfully interwove psychological, ethical, narrative, and even metaphysical levels of discourse.

Of course, most social scientists today would say that good psychological concepts should not range so widely. They should, according to current fashionable views, avoid the ethical, the narrative, and the metaphysical. Hence, to say that Erikson's view of generativity indirectly made assumptions at these various levels would be, in the eyes of many social scientists, enough to dismiss him as a serious psychologist. But I don't agree. My argument has been that psychological views of the person, espe-

---

1. Don Browning, *Generative Man: Society and the Good Man in the Writings of Philip Rieff, Norman Brown, Erich Fromm, and Erik Erikson* (Philadelphia: Westminster, 1973 [second ed. by Dell, 1975]).

cially moral psychological concepts, cannot avoid this wider range of concepts and ideas. Furthermore, I am convinced that his idea of generativity was philosophically defensible from an ethical point of view, even though Erikson never attempted to test it from that perspective.

In this chapter, I plan to use the framework of Ricoeur's moral philosophy and theory of hermeneutics to show just how rich and complex Erikson's moral psychology actually was. It was far more than straightforward empirical psychology. This boundary-breaking richness was a strength, not a weakness. It did not make his ideas on generativity bad psychology; it made them good psychology that was implicitly set within unwitting but very sound wider frames of meaning. The concept of generativity did indeed transgress boundaries and lapse into ethics, morality, and narratively presented metaphysics. And it did so intelligently — perceptively. This is the reason, I suspect, why Erikson's concept of generativity has from time to time attracted the interest of Christian ethicists, even Reinhold Niebuhr, whom I have used so much in these pages.[2]

But there was a major deficiency in Erikson's moral psychology. This can be found in his poor account of its boundary-breaking moves. It has been my argument that moral psychology needs philosophy and also religious tradition. But if it is to present itself as an academic discipline, it must give accounts of its disciplinary mobility. I believe that Ricoeur's critical hermeneutical model of morality helps us understand some of the moves Erikson made but could not himself explain.

There is more about Erikson's moral psychology that I want to highlight. I have come to believe that the concept of generativity has special relevance for addressing the challenges of modernity and the increased speed of social change, pluralism, and social conflict that often comes in their trail. In this chapter, I will defend my claims about the moral significance of the concept of generativity and its relevance for facing the possibilities and strains of modernity.

Three Competing Models of Morality

Contemporary philosophical ethics has advanced three competing models of the ethical life. These three models have been more or less implicit in the chapters of this book. Each believes it can provide the most satisfac-

---

2. Reinhold Niebuhr, *Man's Nature and His Communities* (New York: Charles Scribner's Sons, 1965), p. 109.

tory account of the field of ethics and be the most compelling guide to the solution of present-day moral and social challenges. They can be conveniently referred to as an *ethics of virtue,* an *ethics of principle,* and a *narrative ethics.* These three approaches have parallels to Ricoeur's view of the process of moral reflection as moving from practices and habits (virtues) that pursue the good, to some principle of criticism (in his case, the deontological test), to an encompassing narrative that endows the first two moves with larger significance. But that is the point: *in Ricoeur, these strands explicitly come together.* I claim that Erikson's concept of generativity implicitly contains elements of each of these perspectives. Although Erikson never consciously identified these different viewpoints nor systematically ordered them in relation to one another, they fit together in his thought and do so without contradiction.

Because all three models are present in his writings, his concept of generativity when fully understood is simultaneously multidimensional, powerful, and susceptible to misunderstanding. It is also quite easy to omit one or another of these three perspectives when discussing his views on generativity. Most interpreters in fact do this. This chapter will attempt to clarify these potential misunderstandings and take steps to show the possible contributions of generativity to an ethic for the twenty-first century, one able to address the processes and challenges of modernization.

Leading representatives of an ethics of principle — at least of the deontological in contrast to the utilitarian kind — can be illustrated with reference to three individuals we have already mentioned: John Rawls, Jürgen Habermas, and moral psychologist Lawrence Kohlberg. All of them agree that tradition is no longer a trustworthy source for ethics in either the modern or postmodern world. These three thinkers also hold that conflicting communities and individuals can no longer agree on the definition of the nonmoral or premoral goods that should be central to our lives together. The best we can do, these scholars insist, is to agree on a procedural morality of discourse — one based on various revisions of Kant's categorical imperative and its implications for an ethic of respect.[3] The rapid dislocations wrought by modernity's increasing reliance on technical reason can be addressed only by the common implementation in our debates of the universal principle of treating others as ends. Coping with modernity, for these philosophers, comes down to socializing individuals and communities to respect one another in their various conflicting processes of deliberation.

---

3. Immanuel Kant, *Foundations for a Metaphysics of Morals* (New York: Bobbs-Merrill, 1959), p. 47.

Ethics of virtue, as we have noted, can be found in the well-known writings of Alasdair MacIntyre and Stanley Hauerwas. They insist that simple rational principles are not enough to either resolve conflicts or guide action toward the future. The dynamics of modernity, according to them, need to be anchored, if not countered, by tested traditions of habits and virtues. Aristotle and Thomas Aquinas — classical theorists of virtue — are their heroes, and they commend this tradition to the modern world.

MacIntyre and Hauerwas also promote the relevance of narrative for the formation of the moral self. They are advocates — along with such diverse figures as Ricoeur, Amitai Etzioni, and Robert Bellah — of the importance of communities of tradition that carry commanding narratives and form virtues in their followers who exhibit these narratives. These thinkers believe, as do the contributors of *Hardwired to Connect*, that the fragmenting dynamics of modernity must be restrained by the renewal and preservation of communities of tradition and the narratives that they carry, especially those that seem most central to the various contemporary world cultures.

Erikson had the wisdom of implicitly bringing these three different perspectives together. Because he was a psychologist who paid attention to the rhythms of biosocial development, however, he contributed a theory of the "good" that is absent from most contemporary proponents of any one of these three alternative models of morality. It is hard to find a coherent theory of the good in the premoral sense in any of the leading theorists of an ethics of virtue, principle, or narrative. For instance, there is, in Ricoeur's language, a strong teleological beginning point for Erikson in his moral psychology. This theory of the premoral good can be found in his view of human development and the cycle of the generations. In short, Erikson implicitly told us that to handle the promises and dangers of modernity we need viable communities of tradition, but ones that actualize the goods of human development as well as exhibit the principle of respect for individuals as they struggle to grow. There is little doubt that Erikson was a source of inspiration for the authors of *Hardwired to Connect* when they wrote that an authoritative community

> is significantly more likely to reflect, as a core part of its identity, the quality of *shared memory,* a key dimension of human connectedness and a vital component of civil society. Shared memory says: This is where we came from. This is what happened. This helps explain why we are who we are. We heard the stories; we tell the children; we remember.

Shared memory can help to deepen identity, and define character, largely by giving the child clear access to lessons and admirable persons from the past. In this way, shared memory can
deepen our connectedness not just to other persons currently living, but also to persons who have died, and also, in some respects,
to persons not yet born.[4]

I will illustrate what this quote implies for a theory of the premoral good
relevant to each of the three dominant models — an ethics of virtue, an
ethics of principle, and a narrative ethics.

Teleology and Deontology in Erikson

Let's first turn to the ethic of principle in Erikson's idea of generativity,
even though this is probably the least visible of the three models in his
writings. Even careful readers of Erikson can easily overlook that he sometimes states a summary principle that has moral meaning and yet is consistent with his larger body of psychological concepts. Ethical systems
that ground themselves on some general principle can be separated, according to moral philosophers, into teleological and deontological points
of view.[5] Even with these distinctions in mind, Erikson's moral thought
does not precisely illustrate either of these alternative ethics of principle.
Rather, it exemplifies features that combine elements of both models into
what moral philosophers sometimes call a "mixed deontological" model
of moral obligation. Here is what I mean.

Teleological views conform to the principle that ethical duty consists
of acting in such a way as to bring into reality increased amounts of
nonmoral or premoral values or goods. These premoral goods, as we have
seen, might consist of anything from food, water, health, shelter, or pleasure to more sophisticated goods such as the development of human capabilities and their refinement through practices such as parental care, education, forms of culture, or even play. The birth of a child is often thought
to be a great premoral good. It would be wrong, however, to say that a child
as such is a moral good; that depends on the kind of will the child develops
and the pattern of habits and virtues that he or she acquires. But most people would say that children are a great good in a basic premoral sense be-

4. *Hardwired to Connect: The New Scientific Case for Authoritative Communities* (New York:
Institute for American Values, 2003), p. 37.

5. William Frankena, *Ethics* (Englewood Cliffs, N.J.: Prentice-Hall, 1973), pp. 14-16.

cause they are beautiful, cute, endearing, continue the species, and have great potentialities for growth into moral responsibility. Teleological principles of ethics are often thought to be associated with the utilitarianism of Jeremy Bentham or John Stuart Mill, the pragmatism of William James or John Dewey, or even the older teleological models of Aristotle or Aquinas. And we have certainly seen a strong teleological dimension in Ricoeur. All of these views share at least one common ethical idea or principle, namely, that moral action should increase the goods of life. Various teleological views of ethics differ in their theory of which goods are the most important; they also vary in their view of how the goods of life (whatever their theory of these goods happens to be) should be justly distributed.

Deontological moral systems, on the other hand, claim to ground moral obligation on reasons or principles that are intrinsically moral and independent of consequences that increase or decrease the premoral goods of life. As I have mentioned several times already, Kant's categorical imperative (which says, "I should never act in such a way that I could not also will that my maxim should be a universal law") is often presented as the arch example of deontological ethics.[6] His second formulation of this imperative instructs us to "act so that you treat humanity, whether in your own person or in that of another, always as an end and never as a means only" and is a further illustration of classic deontological ethics.[7] These principles make respecting the rationality and personhood of both self and other the key to morality, as we saw above with Rawls, Habermas, and Kohlberg. The promotion of other goods such as health, wealth, pleasure, potentialities, or skills cannot, according to Kantian deontology, trump or override respect for the agency, autonomy, and rationality of persons as ends. For example, a mother may sense her son's mathematical or musical skills, but if she attempts to actualize them in ways that deride his personhood and rationality and those of others, even bringing into reality these goods must be seen as proceeding in a basically immoral way. This is true because her action does not conform to the principle of respect for her son as an end who should never be reduced to a means alone.

Erikson was a mixture of both of these perspectives — the teleological and the deontological. But this combination was not caused by confusion. He had a defensible way of relating these diverging styles of ethical thinking. He was not philosophically self-conscious in the way he com-

---

6. Immanuel Kant, *Foundations of the Metaphysics of Morals* (Indianapolis: Bobbs-Merrill, 1959), p. 39.

7. Kant, *Foundations of the Metaphysics of Morals*, p. 47.

bined them, but he did it wisely nonetheless. Erikson was a teleologist in his emphasis on the actualization of the interacting potentialities (premoral goods) that sustain and renew the cycle of the generations. At the same time, he sounded like a deontologist in his concern that these goods be universalized to include each present and future child and to include the personhood of even the young. For instance, he could speak of a "universal sense of generative responsibility toward all human beings brought intentionally into this world."[8] Here we see something in Erikson that is close to Kant's categorical imperative, Ricoeur's deontological test, and Janssens's idea of love as equal-regard.

For Erikson, as for Ricoeur, such universalization should be accomplished in ways that communicate respect for persons. But rather than grounding respect on the human capacity for rationality, as did Kant, Erikson is more likely to speak of the phylogenetic need for "mutual recognition of and by another face."[9] This is a fresh way to ground the ethical demand for respect that even Ricoeur does not quite take. Nonetheless, an ethic of universal justice of mutual recognition pervades Erikson's ethical psychology, giving it at times a Kantian tone if not a technical Kantian substance. Furthermore, communicating respect for the personhood of the other, in the sense of recognizing her or his face and bestowing a sense of validity through this recognition, is for Erikson the great insight of both good psychotherapy and the nonviolent ethic of *satyagraha* championed so effectively by the philosophy and life of Mahatma Gandhi.[10]

The implicit principle of respect for all persons and all children was, however, always qualified by Erikson's principle of generativity. Although one's natural generative interest in the welfare of one's own offspring was never allowed by Erikson to trump a universal obligation to the well-being of *all* children, it was nevertheless important to Erikson for understanding the teleological origins of ethics. In advancing this formulation, Erikson was giving his own twist to the kind of mixed-deontological principle of obligation found today in Ricoeur but also in moral philosophers such as William Frankena, Alan Donagan, Martha Nussbaum, and, as we have seen, the moral theologian Louis Janssens.[11] We also have found it in Ricoeur's interpretation of the Golden Rule and, by implication, the prin-

8. Erik Erikson, *Insight and Responsibility* (New York: W. W. Norton, 1964), p. 131.

9. Erikson, *Insight and Responsibility*, p. 94.

10. Erik Erikson, *Gandhi's Truth* (New York: W. W. Norton, 1969), pp. 437-40.

11. Frankena, *Ethics*, p. 43; Paul Ricoeur, *Oneself as Another* (Chicago: University of Chicago Press, 1992), pp. 219-29; Jürgen Habermas, *Communication and the Evolution of Society* (Boston: Beacon, 1979), pp. 62-68.

ciple of neighbor love. These perspectives share a common feature of containing yet guiding various teleological theories of the good life with a superordinate concern with universal justice and respect for the other as an end, or, as Erikson would say it, as a person deserving of recognition and mutual regard.

The Archeology of Generativity

But now I must go backward and say more about Erikson's teleology — his theory of premoral goods that is *ethically* relevant but not *morally* exhaustive, to use Ricoeur's distinction once again. It should be acknowledged that regardless of the presence of the deontological dimension of Erikson's ethic, from another perspective the teleological aspect is the more fundamental to his thinking. The test of universal respect or recognition comes for Erikson, as it does for Ricoeur, as a second step, after one has advanced preliminary claims about the good. His teleology is immediately evident in his basic definition of generativity as "the concern in establishing and guiding the next generation."[12] The word "establishing" refers to the *goods* of procreation and the actualization of the epigenetic timetable of human potentialities. The word "guiding" refers to the *goods* of education and teaching as cultural acts or practices that give social patterning to these goods. The teleological elements are all the more striking in one of Erikson's many definitions of "care" (the virtue associated with generativity) as "a quality essential for psychosocial evolution, for we are the teaching species."[13] He goes on to say, "Animals, too, instinctively encourage in their young what is ready for release."[14] This raises the question, just what potentialities (or goods in this sense) do parents instinctively try to release or actualize in their offspring?

Teleological perspectives on ethics are also evident in Erikson's reformulation of the Golden Rule, as are deontological elements pertaining to justice, equality, and the recognition of others as ends. Erikson's restatement of the Golden Rule goes like this:

> Truly worthwhile acts enhance a mutuality between doer and the other — a mutuality which strengthens the doer even as it strengthens the other. Thus the "doer" and "the other" are partners in one

12. Erik Erikson, *Young Man Luther* (New York: W. W. Norton, 1962), p. 267.
13. Erikson, *Insight and Responsibility*, p. 130.
14. Erikson, *Insight and Responsibility*, p. 130.

deed. Seen in the light of human development, this means that the doer is activated in whatever strength is appropriate to his age, stage, and condition, even as he activates in the other the strength appropriate to *his* age, stage and condition. Understood this way, the Rule would say that it is best to do to another what will strengthen you even as it will strengthen him — that is, what will develop his best potentials even as it develops your own.[15]

This is a complex passage and a challenge to interpret from the perspective of philosophical ethics. One can say with confidence, however, that this is not a reduction of the Golden Rule to a simple exchange theory. Erikson is not arguing that the Golden Rule is telling us to actualize potentialities in others *if* we can predict that they in turn will actualize us. The Golden Rule, in Erikson's rendition, is not a conditional contract analogous to those created to regulate transactions in the fields of business and law. It is a theory of reversible mutuality built, as we will see, on far more fundamental teleological and deontological grounds. Its reversibility — the fact that it must apply equally to self and other — points to its deontological characteristic. The fact that this reversibility or mutuality interweaves and promotes fundamental developmental goods and human capacities points to its teleological features.

Erikson's reinterpretation of the Golden Rule draws on several aspects of his psychological and moral system. The instinctual grounds of generativity are important, although not exhaustive; the concepts of "cogwheeling" and the "epigenetic ground plan" are also important for Erikson's view of the real meaning of this ancient moral principle. We must remember that Erikson believes that there is, to borrow a term from Ricoeur, an "archeology" to generativity and its associated virtue of care. By archeology, Ricoeur means a set of archaic desires, but desires that are always filtered through a linguistic or symbolically encoded cogito or ego and its cultural practices.[16] This means that we never know our desires directly without symbolic mediation. Ricoeur would say, and Erikson would agree, that our desires are always *interpreted* desires. Our desires become attached to objects and practices that are themselves linguistically mediated. These objects and practices become the teleology of our desires (the direction or aim of our desires), and when we contemplate our desires, we think about them dialectically in terms of both their push *and* their aim —

---

15. Erikson, *Insight and Responsibility,* p. 233.

16. Paul Ricoeur, *Freud and Philosophy* (New Haven: Yale University Press, 1970), pp. 419-30.

in terms of both their archeology and their teleology or objects of satisfaction. This is why Erikson preferred to speak about modes and modalities or biosocial patterns of interaction rather than about instinctual energies as such.[17] And in the case of Erikson, this dialectic between biological tendency and culturally meaningful objects also applied to the desire, need, or inclination — whichever we call it — for generativity.

By employing the idea of archeology, I mean to communicate Erikson's belief that generativity and care have instinctual foundations but also give rise to and interact with a variety of objects, practices, and symbolic meanings. Desire for Erikson is more than what is implied by Freud's concept of *libido* — with all the tension-reduction and pleasure-driven features Freud assigned to it, especially in the middle period of developing his psychodynamic theory. Erikson's theory of instinct is like that found in William James and the contemporary moral philosopher Mary Midgley;[18] there is for them no master instinct from which all other motivations are derived. Even the need for generativity, although casting a gentle claim on the purpose and function of the other psychobiological inclinations, does not in Erikson's psychology exercise dictatorial control over all other tendencies. All basic needs and tendencies find a place in Erikson's theory of the epigenetic principle; it holds that human development evolves out of preexisting potentialities, each of which has "its time of origin."[19]

Erikson broadens Freud's theory of *libido* into a more inclusive theory of psychobiological potentials that have, with the support of what Heinz Hartmann called an "average expectable environment,"[20] phase-specific moments of emergence. These potentials include the pleasure-oriented sucking, holding, and expelling tendencies of the oral and anal phases of development;[21] the wider exercise of muscles and skeleton structure between ages two and five;[22] the emergence of formal cognitive operations during adolescence;[23] increased genital and sexual demands during the early teens;[24] and finally maturing generative needs to procreate and teach

17. Erik Erikson, *Childhood and Society* (New York: W. W. Norton, 1963), pp. 72-80.

18. William James, *The Principles of Psychology,* vol. 2 (New York: Dover, 1950), pp. 338-441; Mary Midgley, *Beast and Man* (Ithaca, N.Y.: Cornell University Press, 1978), pp. 331-44.

19. Erikson, *Childhood and Society,* p. 65.

20. Heinz Hartman, *Ego Psychology and the Problem of Adaptation* (New York: International Universities Press, 1958).

21. Erikson, *Insight and Responsibility,* pp. 72-80.

22. Erikson, *Insight and Responsibility,* pp. 80-85.

23. Erikson, *Insight and Responsibility,* p. 261.

24. Erikson, *Insight and Responsibility,* pp. 263-66.

(or the use of these urges analogously for wider tasks) in young and middle adulthood.[25] These multiple needs and tendencies constitute the foundation of Erikson's theory of cogwheeling — the idea that the needs of the young and those of adults interlock, activate one another, and propel each other through the life cycle. One should think of this less as a calculated exchange and more as an intermeshing of gears that are finely tuned to fit one another. This intermeshing set of potentialities and needs, especially between the very young and their parents, constitutes the archeology of the teleological trajectory of Erikson's ethical psychology.

These inclinations and strivings for the goods of the life cycle constitute for Erikson what humans bring to the ethical task; they make up the premoral foundations of what ethics is all about. But ethics, even the ethics of generativity, involves for Erikson more than this archeology. Disciplined ethics (or, following Ricoeur, "morality") entails, as we have already seen, some guiding principle of justice and universalization that extends our more parochial generative preferences to include but also go beyond our own kin and those closely associated with us. And, as we will see below, such a moral perspective also must give consideration to the virtues and narratives that give meaning to both the objects of our generative desires and the principles designed to order them. But before turning to these additional models of the ethical life, a further word about human generative archeology is in order.

Evolutionary Psychology and Generative Ethics

Erikson's ethics of generativity clearly has similarities to the theory of kin altruism in contemporary evolutionary psychology, sociobiology, and the philosophical efforts to conceptualize the ethical and moral implications of these disciplines. Some ethicists informed by evolutionary psychology believe that kin altruism is the foundation of the moral capacities of humans. James Q. Wilson, whom we discussed earlier, provides a good example of this point of view. Citing the theories of kin altruism and inclusive fitness of biologists W. D. Hamilton and Robert Trivers, Wilson argues that humans have a drive (or at least their genes have a tendency) to replicate themselves.[26] This explains, according to evolutionary psychology, why parents are willing to care for, and sometimes even sacrifice them-

---

25. Erikson, *Insight and Responsibility*, pp. 266-68.
26. James Q. Wilson, *The Moral Sense* (New York: Free Press, 1993), pp. 40-44.

selves for, their offspring; it is really a way of living on into the future through their children as carriers of their genes. This constitutes the grounds of parental care and the love that leads children, in turn, to identify in gratitude with their parents' wishes and values. *Evolutionary psychology thus has its own theory of generativity, and it has analogies to what I have called the archeology of Erikson's view of generativity.* Evolutionary psychology helps ground Erikson's bold but basically unsupported assertion that parents need their children as much as children need them. It also helps support his assertion that humans are teaching animals. Furthermore, it helps amplify the theory of attachment. Children attach to their parents because their parents attach to and need them. Erikson helps us see why kin altruism — parental investment in offspring — also contributes to parent-child attachment as a two-way phenomenon. He helps us see how we can link the kin altruism theories of Hamilton and Trivers to the attachment theories of Bowlby and Schore.

But evolutionary psychology, especially its more sociobiological wing, sometimes presents its theory of generativity in narrowly mathematical terms. The subtleties of Erikson's view of the symbolic levels of generativity are often lost to evolutionary psychologists. For instance, the mathematics of generativity suggests that parents may sacrifice for their offspring (and brothers and sisters for each other) because they share 50 percent of the same genes. In taking care of their offspring, they are contributing to their own inclusive fitness. Or to say it a bit more generously, care for offspring is stimulated by the simple fact that the distinction between self and other becomes blurred in the case of biological progeny. But this biologically shaped tendency to care declines, we are told, as the ratio of shared genes diminishes, with uncles and aunts having less inclination to sacrifice for nephews and nieces since they have fewer genes in common.[27] Kin altruism, according to the theory, soon runs out as the circle of unrelated neighbors and strangers widens. Cooperation and care between non-kin, according to evolutionary psychology, are motivated by reciprocal altruism — the conditional exchange of reciprocal services as conceptualized by forms of economic theory, game theory, and exchange theory so prominent in the social sciences today.

Erikson is more of an instinctual and motivational pluralist than many sociobiologists and evolutionary psychologists. The need to procreate and to care for what one procreates has natural foundations in

27. Peter Singer, *The Expanding Circle: Ethics and Sociobiology* (New York: Farrar, Straus, and Giroux, 1981), p. 13.

Erikson's view, but it is mixed with other motivations that have some degree of autonomy from this central goal. For instance, there are for Erikson relatively autonomous needs to know our world and our place within it, such as the need to have a cohesive yet flexible sense of identity or self-definition.[28] But this need for identity is also fueled by an archaic need, quite biological in nature, for recognition by our primary caretakers — a need or tendency given such prominence in *Hardwired to Connect.* This is a need we never outgrow even as our circles of social interaction expand far beyond the boundaries of our basic kinship units.[29] Erikson's awareness of the interaction between the drive for gene reproduction and other basic needs makes it possible for him not to rely too heavily on kin altruism as a motivational and explanatory theory of our generative capacities. This, on the other hand, is a mistake commonly made in sociobiology, although perhaps less so in the newer evolutionary psychology. Nonetheless, properly used and contained, the theories of kin altruism that come from the discipline of evolutionary psychology complement and enrich Erikson's view of the archeology of generativity.

Erikson, Neo-Aristotelianism, and Thomism: Teleology and the Generative Analogy

Erikson should be understood as standing in a long line of teleologically oriented philosophers extending from Plato and Aristotle to Thomas Aquinas; such a line would also include various contemporary pragmatists as well as many contemporary neo-Aristotelians. Aristotle and Aquinas, as we have seen, were particularly influential for Christian ethics and its *caritas* view of love. Most thinkers standing in this tradition give central place to finding meaning in life through either having and raising children or extending this impulse actually and symbolically to others beyond one's immediate kin. Even Plato did this in the *Symposium* through Diotima's speeches about gaining immortality through our offspring, although in the end he subordinated this impulse to the higher immortality and permanence of abstract contemplation of the good and true.[30] Aristotle, as we have seen, makes a slightly different use of the generative

28. Erik Erikson, "The Problem of Ego Identity," *Psychological Issues* (New York: International Universities Press, 1959), p. 149.

29. Erikson, *Insight and Responsibility,* p. 231.

30. Plato, *The Symposium* (London: Penguin, 1951), pp. 79-94.

analogy when he argues that parental love and preference for kin should not be suppressed in the good city, contrary to Plato's argument in *The Republic*.[31] Rather, we should build on these impulses and extend them to others beyond the circle of immediate offspring. As we saw in Chapter 4, for Aristotle kin preference constitutes the inner glue of society.[32] We have also observed that Aquinas picked up the same line of argument in his Christian ethics. He saw in his theology an analogical link between a parent's preferential love for his or her offspring, God's love of all humans, and the extension of kin altruism to the distant neighbor and stranger.[33] Aquinas followed Aristotle in believing that we have a natural inclination to love our children first; children, in turn, have the same inclination with regard to their parents. But, according to Aquinas, this preferential impulse for our near and dear should be analogically extended to all humans on the belief that they too are children of God, made in God's image, and manifestations of God's goodness — and therefore to be loved as we should love the goodness of God.

In spite of this strong place for the analogy of generativity in Aquinas's thought, and that of his neo-Thomistic followers such as Popes Leo XIII and Pius XI, Catholicism retained into the twentieth century a Platonic sensibility that subordinated in value actual parenthood to the spiritual and symbolic parenthood of the celibate priest. It is important to recognize, however, the cluster of very analogous insights into generativity that can be found in Erikson, Aristotle, Aquinas, late-nineteenth- and early-twentieth-century Roman Catholic social teachings, and evolutionary psychology. Allow me to call attention again to the studies of Stephen Pope as a contemporary scholar actively investigating these congruences.[34] Furthermore, it must be observed that the spiritual world of Catholicism (and other faiths as well) joins with Erikson against the flat naturalism of evolutionary psychology; they both assert in different ways that for generativity to become a cultural work, in contrast to the simple act of biological procreation, it must be elaborated within a worldview that at least finds a place for religious symbolism, if not for the spiritual as such.

---

31. Plato, *The Republic* (New York: Basic, 1968), Bk. V.

32. Aristotle, *Politics: The Basic Writings of Aristotle* (New York: Random House, 1941), Bk. I, iii.

33. Thomas Aquinas, *Summa Theologica* (London: R. & T. Washbourne, 1917), II, ii.

34. Stephen Pope, *The Evolution of Altruism and the Ordering of Love* (Washington, D.C.: Georgetown University Press, 1994).

Generativity, Virtue, and Neo-Aristotelianism

Erikson is not only similar to Aristotle, Aquinas, and certain strands of Christian ethics in understanding the importance for ethics and morality of the analogy of generativity, he also shares their interest in virtue as an aid to the ethical life and to the realization of our teleological aims. An extensive comparison between Erikson and the Aristotelian-Thomistic view of virtue is far beyond the scope of this chapter. The following points, however, should be helpful. First, for both perspectives, virtue builds on and helps realize natural inclinations — extending some natural tendencies while guiding and redirecting others. The American philosophical pragmatist William James, in his *Talks to Teachers on Psychology* and other writings on habits, said the same thing as does the contemporary moral philosopher Owen Flanagan, whom I review in the following chapter. Ricoeur also says virtually the same thing in his discussion of practices: our more refined cultural practices and our individual capacity to carry them out (i.e., our habits and virtues) contain and build on our natural desires but are deemed ethical goods because they pattern our desires toward truly satisfying objects.

Second, Erikson and the Aristotelian-Thomistic school both understand virtue as a kind of synthesis. For Aristotle, a virtue was a *mean* between two extremes;[35] for Erikson, it is a synthesis between conflicting development tendencies.[36] Virtue for Erikson is achieved by a fortunate congruence between a supporting environment and an active ego that attempts to synthesize developmental conflicts (for example, the conflict early in life between trust and mistrust, which is synthesized by the virtue of hope).[37] The life cycle is characterized by many more such conflicts and syntheses.

Hence, Erikson's mixed theory of moral obligation, which subordinates the teleological good to the principle of justice, is made concrete by being supplemented by a theory of virtue and personal formation. But are our quests for the good — our virtues — and our moral principles logically related? This is an issue Erikson, who was not self-consciously an ethicist, never addressed. Ricoeur might be of help in understanding what Erikson was really doing. Ricoeur, of course, would say that ethics is first the quest for the good, but that we first know the goods we seek through the way

---

35. Aristotle, *Nicomachean Ethics*, Bk. II, vii.
36. Erikson, *Insight and Responsibility*, pp. 112-15.
37. Erikson, *Insight and Responsibility*, p. 181.

communities of tradition shape worthy practices, habits, and virtues. Ethics of principle, as Ricoeur suggests, are invoked in situations of conflict when settled teleological goods, practices, and virtues are surprised, overwhelmed, and conflict with the quest for the good by other people.[38] This is when people wanting to do the moral thing should assert more deontological principles of justice and fairness. We do not derive our ethics from abstract principles alone; Erikson knew this. Nonetheless, we need abstract principles to order and refine conflicts in our practices and virtues. Erikson did not know why he had both an ethics of virtue and an ethics of principle, but part of our fascination with his thought, I submit, comes from the fact that he intuited the need for each of these models of the moral life. This is also why his thought is so relevant to the needs of contemporary society and the emerging challenges of modernity.

Just as it has become popular, however, to say that humans cannot live by principles alone, I believe Erikson would agree that we cannot live by either principles *or* virtues alone. Erikson, as we saw, had his ethical principles — for instance, his reinterpretation of the Golden Rule. He also had a theory of how virtue is formed so that people can live well in average, expectable circumstances, and, in addition, be motivated to apply more abstract principles when more serious conflicts arise.

Narrative, Identity, and Ethics

Finally, in addition to Erikson's psychobiology and teleology of generative inclinations, his theory of virtues, and his principle of justice that guides our teleological energies and mediates between our conflicting practices, Erikson also understood the role of narrative in forming the moral life and extending the scope of generativity. In fact, narrativity constituted for Erikson something of a surrounding envelope that oriented and valorized all of these other ethical and moral elements — generative desires, virtues, and principles.

In contemporary philosophical and theological ethics, there are, as I indicated above, many powerful voices claiming that narratives and stories — more than either abstract moral principles, virtues, or the pursuit of the goods — are the true carriers and shapers of the moral life. In order to handle the tensions of modernity, these thinkers insist that we need to revive our narrative traditions and the communities that carry them. In

---

38. Erikson, *Insight and Responsibility,* p. 181.

narrative ethical theory, it is claimed that moral virtues are primarily shaped by stories repeated in the rituals of communities of shared memory. The theological ethicist Stanley Hauerwas believes that narratives form character, and that this narratively shaped character, in turn, organizes our virtues into a functioning whole that exhibits the features of a story with a beginning, middle, and end.

Erikson illustrates how the inherited religious narratives that Luther and Gandhi received and reinterpreted also supported their personal growth toward generative maturity. Religious narratives, Erikson seems to suggest, can do at least two things to consolidate and extend generativity, although it should be confessed that not all religions accomplish these tasks. First, religious narratives can provide us with a faith in the goodness of life — an "ontology of creation," so to speak — that conveys a basic trustworthiness to both our own initiatives and the world's basic tendency to respond to them in supportive and actualizing ways.[39] Second, some religious narratives can, and often do, extend our sense of kinship beyond blood relations to include all of humanity, indeed, in some religions, all of creation. In addition, many religions provide symbols that extend this sense of kinship with others indefinitely into the future.

An example of this first function of religious narrative can be found in the way Luther's sudden realization of the true meaning of the Pauline concept of justification by faith worked to reconnect him with his earliest sense of initiative first awakened by his mother's affirmation and nurture.[40] The theology of justification by faith alone, rather than by works, brought Luther back in touch with the goodness of creation, the goodness of his own agency, the goodness of his sexuality, the goodness of food and close friends, all mediated and witnessed to by his mother's love. A mother's love does not witness to itself, according to Erikson; it witnesses to, or at least can witness to, a deeper trust in the goodness of creation and one's created gifts. This trust in one's basic capacities is fundamental for the successful resolution of later developmental crises, including the crisis of generativity versus stagnation.

An example of the second function of religious narrative can be seen in the fact that both Luther and Gandhi were formed by stories that extended the scope of their generativity to include distant others as well as close kin. In the case of Luther, it was the narrative of how all humans are

---

39. William Schweiker, *Responsibility and Christian Ethics* (Cambridge: Cambridge University Press, 1995), 198-200.

40. Erikson, *Young Man Luther*, pp. 208-9.

children of God, all offspring of the one heavenly Father who was Creator of and Lord over all earthly fathers. And in the case of Gandhi, this divine reality's generative care was extended to all of life, as demanded by the narrative implications of the philosophy of *ahimsa* or nonviolence toward all living things.[41]

These reflections on the role of narrative in an ethic of generativity should leave us with the following generalizations. First, generativity builds on natural psychobiological tendencies to procreate and sustain those who, as Aquinas would say, carry "our substance." This is an important insight of Erikson's, just as it is of evolutionary psychology and the teleological tradition of Aristotle and his followers. *It suggests that although generativity should never be confined to natural parenthood, it must never gain too much cultural and symbolic distance from it.* Second, we must remember that Erikson was an instinctual pluralist. Both he and William James before him understood that our multiple and conflicting natural tendencies require the guidance and stabilization of strong communities of tradition that serve as storehouses of good practices, virtues, moral principles, and narratives. This is the great insight of *Hardwired to Connect* and beautifully reinforced by Erikson's understanding of the possible role of religion in supporting a viable identity. There is no possibility of creating truly generative people without inducting them into a *culture* of generativity with powerful accompanying symbols and communities that carry and reinforce these symbols. Generativity is a tendency of nature, but it needs the support and completion of communities of tradition that contain generatively inspiring narratives.

In spite of this respect for tradition, Erikson understood the importance of the Kantian-like principle of moral respect. Religious and cultural traditions may be carriers of generativity, but they may often seek to apply it only to "those like us" or only to our kin and community. Traditions carrying powerful founding narratives often need critique. Often these principles of critique are contained within the traditions themselves, but sometimes they are not, or at least are not readily available. Erikson knew that the Golden Rule could be used to critique a narrative tradition, and he knew that it was often located within the larger narratives of the world religions. But he also saw it stemming from the primordial cry of our phylogenetic need for recognition. Erikson could appreciate traditions, as he did in the case of Luther and Gandhi. He also had the resources to criticize tradition.

41. Erikson, *Gandhi's Truth*, p. 412.

We must not, however, make the mistake Kant did when he ransacked the world's religious and cultural traditions to affirm those that conformed to his categorical imperative and reject those that did not, as he is thought to have done in his *Religion within the Limits of Reason Alone*.[42] We must not, in analogy to Kant, use the ethic of generativity as a straitjacket that woodenly measures the worth of older traditions and contemporary ideologies only in terms of their compatibility with the ethics and morality of generativity. We can, however, justifiably start a dialogue between the ethics of generativity and all traditions, philosophies, and ideologies that are now vying to guide the future. This dialogue would at least attempt to determine the points of analogy between an ethics of generativity and other religio-cultural perspectives — be they economic, evolutionary, Christian, Buddhist, Hindu, Confucian, or Shintoist — that claim competence to lead us into the future. Discovering webs of analogy between generativity and other philosophies and religions can help provide overlapping communities of meaning and the institutions and people needed to create and maintain the future cycle of the generations. Understanding the levels of Erikson's ethic — his archeology and teleology of developmental goods, his theory of virtue, his mixed-deontological principle of obligation, and his view of the importance of encompassing narratives — should help us proceed with this emerging world conversation and the mutual criticism that it will require.

Erikson can contribute resources that broaden the three alternative ethics I mentioned at the head of this chapter — the ethics of principle, the ethics of virtue, and the ethics of narrative. Here the scope of my inquiry allows me only to be suggestive. First, the ethics of principle — especially as practiced by neo-Kantians such as Rawls, Habermas, and Kohlberg — can be supplemented by a theory of the premoral goods of the human life cycle that every act of justice, and every act of fair communication, should seek to actualize. Erikson's moral vision helps us both to affirm the importance of Kantian justice and to overcome its formalism and potential emptiness.

Second, theories of virtue can be both affirmed and supplemented by Erikson's moral psychology. He provides fresh understandings of how virtues build on and help actualize the epigenetic timetables of the human species. His view of the premoral goods of life helps us understand the natural inclinations and values that our virtues should enhance. This

---

42. Immanuel Kant, *Religion within the Limits of Reason Alone* (New York: Harper and Brothers, 1960).

view of values and virtues can give us more concrete ways of assessing the directions of modernity and determining which possibilities should be welcomed and which rejected, which of them support these important values and virtues and which do not.

Third, Erikson both understood the importance of traditions of narrative for the formation of generative persons and provided frameworks for critiquing the momentary or long-term distortions of such traditions. Narrative traditions that do violence to the cycle of human development or defy the universal principle of mutual recognition (Erikson's analog to the love ethic of equal-regard) are deserving of criticism. Ethicists of narrative, in their drive to balance modernity's rush into the future with the stabilizing resources of a narrative past, are both affirmed and gently criticized by Erikson's additional appreciation for the universals of human development and the universal requirement of justice.

Although Erikson was not a professional ethicist, he had within his thought an important and loosely stated synthesis of most of the elements needed for guiding our ethical trajectories amidst the opportunities and threats of modernity in the twenty-first century.

Chapter 8

Flanagan's and Damasio's Challenge
to Theological Ethics

Throughout the twentieth century, modern psychology has chal-
lenged the ethical implications of Christianity. Along with these at-
tacks have come arguments that ethical systems could be improved if they
took the findings of modern psychology more into account. These two
questions establish the parameters of this chapter: (1) are these challenges
well-grounded, and, (2) does modern psychology have a substantive contribution to make to moral philosophy and theological ethics? I will pursue these questions by examining the contributions of moral psychologist
Owen Flanagan and cognitive neuroscientist Antonio Damasio. Flanagan
will get the most attention because of his more active engagement with
philosophical and theological ethics.

Such challenges from modern psychology accuse Christian ethics of
being both too demanding and too unrealistic. The complaint that it is
too demanding involves psychology's perception of the Christian ethic of
self-sacrificial love as being too rigid and absolutist. The charge that
Christian ethics is unrealistic is the flip side of the argument that it is too
demanding, since it is unrealistic precisely because its rigid ethic of self-
sacrificial love overlooks the realities of human nature — realities that
modern psychology believes it understands much better than does Christian theology. Behind this charge is the even deeper complaint that most
of Christian theological ethics, as well as Western philosophical ethics,
has had an unrealistic understanding of the relation of emotions and feelings to reason or moral rationality.

There is a history to these accusations. Sigmund Freud and Erich
Neumann advanced widely influential psychological critiques of Christian ethics. I want to briefly discuss them both. I will spend, however, the

bulk of this chapter on the criticisms of the rising moral philosopher and psychologist Owen Flanagan.

Freud's complaint, put forth brilliantly in his *Civilization and Its Discontents,* centered on what he believed to be the Christian preoccupation with self-sacrificial love for neighbor, stranger, and even enemy.[1] He develops in this book a variety of criticisms, not the least of which is his belief that the Christian ethic underestimates the aggressive nature of human beings, especially the hostility of those people who do not know us and who are therefore unconstrained by the natural affections of close relations.[2] Notice that Freud's complaint is about both the overly high demands of the Christian faith and its failure to understand the realities of human aggression.

Neumann's argument is somewhat different. He claims in his *Depth Psychology and a New Ethic* that Christian ethics is built on repression. It promotes an absolute ethic that represses and excludes from consciousness all emotions and feelings that conflict with this ideal.[3] This denial of the negative in the human psyche in effect represses what Neumann, following Jung, called the "shadow" — a synthetic psychic reality that combines excluded elements of daily experience as well as inherited traces of the collective evil of the human race.[4] In spite of these different emphases, both Freud and Neumann agree that Christian ethics ends in splitting the human psyche into powerful antitheses of conscious and unconscious. For that reason, it actually promotes violence by losing conscious control over the contents of repression. For instance, many critics of American foreign policy after the destruction of the World Trade Towers on September 11, 2001, felt it was based on just this kind of splitting. When President Bush named Iraq, Iran, and North Korea an "axis of evil," they believed that this projected all evil on these countries and attributed all good to the United States, thus being blind to the darkness lurking in the American unconscious. Furthermore, President Bush's own self-presentation as a born-again Christian has led many critics to believe that such strong distinctions between good and evil are a direct consequence of latent tensions within Christianity itself. These critics were not surprised to see the American image of innocence shattered by the scandals of abuse inflicted by American personnel in Iraqi prisons.

---

1. Sigmund Freud, *Civilization and Its Discontents* (New York: W. W. Norton, 1961), p. 56.

2. Freud, *Civilization and Its Discontents,* p. 57.

3. Erich Neumann, *Depth Psychology and a New Ethic* (New York: Hodder and Stoughton, 1969), p. 35.

4. Neumann, *Depth Psychology,* p. 40.

The Moral Psychology of Owen Flanagan

Owen Flanagan has a slightly different critique of Christian ethics. At a relatively young age, he has achieved distinction in the fields of moral psychology, moral philosophy, and the philosophy of the mind. His *Varieties of Moral Personality: Ethics and Psychological Realism* is a major contribution to moral psychology worth the consideration of all serious theological ethicists.[5] Although he has strong interests in the philosophy of the mind,[6] his interests in moral psychology have continued, as can be seen in his *The Problem of the Soul: Two Visions of Mind and How to Reconcile Them.*[7] Whereas Freud and Neumann attacked Christian ethics for being too demanding and unrealistic, Flanagan voices a similar critique against both Western moral philosophy and Christian views of sainthood and the moral life. Indeed, the major alternative schools of moral philosophy receive from his incisive pen far more criticism than even Christianity, although in *The Problem of the Soul*, Christianity comes in for its share of censure as well. This is somewhat refreshing, I must admit, for those of us used to seeing Christianity singled out as the chief offender. In Flanagan's view, most moral philosophy is too demanding and unrealistic and shares in these respects the faults of Christian ethics.

Flanagan believes that moral philosophy can profit from a major infusion of scientific moral psychology and cognitive science. William James is his hero. John Dewey gets a lot of praise as well. About James and Dewey, and the relatively unknown Mary Caulkins, Flanagan says this, "Along with William James and James's unjustly neglected student Mary Caulkins, Dewey was one of only three people ever to serve as president of both the American Philosophical Association and the American Psychological Association."[8] Not since James and Dewey, he argues, have we witnessed major American intellectuals who have had competence in both psychology and moral philosophy. Since James and Dewey had explicit interest in religion, one might say that not since these two great scholars have we had major intellectuals with competence in psychology, moral philosophy, and the philosophy of religion. Since the time of

---

5. Owen Flanagan, *Varieties of Moral Personality: Ethics and Psychological Realism* (Cambridge: Harvard University Press, 1991).

6. Owen Flanagan, *The Science of the Mind* (Cambridge, Mass.: MIT Press, 1991), and *Dreaming Souls* (Oxford: Oxford University Press, 2000).

7. Owen Flanagan, *The Problem of the Soul: Two Visions of Mind and How to Reconcile Them* (New York: Basic, 2002).

8. Flanagan, *The Problem of the Soul*, p. III.

James and Dewey, moral philosophy largely has ignored psychology. Moral philosophy, Flanagan contends, has worked on the misguided thesis that ethics is autonomous from empirical considerations about human mental functioning. British analytic moral philosophy, Kantianism, utilitarianism, and theologies of revelation have all downplayed the role of psychology in ethics. Flanagan wants to correct this situation. In doing so, he would move moral philosophy (and I would add moral theology) in directions that are more pluralistic, more realistic, and more modest in stating the distance between the ideal and what is genuinely possible in moral behavior.

A moral philosophy should conform, according to Flanagan, to the demands of his Principle of Minimal Psychological Realism (PMPR). Freud and Neumann never developed such a principle, but they were struggling to say something quite similar. Flanagan defines PMPR with the following words: "Make sure when constructing a moral theory or projecting a moral ideal that the character, decision processing, and behavior prescribed are possible, or are perceived to be possible, for creatures like us."[9] Flanagan believes that there are good grounds for "rejecting a normative conception if it depicts a way of life which is psychologically unrealizable — if, that is, the conception violates PMPR."[10] PMPR, however, does more than set limits on how far a moral theory can escalate its demands; it also suggests some of the positive content of our moral ideals. Our psychological makeup provides indirect substance for our moral norms. In making this last point, Flanagan goes beyond anything explicitly stated in Freud and Neumann — but not beyond what can be found in William James. Nor does it go beyond the critical hermeneutical approach to morality found in Ricoeur. For, after all, Ricoeur's critical hermeneutics — with its place for distanciation, diagnosis, and explanation as submoments of the interpretive circle — is a kind of realism; in fact, it is a kind of hermeneutic realism or hermeneutic naturalism.

Flanagan has naturalistic components in his approach to ethics, but he is not a simple naturalist. He holds, however, that social traits (by which he means something close to Aristotle's and Erikson's concept of virtue) do contain within them a range of natural traits or natural inclinations. But these natural traits get expressed in widely varying ways depending on historical, cultural, and social circumstances. Flanagan takes these natural traits (I would call them needs and tendencies and Ricoeur

---

9. Flanagan, *The Problem of the Soul*, p. 32.
10. Flanagan, *The Problem of the Soul*, p. 46.

would refer to them as desires) quite seriously, but does not interpret them to form the basis of a hardened naturalism. He writes,

> Legitimate contenders for natural traits include the six basic emotions of anger, fear, disgust, happiness, sadness, and surprise . . . ; the perceptual input systems . . . ; the propositional attitudes (but not their contents); biological sex, sexual desire, hunger, thirst, linguistic capacity, and the capacities to be classically and operantly conditioned, to reason, and to remember.[11]

Although the inclusion of natural traits within social traits might claim the pedigree of Aristotle, it also can invoke the authority of Aquinas, much of American pragmatism, as well as psychoanalytic ethicists such as Erikson. It gets close as well to positions on the relation of psychology and biology to ethics held by philosophers such as Mary Midgley, Stephen Toulmin, and Peter Singer.[12]

Flanagan applies the PMPR test to a number of classic (and not so classic) moral philosophies. His arguments have implications for the moral theologies which have made use of these philosophies. For instance, Flanagan believes that utilitarianism — and any Christian perspective, such as Joseph Fletcher's situation ethics, that uses a variation of philosophical utilitarianism — is particularly vulnerable to PMPR.[13] The utilitarian believes that for a person to be moral she should "act so as to produce the best possible outcome."[14] The most satisfactory outcome is the maximum welfare for the largest number of people. Flanagan feels that such a view of moral obligation would require, as he says, "an utterly impossible amount of attention to one's action options and to the ranking of outcomes."[15] He insists that this moral principle, whether stated within secular or religious frameworks, puts totally unrealistic virtuoso computational demands on any individual or community trying to live up to it. Under Flanagan's critique, philosophical utilitarianism goes up in flames and so does its Christian counterpart called "situation ethics."

Flanagan's disdain for ethics of principle applies to Kantianism as

---

11. Flanagan, *The Problem of the Soul*, p. 42.

12. Mary Midgley, *Beast and Man* (Ithaca, N.Y.: Cornell University Press, 1978), pp. 165-76; Stephen Toulmin, *The Place of Reason in Ethics* (Cambridge: Cambridge University Press, 1958), pp. 172-76; Peter Singer, *The Expanding Circle: Ethics and Sociobiology* (New York: Farrar, Straus, and Giroux, 1981).

13. See Joseph Fletcher, *Situation Ethics* (Philadelphia: Westminster, 1966).

14. Flanagan, *Varieties of Moral Personality*, p. 33.

15. Flanagan, *Varieties of Moral Personality*, p. 34.

well as utilitarianism, even though the former has no heroic computational feats to accomplish. In the case of Kantian-type moral principle, it is the abstractness of the principle itself that he rejects, whether it be the categorical imperative, John Rawls's principle of justice as fairness, or Jürgen Habermas's principle of intersubjective justice. Flanagan would contend that his arguments apply to Kantian-theological ethics whether it be someone like Gene Outka or the Rawlsian Ronald Green, the latter of whom analogically extends Rawls's principle of justice as fairness to God, thereby seeing God as the perfect exemplification and fulfillment of Rawls's view of justice.[16] It is possible that Flanagan could even be critical of Ricoeur's use of the deontological test, even though, as I have pointed out, that Kantian-like principle does *not* swamp the totality of Ricoeur's theory of morality.

Flanagan has a great deal of sympathy for communitarians such as Alasdair MacIntyre and Michael Sandel. For instance, he acknowledges a role for narrative in the formation of the moral life. Although he does not discuss the writings of Stanley Hauerwas, he doubtless would have a degree of approval for the narrative theological ethics for which Hauerwas is famous. In addition, Flanagan also acknowledges the role of community in a good ethical perspective. In short, rather than being a matter of living by abstract principle, morality is for Flanagan primarily "identity expressive," a matter of manifesting in our practical lives some sense of who we are.[17]

But in spite of his similarity to certain communitarians, Flanagan believes that they overstate humans' need for firm identities nurtured by tradition-saturated homogeneous communities. And he would probably not be too happy with the emphasis on cohesive, identity-forming communities found in *Hardwired to Connect* or, for that matter, in the thought of Erik Erikson. The need to connect, for instance, was not one of the fundamental naturalistic tendencies that Flanagan discusses, and he omits talking about the need for strong communities of tradition to meet, organize, and extend these needs. Pluralistic liberal societies, he claims, can produce workable moral identities if people accomplish healthy early childhood identifications upon which later more fragmented social experience can build. Maybe good parents are necessary, he argues, but strong communities to reinforce and amplify the socialization by parents may

16. Gene Outka, *Agape: An Ethical Analysis* (New Haven: Yale University Press, 1972); Ronald Green, *Religious Reason* (New York: Oxford University Press, 1978).

17. Flanagan, *Varieties of Moral Personality,* pp. 5-6.

not be required. The Principle of Minimal Psychological Realism requires only a certain modicum of self-cohesion and does not require total traditions that back up and reinforce highly consolidated identities. But that, of course, is the issue. Are highly pluralistic societies cohesive enough to provide even those early healthy identifications with parents needed to later give adults the strength to find their moral compass?

Flanagan on Kohlberg and Gilligan

Flanagan addresses the now famous debate between the ethics of justice of Lawrence Kohlberg and the so-called ethics of care advanced by Carol Gilligan. He says, in effect, a pox on both of your houses. Kohlberg's affinities with Kant and Rawls are well known; everything I wrote in the preceding paragraphs about Flanagan's critique of Kant and Rawls would apply to his view of Kohlberg and, by implication, to all religious ethicists and educators attracted to his position.[18] Flanagan agrees with Gilligan that Kohlberg and his followers overemphasize justice and rights in their model of ethical thinking.

But Flanagan believes that Gilligan's ethics of care (and by implication the philosophical and theological feminist ethics that build on Gilligan) is just as one-sided in the other direction.[19] On the basis of recent empirical studies, Flanagan denies that ethical thinking is divided by gender, as Gilligan contends.[20] Men are not rights- and justice-oriented and women care- and relations-oriented in their ethical judgments. Flanagan follows the research of Lawrence Walker and others who suggest that moral thinking follows content.[21] When either men or women think about public issues, they tend to use the categories of rights and justice. When either men or women think about domestic, personal, or familial issues, they think in terms of care and relationality. The differences between men and women are due to their respective socializations and life situations; because society places women in mothering roles, women tend to think more about spheres of life where care models are appropriate. Men, on the other hand, are more often thrust into arenas where rights is-

---

18. See Lawrence Kohlberg, *The Philosophy of Moral Development: Moral Stages and the Idea of Justice* (San Francisco: Harper and Row, 1981).

19. See Carol Gilligan, *In a Different Voice* (Cambridge: Harvard University Press, 1982).

20. It must be remembered that Gilligan herself denies that it is, but much of her own writing and many of her followers continue to talk as if it were. See *In a Different Voice*, p. 2.

21. Flanagan, *Varieties of Moral Personality*, p. 231.

sues are prevalent. Flanagan does grant, however, that care is the more fundamental ethical mode. Why would he say this? Simply because care gets closer to actualizing and preserving basic premoral human tendencies and capacities that provide the framework for PMPR — the Principle of Minimum Psychological Realism. But even then, it is easy to overstate this insight, as he feels is the case in the work of Nel Noddings and Sara Ruddick, prominent champions of the ethics of care.[22]

What is really the case, in my opinion, is that the ethic of care is closer to the actualization (if not nurture) of basic goods in what Ricoeur would call the teleological moment of ethics, while justice is closer to the deontological test that Ricoeur associates with morality. Both are needed for a well-rounded perspective of the various contexts and contents of the moral life. And both are accounted for in the mixed-deontological principles of obligation found in Ricoeur, Janssens, Frankena, and, as we will see in the next chapter, the thought of Martha Nussbaum and John Finnis. Both the teleological ethics of care and the deontological principle of justice are implicit in the Golden Rule, which, as Ricoeur interprets it, should be read to mean we are to do *good* to others as we would have them to do *good* to us. This formulation contains both the teleology of caring for and actualizing the good as well as the reversible logic about the equality of self and other that is typical of deontology. This same mixed-deontological logic can be found, as we should recall, in Janssens's interpretation of the commandment to love the neighbor as we do ourselves. It is not, and should not be, a matter of either/or. The debate between Kohlberg's ethics of justice and Gilligan's ethics of care was flawed and misleading.

Flanagan and Virtue Theory

Classical virtue theory is another aspect of traditional moral theory Flanagan rejects. He would agree with Johannes van der Ven that traditional virtue models must be severely critiqued before they can be rehabilitated. Flanagan dislikes traditional theories because of their idealistic and static qualities. (His criticism of traditional virtue theory is similar to what we found in van der Ven.) Virtues for Flanagan are relevant to particular moral environments and specific ways of life. Most traditional virtue

---

22. See Nel Noddings, *Caring: A Feminist Approach to Ethics and Moral Education* (Berkeley: University of California Press, 1984), and Sara Ruddick, *Maternal Thinking: Toward a Politics of Peace* (Boston: Beacon, 1989).

theory, to the displeasure of Flanagan, lists clusters of basic virtues and holds that the moral person is one who exhibits the full list. Flanagan believes his criticism of virtue ethics is particularly applicable to Christian views of who is and is not a saint.

It is within the context of his discussion of the virtues of saints that we gain the clearest idea of Flanagan's view of Christian ethics. He claims that empirical investigation guided by the standards of PMPR shows that most saints are not directed by some eternal soul unconditioned by impulse or social conditions.[23] They are instead a grab bag of contradictory and unevenly held virtues.[24] Religious virtuosos seldom exhibit the full list of virtues. Furthermore, there are many different types of saints — intellectual saints, ascetic saints, magical saints, and saints such as Mother Teresa who exhibit loving service to humanity. Some are regarded as saints because they show a lifetime of moral acts; others are canonized on the basis of a single heroic deed.

Flanagan believes that there is no categorical difference between saints and ordinary people. Saints, he insists, do not live a single-minded life of obligation; they have nonmoral interests such as friendships, family, and other pursuits. Although Flanagan acknowledges it may be possible to identify a few saints who live moral lives consistent with ethics of principle — such as the Kantianism of André Trocmé or the utilitarianism guiding the abstemious living of the provocative philosopher Peter Singer — many people live similar lives based on very different motivations. In addition, good and bad traits are mixed in saints in ways that often make their worst characteristics essential for their best actions. This was true of Oskar Schindler, whose hedonism, avarice, and womanizing were the very traits that made it possible for him to beguile Hitler's *Sonderbehandlung* and save thousands of Jews.[25]

In accord with these points, Flanagan has some rather strange things to say about Jesus. Jesus, he believes, displayed some "ethically suspect" beliefs and attitudes that, nonetheless, did not undermine his other virtues. He lists Jesus' hatred of the flesh and of close personal ties, characteristics Flanagan mistakenly thinks he finds in Luke 12:49-53, where Jesus talks about bringing "fire to the earth" and division to families. Flanagan overlooks that these passages are more about the social strains created by the decision to follow Jesus than they are about the ascetic denial of the

23. Flanagan, *The Problem of the Soul,* pp. ix-xii.
24. Flanagan, *The Problem of the Soul,* p. 6.
25. Flanagan, *The Problem of the Soul,* p. 8.

flesh. He makes similar remarks about Gandhi, who he believes exploited women by sleeping with them to test his ascetic resolve. In the same way, Martin Luther King Jr. was sexually involved with many women, but Flanagan believes this is "not usually seen as canceling his main ethical merit."[26]

Critique of Flanagan

There are both positive and negative aspects to Flanagan's position. He is certainly right to point to the gap between our moral ideals — whether expressed in the language of virtue or in the language of principle — and the flawed character of our lives, even the lives of saints. But he overlooks, as Christians often have themselves, that the Christian narrative acknowledges this gap between our moral ideals and moral frailties. Christian theology demands the full acknowledgement of our moral faults and sinfulness. An ironic gap exists between Christian ideals and the realities of everyday moral weakness; confessing this requires openness to forgiveness and grace as understood by the Christian story of sin and redemption.[27]

For some years, I have argued that the genius of authentic Christianity is its ability to project commanding ideals and point toward perfection but also to acknowledge that human fallibility and fault ("fault" being Ricoeur's word for actual sin) lead us inevitably to fall short of what is expected. The Sermon on the Mount tells us to "Be perfect, therefore, as your heavenly Father is perfect" (Matt. 5:48). At the same time, when the rich young man called Jesus "Good Teacher," Jesus answered, "Why do you call me good? No one is good but God alone (Luke 18:18-19). There runs throughout Christianity, and especially through the Gospels, a dialectical — in fact, an *ironic* — relation between ideals to which we are called and our finitude, sin, and pervasive inability to conform to them. Jesus' words on divorce are one of the best examples of this tension. On the one hand, Jesus seems to prohibit divorce except for cases involving adultery. On the other hand, he acknowledged that it had been permitted in the past as a concession to reality — "because you were so hardhearted" (Matt. 19:8).

26. Flanagan, *The Problem of the Soul,* p. 9.

27. For a discussion of the ironic character of the Christian faith, with special reference to the Gospel of Mark, see David Rhoads and Donald Michie, *Mark as Story* (Minneapolis: Fortress, 1982).

Flanagan is insensitive to the ironic tension in Christianity between high moral ideals and human fault. Nor does he understand the role of forgiveness. The theme of forgiveness runs throughout the New Testament. One finds it strikingly stated in the Lord's Prayer, which Christians regard as the perfect form of a prayer. Jesus is reported saying, "And forgive us our debts, as we also have forgiven our debtors" (Matt. 6:12). Or again, in Mark, possibly the most ironic of the Gospels, we find these words attributed to Jesus: "Whenever you stand praying, forgive, if you have anything against anyone; so that your Father in heaven may also forgive you your trespasses" (Mark 11:25). This theme of forgiveness recurs over and over throughout the Gospels and the epistles.

Flanagan also is correct in rejecting the widely held modern dogma of the autonomy of ethics from psychology. The capacity of an ethic to both meet fundamental human needs and also fit within the realities of basic human capabilities is arguably a test of its validity. This is a point that Ricoeur argues for in beginning the moral life with our search for the good in ethics before moving to the deontological test of morality. The passions and motivations that move us toward the goods of life are also basic capabilities that limit us in our capacity to act; they provide certain constraints on action that our search for the good must respect. Furthermore, the extent to which an ethic fulfills certain natural human needs and tendencies — although in ways that inhibit some, elevate others, and harmonize the whole both within the individual and in relation to others — is also a relevant test, distinguishable from Ricoeur's deontological text. It should be emphasized that Flanagan's realism is a minimal or weak realism and not a strong one. This is one of his strengths. Hence, he rightly denies being a naturalist in any fully reductionistic sense. He also correctly insists that naturalism cannot provide a full ethic and that more is needed. *But this is where Flanagan comes up short; he gives little insight into the more that is needed and how it would be grounded.*

Flanagan is simply proposing the Principle of Minimum Psychological Realism (PMPR) as a test that various ethical perspectives should pass. In his most recent book called *The Problem of the Soul,* Flanagan shifts from speaking about PMPR to proposing that we envision an "ethics as human ecology."[28] In some ways, Flanagan is proposing what I would characterize as a logically unstable form of critical hermeneutics or hermeneutic realism. Throughout this book, he is trying to reconcile what he calls two images of consciousness and mind. These are the "manifest" or humanis-

---

28. Flanagan, *The Problem of the Soul,* p. 213.

tic image of mind and consciousness (the consciousness that we experience and that is also shaped by our cultural and social world) and the "scientific" image (consciousness and mind explained by evolutionary psychology, cognitive neuroscience, and moral psychology conceived of as natural sciences).[29] Flanagan wants to retain the manifest and humanistic mind; he believes it contains our moral ideals and higher aspirations, and in this he is clearly right. But he wants to repudiate — and with considerable symbolic violence, I might add — the traditional ways of legitimizing the contents and ideals of the manifest or humanistic mind. He certainly wants to reject the idea that these ideals gain their legitimacy, their correctness, because they are revealed or commanded by God. He also wants to reject the idea that our moral norms are uncovered by acts of pure reason, à la Kant. Insofar as our humanistic consciousness contains any moral insights, he argues that such insights must be validated by the empirical disciplines broadly conceived.

By validation, he means employing something close to his PMPR test. In other words, we should look empirically at the common human needs and wants that humans in all cultures have pursued in the past. Then we should examine what evolutionary psychology, cognitive moral theory, neuroscience, and anthropology reveal about which wants and needs seem central and what common environmental conditions (social and natural) are required to help humans flourish. He acknowledges that discovering these needs for the species Homo sapiens — discovering what will satisfy humans and the conditions for their flourishing — is not quite as simple as studying an ecological niche in a patch of wetlands in New Jersey or Rhode Island. But he insists that it has strong analogies. All humans, he says, want pretty much the same things. In this sense, ethics or morality (whichever term you use) has a universal subdimension.[30] Different cultures may pursue these wants and needs in different ways, but the premoral human tendencies are pretty much the same. Furthermore, conflicts between tendencies will arise, but human intuitions about how to justly and fairly adjudicate between the conflicts also have a lot of similarity.

It is clear to me, however, that Flanagan is looking at the manifest consciousness pretty much from the bottom up — from a foundationalist perspective that does not take very seriously either consciousness or its culture- and tradition-created contents. He does not take a hermeneutic view of consciousness. Even though he says our historically shaped con-

---

29. Flanagan, *The Problem of the Soul,* pp. 41-44.
30. Flanagan, *The Problem of the Soul,* p. 286.

sciousness contains our moral ideals, I don't think he fully understands what that means.

Flanagan fails to conceive of the possibility that some of the classical moral ideals — whether in moralities of principle, virtue, or divine command — also might themselves have functioned more as tests of human pursuits of the good rather than as exhaustive and unrealistic theories of moral expectation that exclude our strivings for the good. Flanagan is particularly nervous when he believes an ethical system is so totalistic that it squeezes out the possibility of individuals pursuing nonmoral projects such as becoming a dancer, artist, lawyer, parent, or farmer. Our touchstones Niebuhr, Aquinas, Ricoeur, and Janssens would agree; they would all reject any view of life that denies or represses our wide range of humanistic interests in the goods of life. Flanagan seems oblivious to the many examples of religious humanism that have arisen and flourished in the revival of Aristotelianism in medieval Roman Catholicism (the thought of Thomas Aquinas), Judaism (Maimonides), and Islam (Averroes). He is also neglectful of extensions of these impulses in Christian humanists such as the Protestant Melanchthon, the Catholic Erasmus, and the interactions between Calvinism and the moral philosophy of the Scottish Enlightenment.[31] In addition, he seems unaware of how religious narratives and institutions are often carriers of practical reason that can endure philosophical review and testing. In fact, this has been the goal of much of this book, to demonstrate that religious traditions often simultaneously carry and transmit central premoral values, moral tests, and grounding narratives. God's name may be invoked to lend validity to the moral package of a religion, but the tradition itself may provide additional reasons — additional rationalities — to show why what God wills is also humane and contributes to human flourishing.

Flanagan overlooks the truth that hardly any classical theological moral system functioned to eliminate the actualization of human capabilities as a viable aspect of the Christian life. Sociologist Christian Smith, as we saw earlier, demonstrates how religious traditions contribute to the human and social capital of young people. Such traditions generally encourage the actualization of human capabilities for the good of the religious community. And yes, some traditions have endured periods of dis-

---

31. For an interesting summary of the Christian, Jewish, and Islamic absorption of Aristotle after several hundred years of being lost to the civilized world, see Richard E. Rubenstein, *Aristotle's Children: How Christians, Muslims, and Jews Rediscovered Ancient Wisdom and Illuminated the Dark Ages* (New York: Harcourt, 2003).

torted patriarchy when there reigned a narrow, if not oppressive, view of the capabilities of women. But on the whole, the ideals of these religious systems have worked as tests for the moral review and criticism of life choices rather than as demands crowding out all other pursuits of the goods of life. Theories of virtue may be useful in assessing our actual social traits, and ethics of principle — whether Kantian, utilitarian, the principle of neighbor love, or the Golden Rule — may have a similar testing function. Ricoeur in his *Oneself as Another* captures the essence of this insight. As we have seen time and again, he assigns the Kantian categorical imperative the function of reviewing and testing our teleological aspirations as these are expressed through our narratively defined selves and their various life projects.[32] Flanagan's fear of idealistic ethical systems leads him to overlook the role of principles and elevated goals. He is so bent on providing philosophical space for moral pluralism that he fails to provide us with many tangible moral guidelines. He overlooks the fruitfulness of a position like Ricoeur's that brings together Aristotelianism, Kantianism, and narrative ethics in a single system that bears many of the marks of flexibility and realism that Flanagan values. He fails to see how a philosophical position such as Ricoeur's not only answers many of his objections, but also provides a viable philosophical space for the more explicitly Christian affirmations of a Niebuhr, Aquinas, or Janssens. Allow me to focus on Ricoeur once again to sharpen my appreciative critique of Flanagan.

Ricoeur is close to Flanagan in viewing ethics as primarily dealing with the realization of linguistically encoded human desires and aspirations.[33] But then they begin to differ. Flanagan does not comprehend fully that when desires are confronted with situations of conflict, resistance, and violence, they must pass the deontological test of generalizability and respect for the other before returning to their concrete implementation in practice. Ricoeur grounds respect for the other in a view that sees reflexive narrativity as fundamental to what it means to be a person or self.[34] Because of this, Ricoeur would agree with Flanagan; morality is *identity expressive*. Nonetheless, all narratively expressed desires and aspirations must still, in situations of conflict, pass the deontological test, an insight that Flanagan resists.

---

32. Paul Ricoeur, *Oneself as Another* (Chicago: University of Chicago Press, 1992), pp. 203-39.

33. Ricoeur, *Oneself as Another,* pp. 169-202.

34. Ricoeur, *Oneself as Another,* pp. 113-39.

Ricoeur is enough of a realist to have some appreciation, I believe, for Flanagan's test of PMPR. Ricoeur acknowledged in *Freud and Philosophy* that humans are creatures of desire — of eros.[35] In affirming this, Ricoeur stands with Freud and the entire teleological tradition of philosophy. In his recent *What Makes Us Think?* he shows his openness to a limited contribution to ethics, in contrast to morality, from the thick theory of desire found in evolutionary psychology and cognitive neuroscience.[36] But Ricoeur is frightened of naive realism, just as he is of naive naturalism. Hence, he insists that we know our natural needs and tendencies first of all through the filter of our linguistic and cultural traditions.[37] Ricoeur would be skeptical of imposing too quickly the specific content of Flanagan's PMPR on the cultural construals that various traditions use to represent their teleological aspirations. Ricoeur would start first with the way a tradition linguistically represents these tendencies and needs and then use the PMPR diagnostically. Flanagan misses what is at stake in Ricoeur's subordination of diagnosis and distanciation to tradition — what Flanagan calls manifest consciousness. Hence, Flanagan's naturalism borders on foundationalism. Ricoeur's hermeneutical realism could, however, and indeed *should*, be extended to become a kind of hermeneutically based ecological morality. If that were to happen, the naturalism of the PMPR test would be used diagnostically and not foundationally. Although Flanagan never completely dismisses tradition or the manifest mind, he seldom allows it to speak for itself.

Ricoeur's move to start with a tradition's linguistic expression of these teleological goods is an insight that Flanagan's realism should acknowledge and incorporate. Flanagan derives the content of PMPR entirely from moral psychology and biology conceived as naturalistic disciplines. He overlooks the point that different cultures have different ways of talking about their shared human needs and that these differences are relevant for the moral task. Respecting these differences is crucial to successful dialogue between these traditions and cultures. Nonetheless, Flanagan may have a point that Ricoeur should acknowledge. Ricoeur must acknowledge that even relatively cohesive traditions have conflicts about how to represent pervasive human psychobiological needs. In addition, diverse traditions conflict with one another on these issues. Most

---

35. Ricoeur, *Freud and Philosophy* (New Haven: Yale University Press, 1970), pp. 430-34.

36. Jean-Pierre Changeux and Paul Ricoeur, *What Makes Us Think? A Neuroscientist and a Philosopher Argue about Ethics, Human Nature, and the Brain,* trans. M. B. DeBevoise (Princeton, N.J. : Princeton University Press, 2000), p. 190.

37. Changeux and Ricoeur, *What Makes Us Think?* pp. 434-39.

modern individuals are fed by more than one tradition even if they are primarily informed by a dominant one. Hence, the conflict and potential violence that Ricoeur believes stimulate ethics comes about not only by tension between different needs but also by conflicts about how to interpret, define, and rank these needs to begin with. If this is true, Ricoeur's deontological test of generalizability and respect cannot alone resolve teleological conflicts. *There must be some way to have another test — a test that examines the teleological claims themselves, especially insofar as these claims are about basic regularities in human nature. If this is true, something like Flanagan's PMPR test might be needed to supplement Ricoeur's deontological test. This supplement, however, would function diagnostically and not foundationally or reductively.*

In Ricoeur's theory of ethics and morality, the PMPR test would need to be reworked to function in the following manner: If one had interpreted how conflicting traditions linguistically represent fundamental human needs and had found no analogies or identities between the opposing views sufficient to resolve the conflict, then Ricoeur's concept of "diagnosis" that we explained in Chapter 4 could be used. The idea of diagnosis might use more scientific models of psychology and biology to scan cultural references to human regularities as a means of testing their adequacy. This is a method Ricoeur used to good benefit in his early work, when he turned (as he frequently did in *The Voluntary and the Involuntary*) to experimental psychology and biology to develop his philosophy of the will.[38] As we have seen, he used the concept of diagnosis in strict analogy to how he believed a good doctor works within the context of clinical assessment.[39] The doctor first listens to the way the patient linguistically represents his or her complaints and needs. Then, however, the doctor may use additional technical instruments such as measures of blood pressure, analysis of blood chemistry, or heart examinations with stethoscopes. This more distanciated knowledge (Ricoeur, as we have seen, shies away from the word "objective") is then correlated with the patient's and doctor's tradition-colored linguistic representation of human need, health, and illness.

In this circumscribed sense, the distanciated knowledge may have a role to play in clarifying first-order linguistic traditions of speaking about the teleological goals of health. And by analogy, Ricoeur could conceiv-

---

38. Paul Ricoeur, *The Voluntary and the Involuntary* (Evanston, Ill.: Northwestern University Press, 1966).

39. Ricoeur, *The Voluntary and the Involuntary*, pp. xv-xvii, 87-88, 221-22.

ably turn to Flanagan's PMPR to test conflicts in the wider field of teleological aspirations. But a fully adequate test would require the deontological test as well. And both tests would work within a narrative understanding of selfhood that represents the moral life as more than either of these tests can exhaust.

If Flanagan were to develop something like a real ethic rather than an inadequately articulated partial test, he would have to restore his appreciation for the role of principle in the moral life. A principle functioning like the deontological test is completely lacking in his early *Varieties of Moral Personality* and only makes a weak appearance in *The Problem of the Soul.* Once again, Ricoeur's reformulation of the Kantian test can be helpful. Because Ricoeur believes that morality begins with our teleological aspirations as they are embedded in traditions, he never completely detaches the deontological test from teleology. Hence, he offers a new formulation of the Kantian-sounding Golden Rule. To do to the other as you would have the other do to you really means, as we have seen, doing *good* to the other as you would have the other do *good* to you. He follows Rabbi Hillel's interpretation: "Do not do to your fellow what you hate to have done to you." Ricoeur believes that this "refers to goods which we would love being done to us, and to evils which we would hate being done to us."[40] Ricoeur's theory of narrative selfhood permits the possibility that this principle could be placed within a larger narrative framework, as is the case when the Golden Rule and neighbor love are situated within the Christian narrative of the goodness of creation, its fall, and its redemption in the figure of Jesus Christ. Ethics and morality can be identity expressive — yes, expressive of this narrative — but still contain a place for moral principles as tests. Ricoeur's basic moral principle — his reformulation of the deontological principle to include a subordinate concern with the good — has a flexibility that Flanagan begs for but does not himself provide.

Ricoeur's reformulation of the Golden Rule provides us with a mixed-deontological principle not unlike those found in Louis Janssens's understanding of neighbor love as the *ordo caritatis et bonorum* and in the ethics of both William Frankena and, as we will soon see, Martha Nussbaum.[41] It is a formulation that Reinhold Niebuhr gets close to but fails to fully de-

---

40. Paul Ricoeur, "Teleological and Deontological Structures," in *Contemporary French Philosophy,* ed. Phillips Griffiths (Cambridge: Cambridge University Press, 1987), p. 109; see also Ricoeur, *Oneself as Another,* pp. 219-27.

41. Louis Janssens, "Norms and Priorities of a Love Ethics," *Louvain Studies* 6 (1977): 218-30; William Frankena, *Ethics* (Englewood Cliffs, N.J.: Prentice-Hall, 1973), pp. 43-45.

velop — an unfortunate lack in an otherwise powerful presentation of the Christian narrative and its implications for theological anthropology. When such formulations are used to test teleological aspirations, they can help assess moral situations as different as a mother's care for her infant and the enactment of legislative law in the realm of politics. When a mother cares for her child, considerations of justice are not foremost in her mind. Her primary concern is to do good, to take care of her infant. Nonetheless, the formal requirements of justice may function in the background of her care. It would be immoral of her to disregard the obstacles facing poor mothers in caring for their children or to directly contribute to their difficulties through her own acts. Although concern with her own future welfare will not be foremost in her mind, she may be dimly aware of some principle of generational justice that leads her to expect a degree of mutual care in return when her dependent infant becomes an adult and she becomes old and frail. Indeed, she herself may be caring for her own dependent mother at the same time that she cares for her infant. *A mixed-deontological test of the kind proposed by Ricoeur should be seen as having both a foreground and a background at any one moment in history and in any particular situation.* Whether the deontological or the teleological element is in the foreground would be determined by context and the type of issue being confronted. Both dimensions, however, should be present to some degree in all moral judgments. When the teleological element — the doing of good — is in the foreground, we are likely to call it love and care. When the deontological element is in the foreground, we are likely to call it justice. In reality, we must hold love and justice in dialectical tension. In many acts, they are one and the same. Sometimes they appear to be separate, but for justice to be efficacious, the teleology of actualizing human premoral goods must be somewhere in the background. And for love to have form and endurance, the deontological test of justice must never be absent.

A mixed-deontological principle of justice or love in which foreground and background shift in accordance with the issues at stake can resolve the impasse of the Gilligan-Kohlberg debate. It can make sense of the empirical research by Walker and others showing that men use an ethic of care when meeting the needs of children, and women use an ethic of justice when deliberating about large-scale social and political issues. Furthermore, a mixed model of obligation could find a place for Flanagan's PMPR; it could test and refine conflicts within and between traditions about our teleological judgments. On the other hand, without something like Ricoeur's deontological test, Flanagan's PMPR leaves us with a moral pluralism that borders on out-and-out relativism. The Principal of Minimal Psychological Realism would become, in effect, the principle of maximum ethical pluralism. Such a consequence undercuts the weight of Flanagan's claim that moral philosophy (and, I would add, Christian ethics) needs the substantive contributions of psychology.

Damasio, Neuroscience, and Christian Ethics

Antonio Damasio is a clinically oriented neuroscientist. His major books have been a sensation. They have been widely read throughout the world and translated into over a dozen languages. While Flanagan is basically a moral philosopher who reads psychology, Damasio is head of a department of neurology at a major Midwestern university who also happens to read and address philosophy. Although he is a respected clinical neuroscientist, his fame has been established by his capacity to write about complex issues in neuroscience in such a way as to cross disciplines, discuss issues in philosophy and religion, and do this for a very wide readership. Neuroscience — the science of the brain — is one of the most sensational fields of academic study today. Because of new techniques such as magnetic resonance imaging (MRI) for observing the processes of different parts of the brain, scientists now have ways for determining which parts of the brain are largely, although seldom completely, in control of different mental functions. This has been particularly useful for studying brain-damaged or impaired patients who come for help to neuroscientists such as Damasio.

Damasio's three widely read books — *Descartes' Error, The Feeling of What Happens,* and *Looking for Spinoza* — are primarily concerned to explain the relationship of emotions and feelings to human consciousness.[42] But in the process, he also makes interesting remarks, highly parallel to those of Flanagan, on the relationship of body, emotions, and feelings to moral sensibilities, moral virtues, and moral decision-making. In short, he makes points similar not only to Flanagan but also to at least part of the argument I have been advancing. Higher levels of moral reasoning are informed by bodily, emotional, and feeling states pertaining to the experienced goods and evils, pleasures and discomforts, joys and sorrows of ev-

---

42. Antonio R. Damasio, *Descartes' Error: Emotion, Reason, and the Human Brain* (New York: Putnam, 1994); *The Feeling of What Happens: Body and Emotion in the Making of Consciousness* (New York: Harcourt Brace, 1999); *Looking for Spinoza: Joy, Sorrow, and the Feeling Brain* (Orlando, Fla.: Harcourt, 2003).

eryday life. He is making, as is Flanagan, nothing more or less than the point made by Ricoeur, that ethics begins in the teleological strivings of humans toward the goods of life — an insight that Ricoeur thinks he gets from Aristotle. Both Flanagan and Damasio are aware of their Aristotelian credentials as well. Damasio also turns to Spinoza, and both Flanagan and Damasio acknowledge their indebtedness to William James. But there are still important differences between Flanagan, Damasio, and Ricoeur, as we will also see.

In Damasio's intriguing book titled *Descartes' Error,* he rejects Descartes's separation of *res extensa* (material objects in time and space) from *res cogitans* (the mind and thoughts), which do not share these physical properties.[43] In other words, Damasio rejects the separation of mind and body. Flanagan agrees.[44] But Damasio develops this point with marvelous flare. Through analyzing stirring cases of his own brain-damaged or impaired patients, case studies of the patients of other neurologists, and the famous story of Phineas Gage — the mid-nineteenth-century twenty-five-year-old New Englander who had a three-and-a-half-foot steel rod blown through his brain and lived to tell about it — he makes some very interesting generalizations about how the human mind actually works.

Here are some of his main points. The body and the brain are intimately connected; in fact, there is a sense in which every part of the body is sending messages to the brain, and the brain is sending messages back to every part of the body.[45] In many ways, it is accurate to say that the brain is extended throughout the body and not just located in the head. The lower parts of the brain — for example, brain stem, limbic system, thalamus, and hypothalamus — produce *primal emotions* such as fear, anger, disgust, surprise, sadness, and happiness. They also produce *social emotions* such as sympathy, embarrassment, shame, guilt, pride, jealousy, envy, and gratitude.[46] Damasio would agree with the evolutionary point of view; these emotions have been produced by free variation and selected for retention because they have contributed to the survival of individuals and their progeny. In this sense they are premorally good. They contribute to the homeostatic balance and wisdom of the organism. At this point, I should observe, Damasio almost sounds like the organismic romanticism that one associates with the older humanistic psychology of Abraham

---

43. Damasio, *Descartes' Error,* p. 124.
44. Flanagan, *The Problem of the Soul,* pp. 80-81.
45. Damasio, *Descartes' Error,* pp. xvii, 90.
46. Damasio, *Looking for Spinoza,* pp. 44-45.

Maslow and Carl Rogers (reviewed in Chapter 2). In fact, this fundamental level of emotionality contributes, he insists, to higher levels of core consciousness, feelings of selfhood, rationality, and decision-making. They are like Spinoza's concept of *conatus;* they constitute the "aggregate of dispositions laid down in brain circuitry that, once engaged by internal or environmental conditions, seeks both survival and well-being."[47]

Cut people off from their lower-order emotions through some disturbance in the brain — as happened to the brain-damaged Phineas Gage or to Elliot, one of Damasio's own patients — and they may seem deceptively rational in almost every sense. At the same time, however, they exhibit new limits, in contrast to their pre-damage lives, in enacting responsible moral behavior.[48] Phineas was still logical but became impulsive, self-indulgent, and socially inept. In the case of Elliot — the more intriguing case for my purposes — a brain operation had left him with damage to the ventromedial area of his frontal lobe, an area that seems to control communication between the primal social emotions and consciousness.[49] In spite of the damage, Elliot had high levels of abstract and formal moral thinking capacities as described and measured by the moral reasoning tests of Lawrence Kohlberg.[50] But when it came time for Elliot to think about his *own* personal moral decisions, he could not successfully deliberate and act. As a consequence, he could not conduct the normal affairs of his life such as hold a job, work well with people, or conduct his own business transactions. His kind of brain damage had cut his higher levels of moral rationality off from his own emotions.

Ricoeur's appreciation for the place of affect, striving, and emotion in the ethical life would lead him to agree with all of this, as he does in his dialogue with neuroscientist Jean-Pierre Changeux in *What Makes Us Think?* That is, he agrees that "ethics is rooted in life and that normative ethical behaviors find their origin in the impulses of life."[51] But it is, for Ricoeur, life first as experienced phenomenologically by the experiencing self; knowledge of the brain at best would only correlate with and help diagnose what we know by experience. From this point on, Ricoeur and Damasio would begin to depart even more, or at least make their points with considerably different degrees of emphasis.

Damasio makes a distinction between emotions and feelings. In fact,

47. Damasio, *Looking for Spinoza,* p. 36.
48. Damasio, *Descartes' Error,* pp. 31-44.
49. Damasio, *Descartes' Error,* pp. 32-33.
50. Damasio, *Descartes' Error,* p. 48.
51. Changeux and Ricoeur, *What Makes Us Think?* p. 20.

the higher levels of reason, including practical moral reason, are informed by feelings that interpretively perceive emotions in light of certain contents of selfhood and consciousness. A feeling is a perception — in fact, an interpretation — of an emotion.[52] But this raises the question: where does this interpretive perception come from? It seems to come from experiences which affect our evaluations of our emotions — experiences from which we learn about dangers, pleasures, and the satisfactions of various practices. In other words, feelings are partially shaped by the higher moral accumulations of a culture — even the religious dimensions of a culture. Feelings perceive and interpret emotions in light of some *point of reference.* With this idea, Damasio unknowingly begins to make a point similar to Ricoeur when he says our strivings for satisfaction in life invariably get interpreted *with reference to* inherited practices, ideals, narratives, and language. His point about the mixed role of feelings also could bring us back to the interpretive role of Christian practices and narratives as understood by theological ethicists such as Niebuhr, Janssens, Aquinas, Pope, and the theological feminists I have addressed. All of them take natural emotions seriously but also perceive and interpret them from the perspective of Christian doctrines of creation and salvation.

Basically Damasio is using the discoveries of neuroscience to make the simple distinction between premoral and moral goods, between ethics and morality. Emotions and feelings contribute to the premoral good and to ethics; I think Damasio would have to accept something like the distinctions between premoral goods, ethics, and morality, along the lines opened by Ricoeur. Damasio is simply trying to knock down any moral system that seems to rely on a sharp distinction between body and mind, emotions and rationality such as he thinks has been the case with much of Western theology and philosophy, most notably Descartes and Kant. But he also believes that our premoral emotional evaluations of the good — as important as they are for ethical rationality — are not enough for a full moral rationality. Reason, consciousness, various levels of the self (especially what he calls the "autobiographical self"),[53] and "extended consciousness"[54] also are necessary for a full ethical system.

Extended consciousness seems to be, for Damasio, the consciousness that is constituted by history, tradition, and language. He grants that this tradition-laden level of consciousness "allows the human organism to

52. Damasio, *Descartes' Error,* p. xiv.
53. Damasio, *Looking for Spinoza,* p. 270.
54. Damasio, *The Feeling of What Happens,* pp. 230-33.

reach the very peak of the mental abilities."[55] For instance, it gives us our "sense of the minds of the collective; the ability to suffer with pain as opposed to just feel pain and react to it; the ability to sense the possibility of death in the self and in the other; the ability to value life; the ability to construct a sense of good and evil distinct from pleasure and pain."[56] Although Damasio never quite says it, extended consciousness is the consciousness that permits us to base our selfhood on classic and critically appropriated practices transmitted by a tradition — practices that provide us, as MacIntyre and Ricoeur would say, with tested ways to pursue the ethical and moral good. Ricoeur would say that extended consciousness shapes our emotion-tinged feelings to look backward from what we have learned about morals to evaluate which of our emotions support our moral norms and which are in tension with them. As Ricoeur says in his dialogue with neuroscientist Changeux, it is only because we already are moral creatures that we can look back to either the history of evolution or the analysis of brain functions and find analogues and precursors of our present moral capacities. He writes, "it is because we are here, as human beings, posing the question of the meaning of morality, that we can read the spectacle offered" by the sociobiologist or brain researcher and then discover analogs to our moral capacities today.[57] Nonetheless, I would say, maybe even more emphatically than Ricoeur, that such diagnostic knowledge is morally useful and stabilizing.

But Damasio is fearful of going too far toward what I call a critical hermeneutics. He approaches things mainly from the bottom up, from body to consciousness, from brain to culture and religion, not the other way around. He wants to remind us that our tradition-saturated consciousness rests on somatic foundations. He writes,

> The enchainment of precedences is most curious: the nonconscious neural signaling of an individual organism begets the *protoself,* which permits *core self* and *core consciousness,* which allow for an *autobiographical self,* which permits *extended consciousness.* At the end of the chain, *extended consciousness* permits *conscience.*[58]

Damasio is a neurologist and neuroscientist. We must allow his interest in building consciousness from the bottom up. Of course, he is partially

---

55. Damasio, *The Feeling of What Happens,* p. 230.
56. Damasio, *The Feeling of What Happens,* p. 230.
57. Changeux and Ricoeur, *What Makes Us Think,* p. 181.
58. Damasio, *The Feeling of What Happens,* p. 230.

right; consciousness does have certain roots in the body, nervous system, and brain. But we must not permit him to miss the dialectic between bottom and top — between body and a tradition-constituted consciousness.

Once history, tradition, language, and narrative evolve, the logic and causality change. Feelings (to use the category of Damasio) convey new meanings backward and deep down to our emotional and somatic regulatory systems. Damasio admits as much in the way he defines the nature and function of feelings. It may be entirely justifiable to say, along with Ricoeur and Niebuhr, that just as humans are embodied creatures of nature through and through, we are also historical creatures in dialogue with the traditions and narratives that shape our extended consciousness from that direction. And this history defines our emotions just as our emotions render all history and culture as embodied.

As we have seen, both Flanagan and Damasio minimally and reluctantly recognize that, in a way, we are historical and tradition-laden creatures. But they are afraid that tradition must always be equated with a form of dogmatic revelation that will blind us to nature's tendency toward the proto-ethical impulses of sympathy, attachment, balance, kin altruism, and care. In the end, Damasio seems attracted to the pantheism and nature romanticism of Spinoza, even though he acknowledges it may be lacking in ways he has difficulty articulating.[59] Strangely, he seems to both understand what tradition contributes to morality through our extended consciousness and yet be reluctant to critically interpret and retrieve it. Both Flanagan and Damasio can be thanked for helping us clarify some of the premoral aspects of ethics and morality. Finally, however, we must reject them for their failure to place these insights into the service of a full hermeneutic circle designed to critically reclaim the richness of our religious and philosophical, Jewish and Christian, traditions.

---

59. Damasio, *Looking for Spinoza*, p. 275.

Chapter 9

Christian Ethics and the Premoral Good

Throughout the preceding chapters, I have been implicitly developing a multidimensional view of human nature. Part of this multidimensionality has been the concept of human premoral good. I have been claiming that both moral psychology and Christian ethics need a concept of the premoral good. Indeed, this concept points to one of the crucial links between modern moral psychology and theological ethics from a Christian point of view.

In this chapter, I will investigate further the idea of the premoral good. I will do this, however, within the context of a general discussion of the multidimensionality of the human, especially as this relates to the concepts of dignity and respect. I begin with dignity and respect largely because they are commonly recognized in secular thought to point to the core of morality. And this is true; to be moral is to treat others and self with dignity and respect. But I will gradually show how these concepts are more complex than often thought and can, in addition, benefit from being placed within a wider theological context.

In concentrating in this chapter on the premoral good, I am reasserting its crucial role in ethical and moral reflection — even in the disciplines of moral theology or theological ethics, whichever term you prefer. Part of my argument throughout this book has been that the discipline of moral psychology has something significant to contribute to the premoral or teleological dimension of moral reflection. Now it is time to say more about why that is the case and why Christian ethics has something to gain by attending more carefully to the question of the premoral goods of life.

In coupling the word "respect" with the word "multidimensionality,"

I am broadening the dimensions of the human commonly thought to be appropriate objects of respect. In contrast to Kant and his followers, I contend that the object of respect includes but goes beyond the rational and moral capacities of individual humans.[1] There are several dimensions to the human that deserve respect. Because of this, the word "respect" should have different meanings depending on the dimension under consideration. The dignity of humans today is threatened at many different levels — by tyrannies that deprive humans of rational control over their lives, by poverty that robs them of the necessities of life, and by spreading technologies that render them means to ends over which they have no control. What is common to these diverse assaults on human dignity? They all fail to *respect* the multidimensional character of the human being.

Multidimensionality within Theological Anthropology

Most secular academic disciplines have attempted to overcome the fragmentation of human nature by reducing it to any one of a variety of incomplete perspectives. Behaviorism, rational-choice theory, sociobiology, psychoanalysis, Marxism, and social constructivism are all current aggressive attempts to achieve a unitary view of human nature by reducing it to a single narrow perspective.

In contrast, most great theological anthropologies implicitly acknowledge the multidimensional character of the human, although only a few make this an explicit feature of their program. In our time, Paul Tillich is known for introducing multidimensionality directly into his thought. Using the insights of phenomenological description, Tillich listed the inorganic, the organic, the psychic, and the spiritual as the fundamental dimensions of the human.[2] William Schweiker, in an effort to develop a responsibility ethic for a new Christian humanism, lists three dimensions of basic human goods: premoral, social, and reflective goods.[3] The natural law theorist John Finnis and the neo-Aristotelian Martha Nussbaum acknowledge multidimensionality by distinguishing between moral and premoral goods and proposing detailed lists of the latter.

---

1. See Immanuel Kant, *Foundations of the Metaphysics of Morals* (Indianapolis: Bobbs-Merrill, 1959).

2. Paul Tillich, *Systematic Theology*, vol. 3 (Chicago: University of Chicago Press, 1963), pp. 22-23.

3. William Schweiker, *Responsibility and Christian Ethics* (Cambridge: Cambridge University Press, 1995), pp. 120-21.

These last two positions, which I soon will address more completely, have importance for my primary thesis. I argue in this chapter that an adequate moral psychology and Christian ethic requires a religious and cultural program that *not only respects the full multidimensionality of the human but also protects one frequently neglected strand of it, the dimension of premoral goods that enhance human life.* But to do this requires properly locating the premoral within the other dimensions of human life. The disciplines of moral psychology have a limited but important contribution to make to clarifying the premoral dimension of moral reflection.

I already have discussed the meaning and definition of the concept of the premoral good. But many people complain that the concept is obscure and difficult to understand. So, let me amplify what I have said. By the word "premoral," I mean the many ways we use the words "good" and "value" to refer to experiences and objects that are considered pleasant, fulfilling, agreeable, healthy, or in some way enhancing to human life. The premoral good, as I have indicated, is close to what Ricoeur means by the teleological goods of life. I see no problem in associating the word "premoral" with the field of ethics as Ricoeur defines that term. Premoral goods, like his view of the field of the ethical, are never considered as fully moral goods even though they are morally relevant.[4] Here are some examples. Education is a premoral good; it extends our cognitive powers and often leads to higher earnings, but it is not necessarily a moral good. Whether the good of education is moral depends upon the human will that guides it, the purposes to which it is put, and who is included or excluded and why. Health is a good, but not necessarily a moral good. Some people who are physically and mentally healthy are quite immoral and some unhealthy people are moral exemplars. Automobiles, trains, good roads, and clean air and water are premoral goods, but not necessarily moral goods.

Premoral goods, as I have argued, can conflict with one another. Good things can often compete with and stamp out other good things. Good food can damage the good of health if we eat too much, and the good of money can destroy the good of love and family if we work too hard and long to get it. Reconciling conflicting goods — as Ricoeur, William James, and Louis Janssens all have said — is generally viewed as a dis-

4. William Frankena makes a distinction between nonmoral and moral good. See William Frankena, *Ethics* (Englewood Cliffs, N.J.: Prentice-Hall, 1973). Janssens makes what I think is the more helpful distinction between moral and premoral good. It communicates that premoral goods are morally relevant but not morally definitive. See Louis Janssens, "Norms and Priorities of a Love Ethics," *Louvain Studies* 6 (1977): 207-38.

tinctively moral task. Premoral goods may be relevant to judgments about the moral good, just as teleology is relevant to morality à la Ricoeur, but they are not in-and-of-themselves moral goods.

Contemporary theology has had difficulties addressing the premoral level of the multidimensional nature of the human. This dimension of life is increasingly being clarified by social sciences such as economics, evolutionary psychology, and the health sciences. This turn to the social sciences has led to the exclusion of theology as a resource for the clarification of public issues. More and more, society is trying to solve its problems through the use of interdisciplinary panels and research teams. Increasingly, theology is absent from these teams. Frequently these teams are weighing and balancing judgments about the premoral goods vital to human flourishing and searching for the most efficient and effective means to actualize them. Christian ethics is perceived more and more by other disciplines as having little to say on these issues, or at least little it can argue for effectively in the public forum.

I will illustrate further the nature of premoral goods by locating them within a larger view of the multidimensional nature of the human. In a series of essays and books stretching from the early 1980s and in previous chapters in this book, I have identified five levels or dimensions of the human.[5] I have argued that these dimensions are also implicit or explicit in all acts of moral thinking or practical reason. In fact, I claim to have found these five dimensions not by looking directly at the stationary individual but by analyzing a particular kind of action, namely, reflective moral action. To be honest, I had arrived at this list of five long before I found them implicit in Ricoeur.

But indeed I also have found them in Ricoeur's analysis of praxis, so let me begin there. The order of the five dimensions follows Ricoeur's description of the thickness of human action or what he prefers to call praxis. We have seen bits of this description earlier in the book. Possibly the reader will remember the analysis of the father searching for milk to feed his hungry children that I set forth in the introduction to this book. Now I invite you to think about it in terms of our discussion of the multidimensional character of being human. Here, I think, would be Ricoeur's order of the multidimensional thickness of human action: (1) Humans are desiring creatures in quest for the premoral goods of life, (2) who pursue

---

5. Don Browning, *Religious Ethics and Pastoral Care* (Minneapolis: Fortress, 1988), pp. 53-71; *A Fundamental Practical Theology: Descriptive and Strategic Proposals* (Minneapolis: Fortress, 1991), and *Marriage and Modernization* (Grand Rapids: Eerdmans, 2003), pp. 160-63.

their desires and needs through practices and habits that consolidate their experiences of the good, (3) assign meaning to these practices through ideals and narratives about life's purpose, (4) test resolutions of conflicting wants and practices through general principles (in Ricoeur's case, a fresh interpretation of the Golden Rule and a slight amendment to Kant's categorical imperative), and (5) refine these ideal solutions with attention to the social and natural constraints of concrete situations (Hegel's *Sittlichkeit*). Ricoeur's ground-up way of organizing these five dimensions is probably more useful than the more hierarchical way I spoke about them in some of my earlier formulations.[6] I am not saying the five dimensions are always explicit. In fact, they are often explicitly denied, as in the case of the positivistic scientist who denies his investigations assume any overarching narrative that gives them meaning. Part of what I will be doing in this chapter is showing that even when these dimensions are denied, careful analysis can nonetheless often uncover the presence of such narratives and the other dimensions as well.

Whether thought about bottom-up (from practices to overarching narratives) or top-down (from narratives to more specific practices), it is important to think of these dimensions as interactive and mutually qualifying. Certainly practices are influenced by narratives and assumed principles. But the reverse is also true; encompassing narratives and the implementation of moral principles are influenced by practices and social and natural constraints on practices. Furthermore, fresh and critical moral thinking entails working on all five of these levels. Since the dimensions are implicit or explicit in all human praxis, Ricoeur's view of its thickness actually ends by depicting all praxis as forms of human practical reason or *phronēsis*.

These five dimensions have implications for theological anthropology. To illustrate this, I tentatively will give them a more hierarchical order. They go like this. First, we are creatures that get oriented to life through ideals and narratives about the nature of *Being*, the ultimate context of life. The narrative of God's action in relation to the world gives us our basic orientation toward Being. Second, we are also creatures who must have general principles for mediating between self and other and the conflicting goods of life; our grand narratives qualify, ground, and generally contain such principles within their overarching framework or sym-

6. I have derived these five dimensions from Ricoeur's analysis of praxis in his "Teleological and Deontological Structures of Action: Aristotle and/or Kant?" in *Contemporary French Philosophy*, ed. A. Phillips Griffiths (Cambridge: Cambridge University Press, 1987), pp. 99-112.

bolic canopy. For example, the Gospel story of Jesus' birth, life, death, and resurrection contains within it his teachings on the Golden Rule and the principle of neighbor love; these principles do not stand alone but are elements within a larger narrative plot. Third, we are creatures with wants, needs, and pervasive tendencies who pursue various premoral goods, often sinfully, that will satisfy them, but within a world of meaning defined by our religio-cultural narratives and mediated by whatever general principles they hold. Fourth, we are creatures who live in the context of social and natural systems; they constrain and guide our wants, but within the context of our basic stories and the principles we use to make decisions. And, finally, we are creatures who live by practices, habits, virtues, rituals, and rules that reflect judgments made at the other four levels. This, I submit, is one view of the multidimensional nature of the human — a view from the top down, which is the way most dogmatic theology is written. It is a view gained from an analysis of our most distinctive human characteristic — the truth that we are creatures of practical reason or *phronēsis*.

Now, to be honest, we humans may not always live faithfully according to these inherited classic narratives, principles, or practices. We also may fail to understand them properly. We may try to evade their obligations. We may consciously or unconsciously cheat. Because we are finite, we are, as Ricoeur would say, fallible; we can overreach or under-reach — we can err. Because we are, as Niebuhr would say, anxious finite creatures, we willfully and intentionally try to secure ourselves by exploiting our neighbor — by sinning. We are, in the language of Ricoeur, creatures of actual fault. Furthermore, we may get confused by conflicting interpretations of our own tradition and the contradictions between inherited traditions and new ideological competitors. After all, we live in a pluralistic society where, increasingly, multiple traditions vie for the mentality of people, both traditional ones that are already deeply a part of their effective history and new ones that would like to convert people and displace inherited classics. *But I hold that regardless of these complicating factors, when we think or deliberate about what we are to do, we will be implicitly or explicitly making judgments at all these different levels or dimensions. That is my claim in asserting the multidimensional structure of human nature and moral action.*

It is my belief, as I indicated above, that the contemporary crisis of theological anthropology is due to its inability to be articulate about the premoral wants and goods that humans strive for and how they should be qualified and refined by principles consistent with the Christian narrative. It is thus the middle territory between our concrete practices and our overarching narratives and principles — in other words, the theory of teleological or premoral goods — that constitutes the heart of our crisis. Christians who sometimes tell the same theological narrative, hold the same general moral principles, and practice the same rituals frequently make drastically different moral judgments. These differences, I submit, come from holding conflicting views of life's central premoral goods and how they can be actualized within the constraints of the social and natural environment in which we live.

Distortions of the Human in Contemporary Discourse

Most of the powerful contemporary secular anthropologies concentrate on one of these five dimensions to the neglect of others. I use the word "neglect" intentionally. Many of the current reductive anthropologies do not take *explicit* responsibility for judgments at each of the levels of practical reason, but they often unwittingly make *implicit* judgments at levels for which they do not take public responsibility. In the process, they sneak these judgments indirectly into their theories and discourses. In what follows, I will summarize research, mainly on the social sciences, that I have reported at length in past publications.

Modern Psychologies and Premoral Goods

Selected modern psychologies come to mind. Many of them aspire to advance scientific understandings of motivation and health, hence primarily concentrating at dimension three of the five levels — the dimension of premoral tendencies and goods. Even then, their theory of premoral tendencies and goods is often narrow and incomplete. Furthermore, these psychologies often unconsciously project theories of obligation as well as implicit visions, metaphors, or narratives with metaphysical overtones. Consider the humanistic psychologies of Rogers and Maslow, which I touched on in Chapter 2. Health for them had to do with self-actualization. They were unaware, however, that without some further qualification, the premoral value of health defined as the actualization of one's potentialities can easily be turned into an ethical-egoist theory of moral obligation.[7] The logic goes like this: to be healthy is to self-actualize, therefore you have an

---

7. Don Browning, *Religious Thought and the Modern Psychologies* (Minneapolis: Fortress, 1987; rev. ed. 2004).

implicit moral obligation to actualize first of all your own potentials. Ethical egoism, however, is generally thought by moral philosophers to be an inferior theory of obligation; it cannot solve conflicts without assuming that sooner or later the other person will give up his or her demands and yield to your self-actualization. Or even worse, ethical egoism tries to avoid recognizing conflict by resorting, unaware, to a metaphysical judgment holding that at the depths of things, all genuine self-actualizations are harmonious and in fact cannot legitimately conflict.[8]

Humanistic psychology is the psychological theory that undergirds much of contemporary popular psychotherapy. It goes beyond a scientific theory of motivation and health by making moral judgments of an ethical-egoist kind and implicitly makes metaphysical judgments about the ultimate harmony and nonconflicting nature of all authentic and undistorted self-actualizations.[9] It may well be that the influence of humanistic psychology also goes well beyond the confines of formal psychotherapy. It is a decent hypothesis to think that humanistic psychology, in tandem with other social and cultural forces, is one of the sources for the new turn to "life," "my life," and "my experience" in contemporary spirituality.

Freud also went beyond psychology's concern to describe our basic tendencies, needs, and premoral inclinations and delved as well into the other dimensions of practical reason. His mature theory of motivation was built around the dual instinct theory of *erōs* and *thanatos*. Freud, in contrast to Rogers and Maslow, recognized the conflicting and dangerous nature of our fundamental motivations. But, in the end, his theory of health was also an implicit ethical egoism, but one based not on actualizing our potentials but on directing our instincts toward gaining various kinds of premoral pleasurable satisfactions, as Philip Rieff points out, but in safe and realistic ways.[10] Freud too, in his later theory, went beyond talking about health as the prudent release of premoral pleasures and drifted into the area of metaphysical narratives; he speculated that his dual instinct theory of life against death might reveal the fundamental dynamics of the cosmos — the conflict between *erōs* and *thanatos*, life and death.[11]

If space permitted, I could extend these illustrations about the unwitting visional and obligational fringe of the modern psychologies with ad-

---

8. For William Frankena's critique of ethical egoism, see his *Ethics*, p. 19.

9. Browning, *Religious Thought and the Modern Psychologies*, p. 81.

10. Philip Rieff, *Freud; The Mind of the Moralist* (New York: Viking, 1959), and his *The Triumph of the Therapeutic* (New York: Harper and Row, 1966). See also Browning, *Religious Thought and the Modern Psychologies*, pp. 41-43.

11. Browning, *Religious Thought and the Modern Psychologies*, pp. 41-43.

ditional references to B. F. Skinner, Carl Jung, Erik Erikson, and Heinz Kohut, as I have done in *Religious Thought and the Modern Psychologies*. Other scholars have extended this mode of analysis to psychologies other than those I have examined. From one perspective, the psychologies I have examined have reduced the human to narrow concepts of motivation and theories of health. From another perspective, their reductions do not remain reductions; they flow surreptitiously into moral and metaphysical judgments which are neither acknowledged nor defended. Hence, they begin to lapse unwittingly into the wider ranges of the five dimensions of practical reason.

Rational-Choice Economics and Evolutionary Psychology

The fields of economics and evolutionary psychology can also be cited as reductionist. Like humanistic psychology and Freud, they develop powerful but narrow theories of premoral good, generally around concepts of psychological motivation. Hence, they too specialize in the dimension of premoral tendencies and goods, the teleological dimension of life. Even then, their theories of the premoral are, from my perspective, too narrow. From another viewpoint, they are casual wanderers into the fields of morality and general metaphysical visions of the world. Rational-choice theory, often called neoclassical economics, is the dominant model of economics in the United States and has also gained enormous influence over the social sciences in general. It is built on a parsimonious theory of human motivation and a minimalist theory of rationality. Human beings, according to this view, are motivated by a limited number of hardwired bio-psychological wants and needs. In the terminology of this book, these wants and needs would be premoral and close to what Ricoeur calls teleological aspirations toward the good. But the rational-choice list is narrow, and it leaves out the crucial need for attachment, even though it does include a gesture toward the premoral good of kin altruism. Gary Becker — a leading rational-choice theorist and Nobel Prize Winner — includes in his list inclinations toward "health, prestige, sensual pleasure, benevolence, or envy." Benevolence refers to parents' concern for their own children and blood-related kin, who are both sources of emotional satisfaction and carriers of their parents' genes.[12] This is close to evolutionary

---

12. Gary Becker, *The Economic Approach to Human Behavior* (Chicago: University of Chicago Press, 1991), p. 5.

psychology's concept of kin altruism. Rationality in economic activity, and other forms of action, entails choosing the most efficient means to the satisfaction of these basic inclinations. Furthermore, rational-choice theory holds that all objects that satisfy these inclinations are commensurate; whether we decide to buy a car, invest in art, get married, or have a child is based on rational calculations about which of these choices will yield overall the greatest amount of satisfaction. If the costs of having a child have gone up and the satisfactions have gone down, we might instead choose to invest in a Mercedes or take a European vacation.[13]

Rational-choice theory, even more directly than humanistic psychology and Freudian psychoanalysis, elevates an ethical-egoist theory of motivation toward a variety of premoral values into a normative theory of ethical obligation. In reading rational-choice theorists, one cannot avoid a message that goes like this: We *are* ethical egoists. We are wired to satisfy certain premoral needs and to pursue certain premoral values. Therefore we *should* conform to this theory of motivation and to this theory of moral obligation in all of our actions.

But rational-choice theory may have an implicit narrative and ethical horizon that is not captured by its explicit theory. In closely reading the texts of this school of thought, one is struck by how rational-choice theorists end in celebrating the virtues of industry and efficiency and indirectly tell stories about the meaning of life that justify these virtues. This leads economist and social philosopher Donald McCloskey — who as an economist is in fact a rational-choice theorist — to render a very interesting judgment about the assumed narrative background to this perspective in economics. McCloskey says rational-choice theories assume a moral and narrative background not unlike the Protestant ethic that has shaped so much of Western cultural life. The rational-choice vision of life and morality does not emphasize a lazy and passive economic consumerism but rather an active and energetic economic productivity.[14] Rational-choice theory unwittingly exhibits almost all of my points made so far: that human nature is a multidimensional reality, that much of modern intellectual life (including rational-choice theory) tries to deny this, and that nonetheless judgments about the omitted dimensions unknowingly creep back into these theories without the supports of responsible justifications.

13. Gary Becker, *A Treatise on the Family* (Cambridge, Mass.: Harvard University Press, 1991).

14. Don McCloskey, *If You're So Smart: The Narrative of Economic Expertise* (Chicago: University of Chicago Press, 1990), pp. 135-40.

Increasingly, there is in academic circles something of a marriage between rational-choice theory and evolutionary psychology to create a general bio-economic view of the human. Although I have found much of value in evolutionary psychology, it, like all of the social sciences, needs interpretation and placement within larger frameworks. When it gets absorbed into the grim worldview of rational-choice theory, its positive contributions get lost. When these two conceptual systems are synthesized, analogies are often drawn between the demands of markets in economic theory and the idea of natural selection in biology; human behavior is variously rewarded or extinguished depending on the selective power of markets and/or the selective pressures of natural environments.[15] Furthermore, evolutionary psychology, like some rational-choice theory, assumes that humans have hard-wired inclinations, the most important of which are captured by the twin concepts of kin altruism and inclusive fitness. These concepts suggest that the core of human altruism is derived from our preferential treatment of those who share, preserve, and pass on our genes.[16] As we saw above, much of rational-choice economic theory has incorporated this element of evolutionary psychology as one of the central components of its view of the human. This emerging bio-economic view of the human is one of the dominant intellectual trends of our time and constitutes a major challenge to the relevance of a Christian theological anthropology.

Evolutionary psychology itself also lapses into the ethical dimension of the human, but it does so intentionally. As we have seen, E. O. Wilson, Richard Alexander, Robert Reich, and Frans de Waal are just a few of the sociobiologists and evolutionary psychologists who believe that these disciplines hold the key to a viable theory of ethics for our time. Nonetheless, evolutionary psychology is similar to most of the modern psychologies and to rational-choice theory in proffering an important yet still overly narrow theory of premoral values and also an essentially ethical-egoist theory of moral obligation. Evolutionary psychologists believe that humans are basically motivated to enhance the present and future viability (indeed, immortality) of their own genes. They extend this ethical egoism into complicated theories of kin altruism and reciprocal altruism, however. Kin altruism, as we have seen, gives birth to empathy; in loving our children as parts of ourselves, we also feel their pains and joys as we would

---

15. Richard Posner, *Sex and Reason* (Cambridge, Mass.: Harvard University Press, 1992).

16. Donald Symons, *The Evolution of Human Sexuality* (Oxford: Oxford University Press, 1979), and Martin Daly and Margo Wilson, *Sex, Evolution and Behavior* (Belmont, Calif.: Wadsworth, 1978).

our own pains and joys. This is the core of our capacity to empathize with offspring, and (through the analogical extension of these capacities) to empathize with others outside the family line. Our more expansive adult capacity to generalize this empathic concern for others, according to Frans de Waal and others, is born out of this crucible of kin altruism in intimate family settings.[17] Nonetheless, kin altruism — as the concept is handled by most contemporary evolutionary ethicists — is still a form of ethical egoism; we advance the lives of others as a way of advancing our own lives. Elaborate forms of reciprocal altruism are also basically complicated forms of ethical egoism. We learn to help others, as Richard Alexander claims, because this stores up capital for the day we need help in return. Sometimes we help others, according to Alexander, not with the expectation that they will return the favor in our lifetime but because we expect them to help our progeny (the carriers of our genes) sometime in the distant future.

Evolutionary psychology has the advantage of intentionally moving into ethics; it has not backed into it unwittingly and implicitly as so much of social science tends to do. It has both advanced descriptive accounts of morality and projected normative ethical theories. It is, however, less explicit about its general vision of life. Nonetheless, an analysis of the horizons of evolutionary psychology suggests that it assumes an agonistic vision of life — a metaphysical narrative that implicitly holds that strife and violence are the fundamental qualities of being. John Milbank in his provocative *Theology and Social Theory* has argued that much of modern economic and social-science theory assumes such an agonistic ontology, mainly influenced by Nietzsche and Darwin.[18] I think his critique applies to most of evolutionary psychology as well. Although some forms of evolutionary psychology use the doctrine of kin altruism to show the origins of our capacity to empathize with offspring, brothers, and cousins, and from there analogically to those beyond the family circle, these theories never actually deliver empathy beyond the logic of self-interest. Hence, it is easy to see why rational-choice economics and evolutionary psychology are joining forces to create a powerful, new, and relatively unified form of reductionism with an overly narrow view of premoral values, an ethical-egoist theory of obligation, and an implicitly agonistic life narrative and ontology. In an effort to avoid a multidimensional view of the human, they together unknowingly have injected a strife-ridden materialism into

---

17. Frans de Waal, *Good Natured* (Cambridge, Mass.: Harvard University Press, 1996).
18. John Milbank, *Theology and Social Theory* (Oxford: Basil Blackwell, 1990), pp. 5, 27-45.

the fields of both ethics and metaphysics. For evolutionary psychology to be morally productive, it needs to realize it only gives insight into Ricoeur's premoral and teleological aspect of a critical hermeneutic perspective on morality, and cannot itself provide the deontological test or the larger narrative context that an adequate morality requires. This is precisely what I have tried to do with evolutionary psychology when I have used its concepts diagnostically in my constructive practical theological ethics without accepting as well its own reductive ontology and morality.

When a full analysis is made of the assumed foreground and background of the so-called secular disciplines, one often discovers within them an implicit multidimensionality. But it is largely assumed, unargued, and morally and metaphysically questionable. Many of the disciplines concentrate on theories of the premoral good, but often inadequately. When the full reality of these disciplines is uncovered, they often look more like theology than is generally recognized. Thus, *the basic difference between theological anthropology and the anthropologies of other human sciences is not that theology is morally and metaphysically freighted and the others are not; the difference is rather that theological anthropology takes responsibility for its moral and metaphysical judgments while many other contemporary anthropologies do not.* If this observation holds, then theology and the secular disciplines are on far more equal ground than is generally recognized. For this reason, theology should regain the confidence to enter into a full critical conversation with competing contemporary views of the human.

The Premoral Good and Christian Narrative

So far, I have argued for the multidimensional richness of Christian theological anthropology, at least the theological anthropology of Reinhold Niebuhr. Although I have made much of the theory of moral obligation found in Janssens's love ethic of equal-regard, I have used Niebuhr to illustrate the richer multidimensionality of Christian anthropology. Ricoeur helps us grasp multidimensionality as a philosophical perspective on praxis; he does not himself, in spite of his Christian sensibilities, actually fill out his thick theory of human action with a robustly Christian content. He is a very helpful philosopher, perhaps a philosopher of religion. But Ricoeur is not explicitly a Christian theologian. For the fullness of Christian theology, we must look beyond Ricoeur.

I have not, it should be noted, so far argued for the excellence or correctness of Niebuhr's view of the multidimensional nature of Christian anthropology. That is another task. I have observed, with favorable comment, that these dimensions in Niebuhr reciprocally qualify each other; the moral, premoral, social, and natural are not derived deductively from the visional and narrative dimension even though they are all qualified and informed by that dimension. This gives Niebuhr a flexibility and power in interdisciplinary conversations that many theologians have difficulty achieving.

Allow me to remind you of Niebuhr's multidimensional Christian anthropology that I set forth in Chapter 1. First, as I have mentioned before, Niebuhr was a keen observer of actual concrete practices in modern secular and ecclesial societies. He fully understood the thickness — the multidimensionality — of our various practices, whether they be business practices, labor practices, educational practices, or the mundane everyday practices of marriage and family life. He could see the implicit premoral values that these practices were striving for, their different implicit moral theories, and their various deep narratives — both idolatrous and genuinely life-giving.

Second, we should recall how Niebuhr understood the teleological and premoral dimension of humans. He viewed humans as creatures of nature with a range of desires for survival, attachment, sex and procreation, acquisition, and group affiliation. These inclinations are good in the premoral sense and viewed as such ontologically from the perspective of God the Creator. Humans are also creatures of cognition and imagination who, made in the image of God, transcend nature yet become anxious over their finitude and vulnerability. Unable to hold this anxiety in faith, they grasp idolatrously at finite securities instead of placing their ultimate trust in the reliability of God as Creator, Governor, Redeemer, and Sustainer.

Third, Niebuhr finds a complex narrative structure in the Christian faith — a narrative about the action of God in relation to finite and sinful humans. In addition to the story of God as Creator, we see emerge the narrative of God as Governor, God as Redeemer (manifest in the life and death of Jesus the Christ), and finally God as Sustainer (manifest in the ongoing witness and action of the Holy Spirit). God the Governor upholds God's moral intentions even in the face of sin. It is God the Governor who brings judgment to human sinfulness even when God also continues to sustain creation with creative love and power. It is God the Governor who requires, at least in the reconstruction I have given to Niebuhr, the deontological test. From the standpoint of the Christian life, the deontological test has behind it the power and authority of both God the Governor (who measures our sins) and God the Creator (who assigns ontological worth to all humans). This story of God's action constitutes the deep narrative dimension of Christian ethics. Freud, humanistic psychology, evolutionary psychology, and rational-choice theory have their respective deep metaphors and narratives. The Christian faith does too, and one that has received and endured much more testing and ascent over the long span of history than the implicit narratives of these newer, allegedly metaphysically neutral and narrative-free social-science disciplines.

The fourth dimension can be found in Niebuhr's development of an identifiable principle of moral obligation. It is rooted in the impossible possibility of a human living the life of full self-sacrificial love which Niebuhr finds in the life and death of Jesus on the cross — the Christian doctrine of the atonement. Although Niebuhr saw this as the moral ideal by which to measure all acts of the Christian life, in reality he thought that under the conditions of finitude and sin even Christians can accomplish little more than a sustained reciprocal justice. It is precisely this theory of moral obligation that I tried to reconstruct, using what I consider to be the far more adequate theory of love as equal-regard articulated by Janssens. This is a view of Christian love that sees the self-sacrifice of the cross not as the goal of Christian love but as a transitional ethic — something, to use the phrase of Timothy Jackson, that we have to be "open to" — in our struggle to return broken relations to the community of love and mutuality central to the strenuous ethic of equal-regard.

We find the fifth dimension in Niebuhr's way of conceptualizing the contextual channels and constraints of a faith-informed practical reason. In his own way, he was a theologian fully aware of the pressures on both secular society and the Christian life of the practices of modernization. He generally spoke about these pressures in terms of the practices of industrialization, with all of its promises and threats to men and women embedded in the wage economy. He also spoke about social constraints in terms of competing centers of power that strove to control economic and democratic processes to their own advantage. These factors constituted constraints to practical action, but constraints that were also often amenable to realistic action — and some compromises — in an effort to enhance justice and the goods of life.

I believe that Christian practical reason and anthropology, when properly understood, have the potential of being more explicitly multidimensional than the reason and anthropology of other disciplines. It is also my conviction that Christian ethics can both confess its multidimensional views with power and defend them in open critical conversation; its view of morality and human nature can be shown to be emotionally convincing and morally and metaphysically plausible. But demonstrating why this is so is not my main goal. Rather, I want to conclude this chapter by arguing that Christian ethics must do more to strengthen and differentiate its theories of premoral goods and demonstrate more convincingly how these goods are related to its view of life and theory of moral obligation. It must do this without losing the richness of the other dimensions of the human — especially what I have called the narrative or visional dimension.

Strengthening the Premoral in Christian Ethics

Niebuhr had a slot, a place, for the premoral dimension of life. Implicitly, many other theologians have this as well, as we saw in the thought of Thomas Aquinas, Louis Janssens, and Stephen Pope. But to have a place for or a formal way of handling the category of the premoral does not give Christian theology all that it needs to handle this dimension in public moral deliberation or the moral education and formation of children, adolescents, and adults. Understanding and differentiating the premoral goods of life is a demanding new task for Christian ethics in the twenty-first century. The premoral good, the reader will recall, refers to all of the ways we speak of the goods of life without necessarily saying something about the distinctively moral good. Much of contemporary discourse about public policy is discourse about premoral goods and evils. Is the water contaminated? How much mercury can the human body really tolerate? How much vitamin C or E is it good for the human body to have? Is there something intrinsic about single parenthood that makes this arrangement for child care less effective? Or do single parents have more difficulties with their children because they lack other premoral goods such as money, time, or outside help? Are fathers necessary for healthy children or are they dispensable if their premoral contributions of money and practical assistance can be replaced by other sources? Should the United States protect itself from nuclear attack from rogue nations? Would it be "good" to have a missile defense program, that is, would it be good in the sense of being effective in protecting life and limb? Most of us would agree that life and limb are premoral goods and that the things that protect our lives are premoral goods as well; but to have my life and all of my limbs does not mean I am a morally virtuous person. Nor does protecting my life necessarily mean that I am protecting it morally. Notice, the question of single motherhood and the relevance of fathers can be discussed independently of making judgments about the moral qualities of particular mothers and fathers. Many very moral single mothers may still have difficulties raising their children for a variety of reasons — lack of money, time, a biologically invested mate, or wider family and community resources. They may be morally virtuous, but their situation is premorally disadvantageous.

Much of the energy of the contemporary social sciences is spent in calculating the consequences of various arrangements of premoral goods. Much of this work is limited to economic considerations that are, on the whole, easier to control than other variables. These have to do with such variables as income, housing, nutrition, and minimum standards of health. Because economic theory in the work of Gary Becker and James Coleman has moved into the arena of "human capital" and "social capital," economics and sociology now often calculate what the variables of education and the customs of certain institutions can add to the wealth and well-being of both individuals and society.[19]

Such discussions also proceed in the field of medicine. The growing use of reproductive technologies and what is called the "new eugenics" is often justified on premoral grounds. People want children, and children are a basic premoral good. Healthy and bright children are even greater premoral goods. This says something about the delightful qualities of promising newborn infants but speaks not a word about the moral qualities of such infants or the morality of conceiving them through the selective procedures of the new reproductive technologies. Children can be conceived in moral or immoral ways; traditionally, having a child out of wedlock has been thought to be an immoral way to have and enjoy the good of children. The Roman Catholic Church has taught that certain reproductive technologies are immoral, but it has never taken a stand against the goodness of conception and children as such.

For the most part, Protestant theological anthropologies have been weak in contributing to public discourse about premoral goods. Roman Catholic moral theology, because of its tradition of natural law and philosophical anthropology, has been better at addressing issues pertaining to premoral values, but often in ways widely thought to be inadequate or, at least, incomplete. As I pointed out above, rational-choice theory, for the most part, assumes a relatively short list of hardwired desires that propel

19. Gary Becker, *Human Capital* (New York: Columbia University Press, 1975); James Coleman, "Social Capital and the Creation of Human Capital," *American Journal of Sociology* 94 (1988): 95-120.

humans toward a range of satisfying goods. These are, as I indicated above, "health, prestige, sensual pleasure, benevolence, envy." Implicit in this approach is not only an ethical-egoist ethic, but a concept of the commensurability of premoral goods. In the rational-choice view, these goods are fungible; it is the overall satisfaction that is aimed for. Health may be sacrificed for prestige or prestige for a boatload of pleasure. Having children, we are told, can be sacrificed easily for more nights at fine restaurants. The aggregate theory of premoral goods — the idea that we aim for overall satisfactions and pick, choose, and exchange between such goods in an effort to gain the greatest overall balance — is also a fundamental tenet of all utilitarians, from Bentham and Mill to contemporary utilitarians such as Russell Hardin or Peter Singer. Roman Catholic proportionalists, such as Bruno Schüller and Richard McCormick, also are thought by some critics to exhibit variations of the belief that premoral goods are commensurable.

John Finnis and the Catholic Natural Law Theorists

Various contemporary natural law theorists (sometimes called the new natural law theorists) such as Germain Grisez, John Finnis, and Robert George have formulated theories of basic premoral goods, made them fundamental to their ethics, but have tried to avoid a variety of pitfalls associated with other teleological ethical positions. For instance, they reject the idea that goods are commensurate, exchangeable, calculable, and perhaps reducible to some basic motivation such as pleasure (Freud), self-actualization (humanistic psychology), or a relatively short list of fungible desires (rational-choice theory). It is offensive to them to think that having a child might range on the same scale of satisfactions as a new car or a trip to the Bahamas and that one might justifiably forgo having the baby, possibly even intentionally abort it, if the costs were too high and the satisfactions of the alternatives more promising. Basic premoral goods for them are incommensurate, and it is immoral to sacrifice intentionally any of them. John Finnis's list of basic goods is similar, with only modest modifications, to the list found in Grisez and George. He argues for seven basic goods that are, he believes, fundamental aspects of human flourishing: "life, knowledge, play, aesthetic experience, sociability (friendship), practical reasonableness and religion."[20] These

20. John Finnis, *Fundamentals of Ethics* (Oxford: Clarendon, 1983), pp. 120-23.

goods are not derived from an analysis of human potentialities; they are self-evident "insights" into the overall experience of our inclinations in relation to truly satisfying objects. These goods are fundamental to fully formed ethical judgments; they require a theory of moral obligation in order to fairly take into account the basic goods of others. Hence, Finnis expands Kant's second formulation of the categorical imperative. Kant's principle of treating the humanity of other and self as an end and never merely as a means now contains in Finnis's reformulation an enlarged view of humanity. Humanity is more than rationality; it now includes practical reasonableness but also all the other basic premoral goods necessary for human flourishing.[21]

Since no one of these basic goods should ever be sacrificed intentionally on behalf of another, Finnis rejects all ethical egoist, utilitarian, or proportionalist perspectives that entertain the possibility of intentionally sacrificing in oneself or another person aesthetic experience for knowledge, or friendship for practical reasonableness.

One should note that natural law theorists such as Finnis, proportionalists, and utilitarians are all kinds of teleologists; they share the belief that rational discourse about the basic premoral goods of life is possible and that the task of morality is to actualize these goods. In Ricoeur's terms, they all see ethics as beginning with the search for the goods of life. On this point, they are different from strict Kantians, strict divine command theorists, and even intersubjective Kantians such as Habermas.[22] Since so much of public policy discourse is about choices in the realm of premoral goods, these natural law theorists at least have resources to join this conversation and often can compete with utilitarians in trying to shape public life. But Finnis and his colleagues are perceived as rigid. Neither their list of basic goods nor the idea of the incommensurability of goods has been successful in finding much acceptance in the larger public debates. But this does not necessarily mean that they are wrong; it may simply mean that sociologically, Americans are incurable consequentialists.

In spite of the seriousness of their insights about the role of basic premoral goods in ethical theory, the new natural law theorists make at least one major error. As Stephen Pope writes, "Grisez and Finnis fail to recognize that basic goods can conflict."[23] One can readily acknowledge

---

21. Finnis, *Fundamentals of Ethics*, p. 51.

22. Finnis, *Fundamentals of Ethics*, pp. 120-23.

23. Stephen Pope, *Human Evolution and Christian Ethics* (manuscript), chap. 10, p. 9.

with Grisez and Finnis, as I do, that life, knowledge, play, beauty, friendship, practical reason, and religion are basic goods and therefore should be respected and never freely or lightly infringed upon. But Pope is right: this overlooks the truth that under the conditions of finitude and sin, these goods are sometimes *forced* to conflict. For instance, under the conditions of material scarcity, the good of life can sometimes conflict with beauty and sometimes with play. Play can conflict with friendship if our friend is ill and needs our continuous care, which interferes with my weekly tennis appointment. The new natural law theorists use this position to take a stand against birth control by married couples, saying that couples should never use artificial birth control, even in cases where the wife's life is at risk. They see no conflict because one may never directly attack the basic goods at stake. But Pope writes,

> The "new natural law theory" takes as "self-evident" what many critics simply deny: that basic goods ought never be violated and that they cannot be subordinated to one another with ethical integrity. It is not apparent to many ethicists, for example, that procreation is a good that ought never be subordinated to the good of responsibly spacing the births within a family. Nor is it apparent to all responsible people that any and every use of artificial birth control damages the moral integrity of those married couples who use it.[24]

Grisez and Finnis may be right that none of these goods should ever be freely or flippantly sacrificed, but they are wrong in believing that responsible moral action does not, at least at times, call us to subordinate one basic good to another or to organize them in some working hierarchy.

Furthermore, the new natural law theorists, although right about their understanding of the role of basic premoral goods in moral theory, overestimate the self-evident nature of these goods. They also underestimate the role of history in transmitting them and science in helping us clarify them, especially when they conflict under the strain of various social contexts. In addition, Finnis's list leaves out a basic good that I have been pushing throughout this book — the good of attachment and connectedness and the role of kin altruism in bringing it about, or at least bringing it about in consistent and dependable ways. History and experience testify to the centrality of this good. In this sense, it is self-evident, as Finnis seems to believe that all basic goods are self-evident. But, as we have seen throughout these pages, science in the form of evolutionary

---

24. Pope, *Human Evolution and Christian Ethics* (manuscript), chap. 10, p. 10.

psychology, psychoanalysis, and other branches of moral psychology has a great deal to contribute to clarifying just how central this good happens to be for human flourishing.

Martha Nussbaum and Capabilities as Goods

A more successful view in academic and public policy circles can be seen in the moral philosophy of Martha Nussbaum. Nussbaum, like Finnis, is a neo-Aristotelian. This means that she is a kind of teleologist in that she believes the task of the moral life is to actualize within a moral framework the premoral goods of life. But her list is both similar to and different from that of Finnis. Nussbaum talks more about capabilities than goods; but that is the point — capabilities *are* basic goods. Her list includes life; health; bodily integrity; senses, imagination, and thought; emotions; practical reason; affiliation; other species; play; and control over one's environment.[25]

It is not my goal to give detailed discussions of either the rational-choice list, Finnis's list, or the list of Nussbaum. It should be noted, however, that they all affirm the goods of life and health. Finnis and Nussbaum also both mention practical reason; this good is conspicuously absent from the rational-choice list of economist Gary Becker. Finnis lists aesthetic experience and Nussbaum lists an analogous good which she calls play. Finnis lists friendship and Nussbaum affiliation; the rational-choice model ignores both friendship and aesthetic experience.

Nussbaum derives her list of capability goods from a combination of sources but mainly from the history of philosophy and recent trends in modern psychology. Her moral philosophy is highly dependent on the ancient tradition of philosophical psychology and the modern clinical and experimental psychologies. Her list of capabilities functions somewhat like Flanagan's Principal of Minimum Psychological Realism (PMPR). And, indeed, she uses modern psychology somewhat in the way that Ricoeur uses modern science in its distanciating and diagnostic modes. The logic of her argument is this: These are the goods of life. They should be pursued, but under the guidance of the Kantian categorical imperative.[26] In bringing together a thick theory of premoral goods contained by

25. Martha Nussbaum, *Sex and Social Justice* (New York: Oxford University Press, 1999), p. 42.

26. For an intersubjective reformulation of the Kantian categorical imperative, see Jürgen Habermas, *Moral Consciousness and Communication* (Cambridge, Mass.: MIT Press, 1990).

and guided by a Kantian universalized respect for others as ends, she has made an analogous move to the one taken by Finnis. Kant has been accepted but thickened to include judgments about human nonmoral and premoral goods.

Nussbaum's mixed-deontological principle of obligation, as William Frankena would call it,[27] has the following logic: I am morally obligated to respect both the selfhood of the other and the other's pursuit of these basic goods. It is also the case that the other is obligated to respect my selfhood and my pursuit of these basic goods. Immorality is defined as the pursuit of some of the goods of life at the expense of intentionally damaging other basic goods or intentionally undermining the ability of others to strive for and gain these goods. According to Nussbaum, societies throughout the world should be judged from the perspective of how they facilitate the pursuit of these capability goods and their actual accomplishment by individuals.[28] Obviously, as I have pointed out, this mixed-deontological view is also quite similar to the concept of equal-regard in Janssens's and Ricoeur's views of the Golden Rule (to do good to the other as one would wish the other to do good to oneself). In other words, Nussbaum and Finnis subject their respective theories of premoral goods to a variation of Ricoeur's deontological test.

Nussbaum interprets her list of capability goods with special interest in the well-being of women. These goods are disproportionately sacrificed by women throughout the world, and societies everywhere should be both critiqued and reformed to support better the attainment of these goods. Nussbaum has partnered with the economist Amartya Sen, who uses a similar list of capabilities, and along with Sen has had substantial influence on the development programs of the United Nations. Her work is increasingly influential on legal and political theory.

But her theories are not without criticism. Roman Catholic moral theologian Lisa Sowle Cahill appreciates Nussbaum's thought yet is critical of it. Cahill's critique of Nussbaum is instructive for illuminating the interaction of tradition and the human sciences in analyzing and ranking premoral goods. Cahill affirms Nussbaum's list of capabilities and their relevance to women, but she complains that Nussbaum excludes the capability of kin altruism — which for women takes the form of motherhood. (It is not clear why Cahill does not criticize Nussbaum also for neglecting

---

27. Frankena, *Ethics,* p. 43.

28. Martha Nussbaum, *Women and Human Development: A Capabilities Approach* (Cambridge: Cambridge University Press, 2000), pp. 73, 159.

the kin-altruistic capability of fatherhood.) Motherhood is a capability, says Cahill, and one that women throughout the world want to actualize. Both tradition (she has in mind especially the philosophical works of Aristotle and the theology of Thomas Aquinas) and the modern evolutionary disciplines, with their insights into the centrality of kin altruism, are together sources of Cahill's emphasis on the capability of parenthood. She asks, should not a society also be judged by and organized to support this capability as well as the other capabilities promoted by Nussbaum?[29]

Furthermore, Nussbaum can be criticized for the rather provincial way she has derived her list of capabilities. They seem to be distinctively Western and couched to meet the needs of educated Western professional women. Ricoeur, as you recall, first of all derives premoral goods from practices, in fact the history of practices of a culture as these would be interpreted in light of the classics of a culture. Nussbaum's method is far more eclectic and less attentive to history, even the history of Western cultures. Furthermore, I think that in addition to giving special attention to a particular culture's effective history, *one must also move into a dialogue with the history of practices and the narratives of other cultures.* Critical hermeneutics would not fault Nussbaum for starting with her own effective history, namely, Western culture and its classics. But it would fault her for interpreting this history too much from the perspective of the modern professional woman and then using her results to measure the needs of women around the world. Should we not have a more open-ended world comparative conversation with other cultures about the basic goods needed for human flourishing, rather than assuming that a list derived from almost exclusively Western sources, and unevenly derived at that, can function to settle these questions around the globe?

And finally, although both Nussbaum and Finnis should be complimented for giving deeper attention to the realm of premoral goods, neither of them has an explicit narrative envelope for their list of basic goods and capabilities. This is a loss since our cultural and religious narratives do a variety of things for our practical reason and its pursuit of the premoral goods of life. I turn to illustrating that point in the next section of this chapter — with special reference to one particular version of the Christian narrative.

---

29. Lisa Sowle Cahill, *Sex, Gender, and Christian Ethics* (Cambridge: Cambridge University Press, 1995).

Niebuhr, Premoral Goods, and the Christian Narrative

Reinhold Niebuhr needs to be brought back into this discussion of the kinds and grounds of human premoral goods. As I pointed out above, Niebuhr was not entirely without his indices of goods, but they were not well developed. I mentioned above how his views of the goodness of God's creation led him to see as ordinate the premoral goods of survival (life), attachment (similar to affiliation in Nussbaum and so important in the *Hardwired* report), material acquisition, group relations such as kinship, and sexual urges (which included for him both pleasure and the desire to have offspring). But he does not develop, and he makes little explicit use of, the goods he does occasionally recognize. It is my theory that this absence of a rich theory of premoral goods and his neglect of the question of incommensurability of goods explains why Niebuhr, in spite of the richness of his theological anthropology, is not used by today's theological ethicists in the close quarters of medical ethics, biomedical research, ecology, business ethics, or, for that matter, the more refined spheres of public policy — an area in which Niebuhr himself was profoundly interested. It is my view that Christian theological ethics (or practical theological ethics, as I sometimes call it) cannot enter those domains and command attention if it does not develop a more adequate approach to the premoral dimension of theological anthropology and moral theology.

I will not try to settle fully the question of an adequate model of premoral goods. I will, however, say this: developing such a model should first of all, following Ricoeur, begin with the demanding interpretive task of identifying how the normative texts of a tradition — in this case, Christianity — have defined and ranked these goods. Christian theology should then encourage other traditions to do the same. Then each tradition should enter a correlational dialogue with other traditions — and with the diagnostic and explanatory clarifications of the human sciences — in an effort to develop heuristic models of what human beings really need or require in order to live and flourish. They should also develop views about how these goods might be weighed and justly prioritized within various social and natural constraints. This view is close to, but finally very different from, the naturalism of what Owen Flanagan called an "ethics of human ecology." It is, rather, a critical hermeneutic or hermeneutic realist approach to an ethics and morality of human ecology — one subject to the deontological test of the love ethic of equal-regard and one both contextualized and relativized by the Christian narrative.

But what is the role of the Christian story, or some respectable version of it, in this daunting task? Notice that Finnis and Nussbaum at least have attempted to address two of the five dimensions that I believe are required for an adequate moral anthropology, namely, theories of premoral goods and a principle of obligation, the latter being acquired by both thinkers through reformulating the Kantian categorical imperative. But Finnis and Nussbaum lack what I have called a "narrative envelope"; they offer no story about the overall view of life and its purposes that they would hold out for human beings. It is my argument that a respectable narrative rendition of the Christian faith can provide needed ontological groundings, energizing motivations, and motifs of recovery that are essential for the realization of the premoral and moral norms of life. *The moral life is more than simply a matter of actualizing premoral values in a way that shows justice and respect to one's neighbor. It entails believing that the moral life is worthwhile to begin with, that one's neighbor is worth respecting, that one should persist when one is failing, and that one should have hope in the face of discouragement.*

At the conclusion of *A Fundamental Practical Theology* I listed and discussed a variety of ways that the Christian narrative influences what I then called "the inner core" of Christian ethics. This inner core of Christian ethics, as I have conceived it, has formal similarities to the mixed-deontological theory of obligation that we have found in Finnis and Nussbaum. It contains indices and hierarchies of premoral values surrounded and guided by a Kantian-like principle of justice. This principle is Kantian-like (rather than Kantian) because it need not be derived and formulated explicitly as Kant did his categorical imperative. It can also — and more profoundly — be based on the revealed New Testament love command or the biblical Golden Rule. I have used Paul Ricoeur and Louis Janssens to formulate the inner core of Christian ethics. Loving your neighbor as yourself means, according to them, doing *good* to your neighbor as you would have your neighbor do *good* unto you.[30] In this formulation of Christian neighbor love, mutual respect and justice guide the subordinate concern with actualizing the premoral goods. Janssens calls this, as we have seen, a love ethic of equal-regard. This mixed deontological view of Christian love as equal-regard is what I call the "inner core" of Christian ethics.

With this in mind, allow me to list the several ways that the Christian narrative envelope enriches the inner core of Christian love to both mani-

---

30. Janssens, "Norms and Priorities of a Love Ethics," pp. 207-38; Ricoeur, "The Teleological and Deontological Structures of Action," p. 109.

fest equal-regard and actualize the premoral goods of life, and to do so for both self and other, our community and other communities. In doing this, I will follow the narrative formulation of Niebuhr.

First and foremost, the metaphor of God the Creator bestows the ontological status of goodness on all the created world.[31] This is a testimony about the nature of being in relation to the finite givens of life. The implication of this is radical; it suggests that all fundamental human needs and tendencies and all basic patterns of the created natural world are good in the premoral sense of that word. "God saw everything he had made, and indeed, it was very good" (Gen. 1:31). Creation included the "waters under the sky" and the "dry land" (Gen. 1:9). It included "every living creature that moves" (v. 21) — "the great sea monsters," "every winged bird of every kind," "cattle and creeping things and wild animals . . . of every kind" (vv. 21, 24). It also included humankind, both male and female: "So God created humankind in his image, in the image of God he created them; male and female he created them" (v. 27). All of these were seen as *good* in the eyes of their Creator. The premoral goods listed in the various systems above, insofar as they can be shown to be truly basic, are endowed with a sacred valence from the standpoint of the Christian narrative of creation. In this sense, these goods deserve to be respected. In their basic status as elementary goods, they are blessed by God and should be respected by humans. The goodness of creation's ontological status before God is the grounds upon which any Christian ethics of human ecology should be based. This is an insight that Owen Flanagan cannot comprehend. Flanagan does not realize that his own advocacy of an ethic (or morality) of human ecology assumes a prior positive ontological valuation of all of creation — an ontological assumption he probably brings from his own childhood immersion in the Jewish, Christian, or Islamic doctrine or story about the goodness of creation. It is also an assumption he does not acknowledge.

The premoral goods of creation — the gifts of the Creator — deserve to be taken seriously as they enter into further moral refinement, prioritization, and organization. But to say that these goods deserve to be taken seriously and in this sense respected does not mean that they should be exempted from further moral organization and testing. Creation is good, but finite goods conflict. The natural conflict of finite premoral goods brings *natural evil*. And humans, who are both finite and free, become anx-

---

31. I develop the following points in Browning, *A Fundamental Practical Theology*, pp. 194-99.

ious and therefore succumb to sin — and this, in turn, brings *moral evil*. Moral evil deepens the conflict of premoral goods.

Second, the metaphor of God the Creator assigns a special status to humans as made in God's image. The core of moral reason requires respect for both other and self as ends in themselves who must never be reduced to means alone, never manipulated, and never commodified. The Jewish and Christian doctrine of the *imago Dei,* it should be noted, gives ultimate seriousness to the status of humans as ends. Kant grounded respect for other and self on the basis of human rationality. This does not necessarily contradict also grounding respect on the *imago Dei.* I hold that both approaches — the Kantian approach and the Judeo-Christian concept of the *imago Dei* — have validity for grounding respect for other and self. I would argue, however, that *grounding respect on the imago Dei is the more profound approach. Furthermore, grounding respect for persons on the primordial relation that all humans have with the divine requires that we demonstrate this respect in our lives with all the more seriousness — a seriousness warranted and required by the divine will. It is one thing to show respect because the other person is a rational animal; it is even more profound to demonstrate this respect because the other is a child of God.*

Third, the metaphor of God the Creator informs the love ethic of equal-regard about the limits of life. The narrative of creation tells us that humans are finite. This means, among other things, that they can never actualize all of life's premoral goods that they might hope for and pursue. One of the central dilemmas of life is that there are more goods to seek than can be actualized within the context of finitude. Furthermore, goods conflict, and in spite of Finnis's point that it is immoral to will intentionally the destruction of one of his basic goods,[32] I argue that the contingencies of life force humans nonetheless to make choices, create hierarchies, and establish priorities among and between the wide range of life's goods. We should not sacrifice the goods of life intentionally except when the relative weight of the various goods and the demands of the deontological test require it. It is partially because Nussbaum, for example, has no narrative that acknowledges life's finitude that she has neither easy answers nor consolation about the tragedy of conflicting goods and unfulfilled capabilities — the reality that actualizing some of our capabilities means almost certainly the sacrifice of others. The story of creation tells us that life is created good; it also tells us that humans are finite and will never know and enjoy all of these goods within the time and space of

---

32. Finnis, *Fundamentals of Ethics,* p. 126.

our this-worldly existence. This story tells us that we must have our theories of the goods of life, but that none of them can be absolutized, and all must be subservient to the principle (or kingdom) of love as equal-regard among all humans.

Fourth, the metaphor of God the Governor is also a part of the Christian story and contributes to the inner core of practical reason. Humans become anxious, and they sin. The premoral goods of life naturally conflict, and this can produce, as Louis Janssens aptly has said, premoral, ontic, and natural evil. But premoral evil — the natural conflict of finite goods in a finite world — is not itself sin and not itself moral evil. Sin and moral evil result from the misuse of our freedom and will. And it is in view of sin and moral evil that God in the Christian narrative emerges as a moral Governor. But I follow those who have spotted a congruence between God the Governor and the abstract character of Christian practical reason and love. God is a God of impartial justice but also a God who wishes for and works for our good in the premoral sense. We confronted this view of God in Chapter 3 in the Parable of the Last Judgment. This told the story of Jesus pronouncing who would be with him in paradise and who would not (Matt. 25:31-45). We are given the picture of Jesus appearing at the day of judgment accompanied by angels. He divides the people of the nations as a "shepherd separates the sheep from the goats" (Matt. 25:32). The good people inherit the kingdom of God and the evil ones do not. How did Jesus know the morally good people — the sheep? Because the morally good had unknowingly given him water, food, clothing, and friendship in his earthly existence when they were ministering to the needs of others. "Truly I tell you, just as you did it to one of the least of these who are members of my family, you did it to me" (Matt. 25:40). Jesus reveals to us a God who identifies with the teleological needs of all suffering persons, demands that we respond to these needs, and is then both the final observer and final recipient of all good deeds. In this way, God as Governor is a model of, perfect exemplification of, and a reinforcement for the inner core of Christian obligation, the mixed-deontological ethic of equal-regard defined as justly respecting both other and self while, and at the same time, actively working for the good of both other and self — indeed all selves.

Fifth, the doctrines of sin, grace, and forgiveness make it possible for the inner core of Christian obligation to become relatively free from the inordinate self-interest and self-justifying maneuvers that typically corrupt and distort human efforts to be just and to do good — to exercise the inner core of practical reason. Knowledge about the reality of sin, moreover, gives the Christian a tool of self-criticism. An awareness of sin should make us suspicious whether our claims to just and enhancing action are as pure as we might think. The acceptance of God's forgiveness and grace should liberate Christians to risk acting in love and justice with the promise that they are justified before God even if they fail and fall short.[33] Here the Pauline message of justification by faith is most relevant to the fulfillment of practical reason. Paul tells the Christian that accepting her justification through faith in God means "not to think of yourself more highly than you ought to think, but to think with sober judgment, each according to the measure of faith that God has assigned" (Rom. 12:3). Paul teaches that Christians when unburdened by the self-inflations of sin will be able to render better judgments — more sober judgments — in life's moral and practical matters. Furthermore, knowledge of forgiveness and grace gives us the courage to act more justly and to do more good than would happen if we were overly burdened with guilt and worried to justify ourselves in our every deed.

Sixth, the Christian narrative of the cross adds an element of supererogation to the practical rationality of a love ethic of equal-regard. The narrative of Jesus' passion — his confrontation with the Sadducees and Roman authorities, his trial and crucifixion, and the mingling of these events with the motifs of the Suffering Servant from Isaiah 53 — add an element of self-sacrificial love to Christian love as equal-regard. Neither a flat love ethic of equal-regard nor a mixed-deontological theory of the kind found in Finnis and Nussbaum can address the reality of the disruptions of sin and evil. The Christian story, as Louis Janssens interprets it, does not tell us to sacrifice ourselves aimlessly.[34] It does not even tell us, according to him, that self-sacrificial love is the center of the Christian life. Instead, it tells a profound story with the following point: in order to live a love ethic of equal-regard, one must time and again be willing to go the extra mile — to work hard, endure, and even sacrifice — not as an end in itself but as a means to restoring love as equal-regard. The Christian story tells about the role of sacrifice in renewing the core ethic of mutuality and equal-regard, the principle of Ricoeur's deontological test. Or, to say it differently, the call for self-sacrificial love helps us to implement and live by the deontological test, *and to do so time and time again,* even in the face of failure and opposition. This, I submit, is the proper meaning of the Christian doctrine of the cross. And this is why the sacrificial giving

33. Browning, *A Fundamental Practical Theology,* p. 198.
34. Janssens, "Norms and Priorities of a Love Ethics," p. 228.

of the cross reinvigorates the Christian life of equal-regard and the exercise of practical reason required to live by that principle. The mixed-deontological principle of obligation found in both Finnis and Nussbaum, devoid as they are of narratives of the cross and theories of forgiveness and grace, has nothing to say about how their ethic is sustained and renewed in light of sin and brokenness.

These six ways in which the envelope of the Christian narrative informs the inner core of Christian practical reason and love help us see the potential power of Christian ethics in public discourse. It is clear that the narrative adds something substantive to Christian love and the reasoning required to implement it. But I have also argued that the inner core of Christian ethics is thoroughly rational and can give public reasons for the positions it advances and defends. The Christian narrative envelope is not like the envelope containing the Christmas messages from our best of friends; it cannot be thrown away after the inner message is read. But the narrative envelope and its core ethic, as mutually qualifying as they actually are, *can be* distinguished from one another. The envelope strengthens and deepens the inner core, but it does not destroy the rationality of the Christian love ethic of equal-regard. That moral rationality can do work in the public arenas of a pluralistic society.

Conclusion

These are some of the ways that the Christian narrative informs and enriches the more directly ethical dimension of human existence. The Christian narrative, all by itself and devoid of the specificity of a principle of obligation and a view of the premoral goods of life, can be vague and indeterminate about what it is that we should do to address the ethical challenges of life. Indeed, it may be the contemporary drift toward a vague narrative ethics that accounts for the church's marginalization in public life. This may also explain the inability of the church to address successfully moral issues such as homosexuality, abortion, assisted suicide, divorce, and marital disruption which beset its own confessional life. *One cannot develop a Christian moral psychology without also developing a substantive Christian theological ethics.* In this chapter, I have tried to fill out and amplify the substantive Christian ethic that seems required by my view of the relation of moral psychology and Christian ethics.

Christian anthropology is multidimensional, and so is the Christian story when properly grasped and told. I have tried to describe this multidimensionality. Most likely, readers will sense that this was a tentative step toward a new Christian humanism — a Christianity that includes within the themes of creation, judgment, and salvation a proximate concern for human flourishing. If this is what readers conclude, they will be right.

Chapter 10

Violence, Authority, and Communities of Reconstruction

I t is now time to return to the issue of authoritative communities. Moral communities form moral people. But what is a moral community and how do they do their work? *Hardwired to Connect,* the study I have been in dialogue with throughout this book, does not use the phrase "moral communities." It uses the concept of "authoritative communities."[1] Implicitly, I have been working to define the connection between authoritative and moral communities throughout these pages. Much of the talk about critical hermeneutics, the thickness of moral experience, teleology, the premoral values of attachment and kin altruism, distanciation and diagnosis, the deontological test, and finally the role of narrativity in traditions — all of these concepts in one way or another are designed to help us understand authoritative communities that are also genuinely productive moral communities forming moral individuals. In this chapter, I will try to make more sense of that concept by both discussing the topic of violence and presenting an illustration of an authoritative community working to cope with violence.

Our primary topic will be youth violence. Two questions will be asked and two hypotheses will be advanced as possible answers to these questions. The two questions are these: (1) What are the features of modern life contributing to the reality of violence by and between youth? (2) What is the most comprehensive solution to this problem in light of the answer to the first question? Of course, I approach these issues not as a social scientist but as a practical theological ethicist — one who uses the social sci-

---

1. *Hardwired to Connect: The New Scientific Case for Authoritative Communities* (New York: Institute for American Values, 2003), pp. 33-34.

ences in close association with the intellectual resources of Western religious traditions. This chapter addresses the scene of youth violence in the United States, but it may throw light on the violence of youth in other countries as well.

The two answers go like this. First, the most comprehensive reason behind violence among American youth is the deterioration of the voluntary and face-to-face institutions of civil society. It should be noted in passing that crime in nearly all categories has declined in the United States over the last seven years, including crime by youth, although it is still significantly higher than four decades ago.[2] Another wave of increased criminal activity by youth is predicted, however, and almost all experts would admit that even with the recent declines, the level is still unacceptably high. The second answer entails the following assertion: The most inclusive strategy for curing youthful violence will entail the revival of the institutions of American civil society — in other words, its authoritative or moral grassroots communities. This renewal necessitates a new theory of authority, what I will call a hermeneutical theory of authority. This renewal must also involve a fresh understanding of how the state and the market should relate to and be nourished by the institutions of civil society.

Civil society is made up of community organizations, clubs, churches, fraternal orders, women's societies, labor unions, political societies, economic societies such as Chambers of Commerce, and families in their conjugal and extended forms. The concept of civil society was first developed by thinkers of the Scottish Enlightenment such as Adam Smith, Adam Ferguson, and David Hume.[3] It was conceived as a realm of communal interaction which created social rules outside of the dictates of state authorities. The rule-making power of civil society was thought to be a defense against the spreading tyranny of the state. When the concept first emerged, civil society was represented as necessarily flourishing alongside the rise of capitalist markets. In fact, it was seen as a source of the moral sensibilities required to constrain the excesses of unchecked market greed. Civil society helped make the market work — indeed, helped make it more moral.

It was soon understood, however, that the market, as well as the state, could be an enemy of the associations of civil society — what we today

2. David Vise and Lorraine Adams, "From Bad to Worse Than We Thought: Despite Reports to the Contrary, a New Study Says Violent Incidents Are Up 40 Percent Since 1969," *The Washington Post Weekly Edition* (December 13, 1999), p. 29.

3. Alan Wolfe, *Whose Keeper? Social Science and Moral Obligation* (Berkeley: University of California Press, 1989), p. 14.

sometimes call the voluntary or private sector. The time pressures, the drive for efficiency, and the relentless means-end logics of market forces can undermine the spontaneous, uncoerced, and reciprocal interactions required to produce workable moral practices and rules governing everyday communal life. Hence, it became increasingly clear that as civil society could function as a defense against the spread of state coercion, it needed also to function as a bulwark against the market's tendency to reduce daily life to the utilities of economic exchange.

Alan Wolfe has built on the work of Jürgen Habermas to show why civil society is in decline.[4] In Habermas's two-volume *Theory of Communicative Action,* he uses the metaphor of "colonization" to describe the process whereby the state from one side and the market from the other are increasingly taking over, at least in the West, the organization of spheres of daily life formerly ordered by civil society.[5] Colonization is a metaphor for a process whereby the respective technical rationalities of market and government increasingly dominate the value and authority patterns of civil society, patterns which have their origin in tradition or in the face-to-face interactions of everyday life.

Wolfe is particularly suggestive in showing how colonization works in the sphere of the family. The United States is his leading candidate for illustrating how market forces increasingly reduce the intimate affairs of family life to the cost-benefit logics of the market. The rational-choice school of economics, which I reviewed in the last chapter, not only is adept at explaining economically induced family change, but, Wolfe believes, is a subtle moral leader in justifying these changes.[6] Rational-choice theorists argue that family changes — increasing divorce, lowering birth rates, rising rates of out-of-wedlock births — are due largely to changes in market forces.[7] The increased participation of women and mothers in the wage market, itself induced by the growing needs of the market, may be the single most powerful explanation of family instability. Their participation produces less economic dependence of women on male breadwinners, and thus makes it possible both to delay marriage and to divorce more freely when difficulties arise. Rational-choice economics demon-

---

4. Wolfe, *Whose Keeper?* pp. 17, 20.

5. Jürgen Habermas, *Theory of Communicative Action,* vols. 1-2 (Boston: Beacon, 1984, 1987).

6. For a closer look at rational-choice economics, see Gary S. Becker, *A Treatise on the Family* (Cambridge, Mass.: Harvard University Press, 1981, 1991), and Richard Posner, *Sex and Reason* (Cambridge, Mass.: Harvard University Press, 1992).

7. Becker, *Treatise on the Family,* pp. 238-76.

strates that the incursion of market patterns of decision-making into family life causes children increasingly to be perceived as economic liabilities. Children are costly; in contrast to agricultural societies where children become farm laborers and old-age insurance, children in market economies make few financial contributions to their parents' welfare. Furthermore, in market economies where both fathers and mothers work outside the home, there is less family supervision of children at all ages. Declining parental presence with their children may be one reason, among many others, why there is so much violence by and between youth in American society.[8]

Finally, market forces have drawn factories away from the inner city, thereby leaving, as William Julius Wilson has argued, males residing in these areas unable to form families because they cannot support them.[9] The increase of violence in American society seems largely to be occurring among young males, and much of this is among the deprived and isolated groups making up the inner city. Father-absence is also a major factor behind this rise in male violence among the young.[10] But behind inner-city fathers' increasing inability to form families and be consistent parents may be the deeper efficiency-driven goals of the market, which led industry to abandon the city in the first place for the greener pastures of a more educated workforce in the suburbs. The separation of fathers from their children also takes the form of migrations by adult males to cities, mining centers, and industrial centers where work is more readily available. This is often the form market forces take in Africa and Central and Latin America.

Wolfe points to an analogous yet different story in Sweden and other Scandinavian countries — his nomination for best example of how state bureaucracy can colonize the family. In these countries, public support of families has increased dramatically since the 1960s. From Wolfe's perspective, this has resulted in a significant transfer of family care to state care and a decreasing sense of intergenerational solidarity between parents and children, old and young. The enormous expansion of day-care institutions, the growth of child allowances, and liberal parental leave programs have contributed to better financial security for single mothers and their children — certainly better than in the United States.

8. Amitai Etzioni, *The Spirit of Community* (New York: Crown, 1993), p. 64.

9. William Julius Wilson, *The Truly Disadvantaged* (Chicago: University of Chicago Press, 1987).

10. Louis Sullivan, "Fatherless Families," *Television and Families* (summer 1992): 34-36.

Valuing such supports, as I do, should not blind us to the way modernization as bureaucratic colonization undermines families and potentially increases violence. The Swedish measures have not enhanced family stability. Divorce doubled between 1960 and 1980 in Sweden, Denmark, and Norway, and in 1984, 46 percent of all children were born out of wedlock in Sweden.[11] The state, no less than the market, may function unwittingly to undermine the cohesion-building and authority-generating interactions of civil society. The spread of the state into the caring functions of families has been accompanied in these countries by a significant rise in teen alcoholism, suicide, murder, and breaking and entering. (Breaking and entering has quadrupled in all three countries from 1950 to 1970.)[12] A recent large-scale Swedish study that tracked about a million children for a decade gives us startling data on the strengths and weaknesses of the health of Swedish children. The children of single-parent families were twice as likely as their counterparts in two-parent families to develop serious psychiatric illnesses and addictions later in life.[13] Experts doubt that the lack of income is the explanation for this difference since Sweden has the best welfare and parental support system in the world. Neither poverty nor gross differences in income can be the explanation. It seems that family disruption itself — divorce and nonmarital births and the difficulties they present single parents — must explain most of the difference. And the increase of divorce and out-of-wedlock births in Sweden may have occurred not as a result of market rearrangement of family dependencies, but because of state interference in these traditional dependencies. Wolfe summarizes the effects of the growing power of the state in the Scandinavian welfare programs when he writes, "In turning some of the functions of the family over to government, Scandinavian societies have strengthened some of its aspects, especially its level of economic support, but weakened others, especially its ability to serve as a source of moral rules."[14]

In summary, the spreading influence of market and state may in many advanced industrial countries be the most comprehensive factor behind the decline of civil society and the rise of problem behavior among the young.

11. Wolfe, *Whose Keeper?* p. 140.

12. Wolfe, *Whose Keeper?* pp. 147-50.

13. Gunilla Ringbäck Weitoft, Anders Hjern, Bengt Haglund, and Mans Rosen, "Mortality, Severe Morbidity, and Injury in Children Living with Single Parents in Sweden: A Population-Based Study," *The Lancet* 361 (January 25, 2003): 289-95.

14. Wolfe, *Whose Keeper?* pp. 146-47.

Civil Society and the Multiple Sources of Violence

To illustrate how the institutions of civil society function to inhibit violence, we must become more concrete about the various forms violence takes. An article titled "Victimization of Children" by David Finkelhor and Jennifer Dziuba-Leatherman develops an interesting typology of victimization done by, to, and between youth. These authors distinguish between pandemic, acute, and extraordinary forms of victimization.[15] Pandemic refers to the range of everyday victimizations such as sibling assault, physical punishment by parents, theft, and peer assault — victimizations which attract little public attention but which children and youth fear. Acute victimization refers to dramatic forms which gain more public attention such as rape, physical abuse, neglect, or sexual abuse. Finally, extraordinary victimization refers to domestic violence, stranger abduction, and homicide — acts which gain great public attention but which, in comparison to other forms of victimization, are less frequent.[16]

These distinctions are useful to illustrate how the weakening of civil society aggravates these various forms of violence and victimization. When civil society declines, there is less adult presence working to nurture and guide the affections and frustrations of youth that give rise to pandemic victimization. Less presence from, less attachment to, and less guidance by trusted adults fails to inhibit the transformation of pandemic violence into acute and extraordinary forms of criminal activity. There is little evidence of an innate drive toward violence of the kind that Freud believed existed.[17] But William James, decades ago, anticipated the direction of recent research when he posited potentials for reactive violence. These reactive potentials are inhibited when strong, affective attachments exist between children and stable adults and peers who are also properly guided.[18] When the institutions of civil society (such as family, church, and adult-sponsored organizations) become distant or nonexistent, affectional connections of youth with parents and neighbors weaken and function to inhibit reactive violence less effectively. This is likely to be the prime factor behind the increase of acute

15. David Finkelhor and Jennifer Dziuba-Leatherman, "Victimization of Children," *American Psychologist* (March 1994): 173-83.

16. Finkelhor and Dziuba-Leatherman, "Victimization of Children," p. 176.

17. Sigmund Freud, *Beyond the Pleasure Principle* (New York: W. W. Norton, 1959), pp. 33-37.

18. William James, *The Principles of Psychology,* vol. 2 (New York: Dover, 1950), p. 397. See also Don S. Browning, *Pluralism and Personality* (Lewisburg, Pa.: Bucknell University Press, 1980), p. 169.

and extraordinary acts of violence done by and between youth. Adolescence and young adulthood are commonly understood in the social sciences as a time when ego controls can be flooded by sexual and aggressive feelings, a time when identity formation is still unfinished, and a time of immense influence exerted by peer groups.[19] Affectional and restraining ties with the figures of civil society have traditionally functioned to inhibit anti-social behavior that flows from such feelings. If civil society is too weak and these ties too anemic, inhibitions will be ineffective. When such institutions are strong, then the youth attached to them and influenced by them will actually flourish, as we saw in Chapter 4 through Christian Smith's research on religious youth in the United States.

Some Inadequate Solutions

A 1994 issue of *The Public Interest* presented a symposium involving a variety of social scientists on the question of youth crime, particularly crime among black youth. The symposium was organized around some provocative proposals advanced by John J. DiIulio, at that time professor of politics and public affairs at Princeton University. Professor DiIulio argued that the main victims of black crime in the United States, much of which is perpetrated by black youth, are other black persons. The main beneficiaries of a tougher policy controlling black violence would be other black people — especially the great host of nonviolent black youth. He wrote,

> At the interracial extremes, the chances that a black male teenager would be victimized by violent crime were 6.2 times that of a white adult male, 7.5 times that of a white adult female, 18.8 times that of an elderly white male (age 65 and over), and 37.6 times that of an elderly white female.[20]

At the time of this symposium, DiIulio turned to law enforcement for the solution.[21] He did not simply mean by this, however, more police on

19. Erik Erikson, *Childhood and Society* (New York: W. W. Norton, 1963), pp. 261-63.

20. John DiIulio Jr., "The Question of Black Crime," *The Public Interest* 117 (fall 1994): 5.

21. It is interesting to note that since that time, DiIulio has come to believe that religious experience mediated by churches is the single most potent force for combating teen violence. In accordance with this, he was appointed as director of the Office of Community and Faith-Based Initiatives in the administration of George W. Bush. He soon resigned, however, for personal reasons and with some frustration over the slowness of the political process.

the streets and more certainty of arrests. He meant more prisons and longer terms so that violent criminals do not quickly return to inner-city communities to prey on poor but law-abiding citizens.[22]

Other members of the symposium were not so happy with this approach. Economist Glenn Loury of Boston University pointed out that black inner-city residents resist such solutions for the simple reason that many of the young boys and men sent to jail would be their own sons, nephews, and next-door neighbors — real people who are also objects of their affections.[23]

Loury's note of caution was reinforced by Northwestern University professor Paul Robinson. Robinson believed that securing the streets of troubled neighborhoods and lengthening the sentences of violent youth would indeed help, but only modestly. Such measures are enormously expensive and concentrate on offenders only after they have committed the violent acts.[24] They do not ask or seek to answer the deeper question: "Why do the vast majority of people, even in difficult situations of need and temptation and even when unlikely to get caught and punished, remain law-abiding?"[25]

Robinson's answer to his question was important but inadequate. He wanted to increase public respect for the criminal justice system's moral authority and to increase the public's internalization of the norms contained in the criminal law codes. He was not out to make people more moral in the religious, cultural, or social sense of that word. He wanted something far more basic. Furthermore, it was something government should do rather than the religious, cultural, and educational institutions of civil society. This modest task would entail having "people internalize the most elemental moral values, by which I mean the prohibitions against violence and dishonesty that have wide support within society."[26]

Robinson's emphasis on a modest role for government in teaching elementary moral respect does not contradict my primary point — that the voluntary institutions of civil society are the primary creators and carriers of both the content of and capacity for civic virtue, even its most elemental forms. Government will have little likelihood of success as moral educator if not reinforced by attachments and connections with family, institutions, and authoritative communities of civil society.

22. DiIulio, "Question of Black Crime," p. 15.
23. Glenn Loury, "Listen to the Black Community," *The Public Interest* 117 (fall 1994): 35.
24. Paul Robinson, "A Failure of Moral Conviction," *The Public Interest* 117 (fall 1994): 43.
25. Robinson, "A Failure of Moral Conviction," pp. 43-44.
26. Robinson, "A Failure of Moral Conviction," p. 45.

Toward a Critical Hermeneutical Model of Authority

How can the institutions of civil society reclaim their authority while simultaneously affirming and limiting the moral logics of both the liberal state and liberal market? In order for the institutions of civil society to be strong, they must reconstitute their moral authority on a new basis. The authors of *Hardwired to Connect* have, as we have seen, argued for the rebirth of authoritative communities. These communities are not just highly cohesive with a great sense of tradition; they must also, according to *Hardwired,* encourage genuine "spiritual and religious development."[27] These communities should be warm and nurturing, thereby facilitating connections and attachments. They should establish clear limits to acceptable behavior. Most of the leadership should be in the hands of nonspecialists — average people who cannot hide behind the guise of objectivity and detachment. These communities should be multigenerational and enjoy a sense of "shared memory."[28] They must be democratic communities which also treat all children and youth as persons of "equal dignity." In short, they should be communities that abide by the "principle of neighbor love."[29] The report acknowledges that this principle can be anchored by reference to the *imago Dei,* thought by Jews and Christians to be reflected in all humans. But *Hardwired* shows surprising sophistication for a statement written primarily by social scientists when it acknowledges that there are also secular ways to ground the dignity of all humans. The study invokes Kant in asserting that neighbor love and the Golden Rule do not necessarily presuppose religious reasoning for their validity. The authors write, "the German philosopher Immanuel Kant, in the second formulation of his so-called 'categorical imperative,' famously insisted that 'all rational beings stand under the law that each of them should treat himself and all others never merely as means but always at the same time as an end in himself.'"[30]

Hardwired struggles to develop a theory of authoritative communities that comes close to what Ricoeur would envision if communities practiced his critical hermeneutics. The report knows that there are examples of "immoral, and therefore harmful" communities in civil society, communities that are authoritarian but not authoritative. "An example," the

27. *Hardwired to Connect,* p. 39.
28. *Hardwired to Connect,* p. 37.
29. *Hardwired to Connect,* p. 39.
30. *Hardwired to Connect,* p. 39.

study suggests, "would be the Ku Klux Klan."[31] Furthermore, the report makes a very important admission which reveals that its authors know there is more to authoritative communities than long and shared memories that pass the deontological test of equal human dignity. It goes on to say, "Many — probably most — real-life authoritative communities will clearly embody and seek to pass on to children numerous other moral norms and specific spiritual and religious values that richly add to, without negating, the foundational moral principle."[32] But that is the point. What more is needed? And does *Hardwired* fully understand the more?

I propose that the report needs a full-blown critical hermeneutics that would provide a model of authority built on the task of interpreting yet critiquing the classics of a religio-cultural tradition. A critical hermeneutic theory of authority would build, as I have argued throughout these pages, on the philosophy of continental thinkers such as Gadamer, Ricoeur, and Habermas as well as that of American pragmatists such as Charles Peirce, William James, John Dewey, and Richard Bernstein.[33] Hermeneutic philosophy sees all human knowing as a type of dialogue or conversation. To understand something is to grasp how we have already been shaped by what Gadamer called the "effective history" of past events, texts, and cultural monuments.[34] As we have seen, by effective history he is referring to how the classics of a cultural tradition (for example, the Bible, Aristotle, Plato, Locke, Kant) shape the experience of individuals within that tradition, even if these individuals have little direct knowledge of them.[35] Interpreting such texts — such cultural monuments — is a process of dialogue and reconstruction. It is also the source of the *shared memories* that *Hardwired* believes must characterize every authoritative community. Interpreting this heritage as a community is in fact a dialogue; it involves bringing our questions as a community of inquiry to the classic texts and monuments of a culture. Since our questions are shaped par-

---

31. *Hardwired to Connect,* p. 40.

32. *Hardwired to Connect,* p. 40.

33. For a general introduction to hermeneutic theory, see Hans-Georg Gadamer, *Truth and Method* (New York: Crossroad, 1982), and Jürgen Habermas, *Knowledge and Human Interests* (Boston: Beacon, 1971). For the more specific idea of critical hermeneutics, see Paul Ricoeur, *Hermeneutics and the Human Sciences* (Cambridge: Cambridge University Press, 1981). For a review of the point of contact between hermeneutic philosophy and the pragmatism of Peirce and James, see Richard Bernstein, *Beyond Objectivism and Relativism* (Philadelphia: University of Pennsylvania Press, 1983).

34. Gadamer, *Truth and Method,* pp. 267-74.

35. Gadamer, *Truth and Method,* pp. 253-58.

tially by how these texts have entered into our experience, our dialogue with the classics is a conversation with meanings and histories to which we already, to some extent, belong.[36]

Finally, this process of interpreting our traditions is, according to the hermeneutical model, also a process of reconstruction. The meanings that rule our lives are always in some way a synthesis between the meanings of past cultural monuments and our present experiences and questions. Our images of authority are always shifting, always a synthesis between current problematics and inherited ideals. Hence, neither the present nor the past rules supreme in the hermeneutic model of understanding. Its model of authority is based on dialogue.

It is the hermeneutical model of authority that should guide the revitalization of the institutions of civil society and the institutions which socialize the young. This model steers a course between the individualism which presently dominates our socialization goals and an emphasis on rigid authority that is now outdated but which certain groups in our society want to reassert.

The organizations of civil society function better when they recognize their tradition-saturated character. In the face-to-face groups of civil society, this process of dialogue and reinterpretation of the classic texts, customs, and rituals of the past can occur with the intimacy and immediacy necessary to appeal to the imagination of the young. Dialogue in the face-to-face situation can elicit their participation and help buffer the transitions from childhood to adulthood and from domestic space to public space.

In addition, more than is often realized, the institutions of civil society help individuals and families confront new problems and reconstruct their traditions to deal with them. They do this by making use of the multiple rationalities which traditions contain. These rationalities can be analyzed and tested in relation to the more articulate modes of thought found in philosophy and the social sciences. The rationalities embedded in traditions are often difficult to detect; they are generally surrounded by narrative and symbolic modes of thinking which obscure their presence. These modes are what I have called the narrative or visional dimension of practical reason. These narratives and symbols package complex rationalities in emotively powerful rhetorical forms which elicit commitment and energy. *Hardwired* has nothing to say about this narrative level of tradi-

---

36. See Paul Ricoeur's discussion of "belonging" in hermeneutic theory, "Hermeneutics and the Critique of Ideology," *Hermeneutics and the Human Sciences,* pp. 64-65.

tion. This is a serious omission if one really wants to understand how authoritative communities become effective.

I am not saying, of course, that all tradition-laden modes of thought contain sophisticated rationalities of a moral and nonmoral kind. Some do not. But many do. This is why they can often speak to and cooperate with more explicitly rational policy perspectives. This is also why their perspectives can frequently conflict with more academically informed policy perspectives. Tradition-saturated rationalities may be different but that does not mean they are any less rational. By tradition-saturated rationalities, I mean, in short, the thick multidimensionality I have been speaking about — the logics of our various practices, the identifiable premoral goods that they contain, the narratives that surround them, the deontological test that they require, and the mediated strategy that Ricoeur associates with the final judgments of wisdom.

An American Black Church as
Tradition-Saturated Authoritative Community

In the paragraphs that follow, I will describe a black congregation located on the south side of Chicago. It is an example of an authoritative community. It also, more than the church members themselves would ever imagine, illustrates features of a community of interpretation guided by a critical hermeneutics in Ricoeur's sense of the term. It has a distinctive way of addressing the violence of young black men and their alienation from families and community. The problem of youth violence in the United States is not simply a black problem. It is well known, however, that discrimination and economic deprivation in the black community have compounded the disruptions of market and state in establishing the conditions for black youth to resort to crime. Many black churches, however, have made exemplary responses to this situation.

To illustrate how affect, narrative, and various rationalities are woven together in communities of tradition, I will analyze this congregation from the perspective of how four popular but competing theories of socialization would interpret what is happening in this church. These are (1) authoritarianism, (2) the psychoanalytic theory of socialization, (3) the distortion-free communicative theories of Habermas and Kohlberg, and (4) the narrative theories of Alasdair MacIntyre and Stanley Hauerwas. I will say more about these alternatives when I use them to analyze this church.

The Apostolic Church of God had approximately four thousand members when I first started studying it during the autumn of 1988.[37] For ten months I attended Sunday morning services, Wednesday evening Bible study, and had long interviews with its pastor, Bishop Arthur Brazier, and many of its lay leaders and members. The Apostolic Church is a member of a rapidly growing denomination called the Pentecostal Assemblies of the World. It practices glossolalia (but only moderately), maintains a strict moral code, and forbids drinking and smoking, premarital sex, and spouse abuse. Divorce is strongly discouraged. It is taught that a person who is "sanctified" by the Holy Spirit — as members of the Apostolic Church are supposed to be — should never resort to any of these behaviors.

Over the last decade, Apostolic Church has grown to over twenty thousand members. It has been a church with a strong social ministry to the Woodlawn and wider Chicago communities. Attention to families is at the core of Apostolic Church's ministry. Within this, a ministry to men — husbands, fathers, young men, and young boys — receives more attention still. When I first studied the church in 1988 to 1989, about 40 percent of the members of this church were males under the age of fifty — an unusually high number. My hunch is that in the meantime, the percentage of younger men has either stayed the same or increased. These ministries to men are supported by a strong family ideology that contains an analysis of the situation of black families and problems of males within the black family. It also contains a theological response to these situations.

Bishop Brazier preaches regularly about the problems of inner-city black families, such as discrimination and what it has done to undercut the economic power of black men and their ability to form families. In addition, he is aware of how market rationality drove many businesses out of the inner city to the easier living and better-educated labor sources of the suburbs.[38] His sermons and writings reveal an accepting yet cautious attitude toward government bureaucracies in the form of welfare programs, but he is also aware of how they can create dependency.

Brazier does not dwell for long in his sermons and writings on any of these external "causes" of the problems of the inner city. He preaches instead a message of empowerment and responsibility. This message is especially addressed to black male youth and young adults.

The heart of Apostolic Church's theology of male responsibility comes

---

37. For the original case study of Apostolic Church of God, see Don Browning, *A Fundamental Practical Theology* (Minneapolis: Fortress, 1991), pp. 243-77.

38. See Wilson, *The Truly Disadvantaged.*

from a passage from the pseudo-Pauline letter to the Ephesians. The verses 5:21-33 are a classic text which informed the family theory of much of Western thought from Augustine and Roman Catholic canon law to the views of Aquinas and Luther. These passages are complex. They begin with the injunction that husbands and wives should be "subject to one another" (Eph. 5:21). Although this egalitarian note is followed by the assertion that the husband is head of the wife as Christ is head of the church, this statement is followed by still another that overturns the logic of antique patriarchy. The male as head is now interpreted as servant rather than dominating agent. "Husbands, love your wives, just as Christ loved the church and gave himself up for her" (Eph. 5:25). Brazier interprets this to mean that the good husband and father should build his authority on servanthood. He is, indeed, to identify with the figure of Jesus and be a sacrificial servant to his wife and family as Christ was to the church.

The phenomenology of religion, as presented by my former colleague Mircea Eliade, throws light on how this religious drama, so often enacted at Apostolic Church, can affect the men of that congregation.[39] The young male — potential husband and father — is asked to identify with the charismatic religious figure, Jesus, who is in turn understood as a human manifestation of the "holy" and "sacred" powers of the universe. Through this identification, the young male recapitulates the *axis mundi* — the dramatic action at the center of the world. In reenacting the Ephesians passage, the ontology of customary male authority is reversed. Rather than being grounded on heroic street virtues of physical strength, cunning, and seductive prowess, male authority is grounded now on an ontology of peace and sacrificial love. Male headship is interpreted as male responsibility. It becomes the idea that husbands and fathers should take the lead in responsible action in family and secular vocation. This emphasis on responsibility in one's secular vocation also frees males to compete in the market — even conform to its rational-choice logics — as long as this competition is constrained by the moral restrictions of Apostolic Church.

Apostolic Church and Four Models of Socialization

My purpose in telling the story of Apostolic Church is not to present an apology for its confessional religious stance. My goal, instead, is to illustrate the socializing power of such authoritative communities in civil soci-

---

39. Mircea Eliade, *Patterns in Comparative Religion* (Cleveland: World, 1963), pp. 3, 99-100.

ety. Furthermore, I want to demonstrate how religious ideologies can function both to articulate and to reinforce types of rationality which can be defended on more directly philosophical grounds. Since Apostolic Church reverses the grounds for male authority, building it on self-giving love and servanthood rather than on physical strength and cunning, it is not incompatible with the liberal moral principles of equality, justice, and mutual respect both between family members and between the family and the outside world. These points will be clearer if we examine Apostolic Church from the perspective of four competing theories of moral socialization.

At first glance, Apostolic Church might appear as an example of an *authoritarian,* rather than an authoritative, religious institution, with powerful devices for producing conformity to doctrinal and behavioral expectations. To make this judgment, however, would be to overlook two important observations: (1) that its sources of authority are the classic texts of a complex religious tradition, and (2) that Bishop Brazier does as much to elicit participation in an interpretive process as he does to set forth an authoritative position that cannot be questioned. Bible-study groups are in abundance at Apostolic Church. Brazier is not the only interpreter, although he is clearly the chief leader of the interpretive process. Because this group interpretive process is visible at Apostolic Church, certain reflective movements occur there which justify using this church as an example of a critical hermeneutical model of authority. I will say more about this below.

Second, the *psychoanalytic theory of identification* accounts for some of the socialization power of Apostolic Church.[40] The power of Apostolic Church is not just its ideals but how it motivates people toward these ideals. Bishop Brazier himself is an attractive and articulate man with whom young black men easily connect and identify. He enters into direct personal relations with black males and encourages a variety of programs (father-son breakfasts, camping weekends with young males and their fathers or mentors, special male worship services) which permit a young male to connect more deeply with his father, if he has one, and also identify with older males who may function as father substitutes. Fatherly affection and attachment are the central motifs of these gatherings. This mirrors the psychoanalytic emphasis on the importance of affective attachments as prerequisites for superego formation.[41] As we have seen, neuroscience and evolutionary psychology have made their own contribu-

---

40. For more on the psychoanalytic theory of identification, see Sigmund Freud, *The Ego and the Id* (London: Hogarth, 1957), pp. 34-53.

41. See Freud, *The Ego and the Id,* pp. 42-43.

tions to attachment theory. Yet, because of the high moral expectations which the fathers at the church hold out for young boys and men, the young clearly sense that certain behaviors on their part will lead to the displeasure of the male leaders of the church. Indeed, certain actions can lead to loss of church membership.

Third, it would be misleading to suggest that psychoanalysis, neuroscience, and evolutionary psychology alone can account for the socializing power of Apostolic Church. It would seem at first glance, however, that Apostolic Church's socialization of young males is completely antithetical to the idea of moral rationality entailed in the theories of Lawrence Kohlberg and Jürgen Habermas or in Ricoeur's theory of the deontological test.[42] Kohlberg, Habermas, and Ricoeur, although certainly not identical in their approaches, share neo-Kantian understandings of moral thinking. In addition, Kohlberg has been directly influential on Habermas's theory of communicative rationality and the socialization processes which bring it about.

But Habermas brings a dialogical perspective to Kohlberg and Ricoeur's deontological test which we need to review in the context of our discussion of Apostolic Church. Both Kohlberg and Habermas play down the role of tradition in developing moral rationality. In addition, both deemphasize the role of attachment or Freudian identification in moral socialization.[43] For them, moral development is a process of differentiating cognitive structures so that successively higher and more comprehensive stages of reversible moral thinking are achieved. Kohlberg believes this occurs in the free-discourse situation in which mutual exchange of claims and counterclaims stimulates increasingly more inclusive stages of cognitive organization.[44] Habermas believes moral socialization occurs in much the same way. Discourse situations where people are relatively equal in power and that presuppose mutual respect between participants constitute the optimal conditions under which moral differences can be resolved.[45] The morally right act is, for Habermas, what can be generalized as acceptable to all interested parties, as this is arrived at in the non-

42. Laurence Kohlberg, *The Philosophy of Moral Development* (San Francisco: Harper and Row, 1981), pp. 161-89; Jürgen Habermas, *Communication and the Evolution of Society* (Boston: Beacon, 1979), pp. 69-94.

43. See especially Kohlberg on this point, *The Philosophy of Moral Development,* pp. 6-28; also Habermas, *Communication and the Evolution of Society,* p. 70.

44. Kohlberg, *The Philosophy of Moral Development,* pp. 29-48.

45. Jürgen Habermas, *Moral Consciousness and Communicative Action* (Cambridge, Mass.: MIT Press, 1990), pp. 43-115.

coercive discourse situation.[46] Kohlberg's principle of the morally right is similar but is stated more from the perspective of what the reflecting individual imagines is generalizable rather than from what is *de facto* acceptable to the dialoging and deliberating parties.[47]

Are there elements of this kind of moral rationality at Apostolic Church? The answer is "yes," but that they are grounded differently. The presuppositions for communicative moral rationality for Apostolic Church are based on explicitly religious assumptions. Rather than following the Kantian assumption that all humans are rational agents, the Apostolic Church assumes all humans are made in the image of God. Both background beliefs — the Kantian and the Judeo-Christian — assume humans are deserving of respect and have the right to be heard. Because of the analogous character of the two sets of assumptions, we should not be surprised to see discussion groups proliferating at Apostolic Church. The reversibility and generalizability of the Kohlbergian and Habermasian theories have analogous expressions in Apostolic Church when small groups attempt to discern the meaning of "loving thy neighbor as thyself" (the principle of neighbor love) or "doing unto others as you would have them do to you" (Golden Rule). Note the reversible logics of both of these classic moral principles. Many of these discussions are open-ended and have the character of inquiry. Of course, as I have pointed out frequently, Kohlberg's and Habermas's principles of generalizability are very similar to Ricoeur's deontological test, although Ricoeur's principle functions within a context that gives much more credibility to tradition.

This leads to the fourth model — the narrative model — of socialization. The narrative features of Apostolic Church inform and animate the more specifically reversible moral logics of treating one's neighbor as one's self. This can be seen in the Ephesians marriage narrative that guides the socialization process of young males. The idea of the husband as a servant ("Husbands, love your wives, just as Christ loved the church and gave himself up for her") empowers the moral capacity of the husband to apply reversible moral thinking to his wife. Notice the principle of reversibility in the following Ephesians passage: "Even so husbands should love their wives as their own bodies" (Eph. 5:28). When asked to specify the mutual obligations of marriage, the members of Apostolic Church invariably go beyond liberal contractualism and its rule that marriage is a fifty-fifty affair. Instead, the men and women of this church say

---

46. Habermas, *Moral Consciousness and Communicative Action,* pp. 60-61.

47. Habermas, *Moral Consciousness and Communicative Action,* p. 65.

that marriage is a "100-100 commitment." Both parties are to give all, not just half. It entails a mutual identification and reversible thinking of the kind implied by treating the spouse as one would one's own body.

The socialization process of Apostolic Church is guided by the narrative embodiment of its tradition-saturated life. The dynamics of attachment-identification and the Kohlbergian-Habermasian dimensions both function within these religious narratives, which are told repeatedly in its services and meetings. Alasdair MacIntyre, Stanley Hauerwas, and Paul Ricoeur are correct in seeing moral socialization as primarily a narrative process.[48] There is no way to understand how many young, black, poor, and sometimes abandoned inner-city males are gradually transformed into responsible fathers and husbands if one neglects the power of the narrative process at Apostolic Church and other congregations like it. At the same time, the stories that are told and the identifications elicited between young males and the servant Jesus would not occur without the mediating presence of real older males (fathers and mentors) who develop affectionate attachments with younger males and use these ties to induct their young sons and friends into the ruling narratives of the church.

In philosophical quarters, there is an ongoing debate between critical-theory perspectives on socialization and the hermeneutical theories that emphasize tradition and often see narrative as the primary carrier of tradition. Habermas is certainly a key representative of a critical-theory approach, while Gadamer, MacIntyre, and Hauerwas, to varying degrees, emphasize tradition and narrative. Ricoeur believes there are ways to bring the two perspectives together into what he calls a critical hermeneutic theory of authority and socialization.[49] Ricoeur, as does Gadamer, puts the priority on tradition. Furthermore, as do MacIntyre and Hauerwas, he believes that narrative is a primary carrier of tradition. Ricoeur, however, develops a theory of authority and socialization that provides, in a secondary way, a role for critical theory's Enlightenment drive toward generalizability or reversibility. Rather than eliminating the claims of narrative traditions, Ricoeur simply demands that all such moral claims be run through the test of their compatibility with the principle of generalizability.[50] But this is done by Ricoeur in such a way as to maintain the

48. See Alasdair MacIntyre, *After Virtue* (Notre Dame, Ind.: University of Notre Dame Press, 1981); Stanley Hauerwas, *A Community of Character* (Notre Dame, Ind.: University of Notre Dame Press, 1982); Paul Ricoeur, *Oneself as Another* (Chicago: University of Chicago Press, 1992).

49. Ricoeur, *Hermeneutics and the Human Sciences,* pp. 76-77.

50. Ricoeur, *Oneself as Another,* pp. 204-18.

importance of motivating desires, affects and attachments (Freud, Erikson, object relations, neuroscience, evolutionary psychology), and orienting narratives (MacIntyre, Hauerwas).

Conclusion

This is basically what we saw happen at Apostolic Church. The marriage narrative of Ephesians was tested for its compatibility with the reversible logic of the principle of neighbor love and equal regard — loving the neighbor (in this case the spouse) as oneself. This same principle is extended by Apostolic Church to the nonfamilial neighbor as well. Apostolic Church is an example of an institution in civil society that exhibits features of a critical hermeneutical theory of authority and socialization. Narrative traditions are not reduced to moral generalizability, but they are at least tested for their consistency with this moral principle.

If youth violence is to be restrained and reversed, institutions in civil society with critical hermeneutical authority must become more numerous and powerful. They must spring up in cities and elsewhere. Policy initiatives on the part of government can support and stimulate such a renewal, but policy cannot itself create such institutions. Such institutions require vision — indeed, require faith. Policy cannot create faith, but it can be sympathetic to it. And through this sympathy, it can at least refrain from undermining such institutions with the acids of official cynicism.

Congregations such as Apostolic Church go beyond the polarities of autonomy and obedience. These standard stereotypical alternatives for articulating the goals of socialization — even among sophisticated social scientists and policy theorists — do not capture the rich resources of this community. Because its models of socialization are more complex than either of these alternatives, this church is surprisingly successful in inducting young males into responsible citizenship in urban environments where violence by and between youth is rampant. Furthermore, such churches illustrate much of what I have been arguing for in this book. The link between moral psychology and Christian ethics can be discerned through the prism of critical hermeneutics when applied to the analysis of authoritative religious communities. Critical hermeneutics, as a possible bridge between scientific moral psychology and Christian ethics, helps us see how such communities actually enable Christians not only to grow in the faith but also to handle the fragmentations of modernity with more power and confidence.

Index